GOLD HUNTER

The Adventures of Marshall Bond

To PAUL LANDELL
MY FRIEND FOR MANY YEARS
WITH BEST WISHES

Marshall Bond Jr.

GOLD HUNTER

The Adventures of
Marshall Bond

by
Marshall Bond, Jr.

UNIVERSITY OF NEW MEXICO PRESS

I DEDICATE THIS BOOK

TO THE MEMORY OF MY MOTHER

AMY LOUISE BURNETT BOND

Foreword

THIS IS the story of my father, Marshall Bond
(1867-1941), who had the good fortune to participate in
many of the colorful and exciting episodes in the final chapter of the opening of the West. He came to Denver in 1875
and, as a boy, rode the open range driving cattle north from
Texas. In 1891 he arrived in Seattle, and six years later
sailed for Alaska to hunt for gold in the Klondike. There he
met Jack London, who based his novel *The Call of the Wild*
on Bond's dog.

He roamed the deserts of Arizona and Sonora and trav-
eled by boat down the Colorado River, camping and examining mines. In 1902 he journeyed to Mexico City on a private
car with a relative of Theodore Roosevelt who was involved
in a bizarre attempt to colonize Mexico with Boers from the
Transvaal. In 1904-05 he lived in a shack in Goldfield, Nevada, reporting for several newspapers on the amazing discoveries of gold. In 1911 he was hunting big game up the
Stikine River in British Columbia with Lord Osborne Beauclerk and the explorer Warburton Pike.

In 1918 Bond went to Chihuahua to examine silver

mines and found himself in the midst of bloody fighting with Pancho Villa. In 1926 he visited Lincoln County, New Mexico, with Governor Miguel A. Otero and interviewed and photographed the survivors of Billy the Kid's gang and the Lincoln County War. In 1927 he journeyed from Cairo to Capetown, viewing Africa at the height of its colonial period. He visited some of the great copper, gold, and diamond mines and went on safari in the Belgian Congo. His final adventure was the gold rush at Mojave, California, in the 1930's.

In 1900 he married Amy Louise Burnett, daughter of Charles H. Burnett of Seattle. They had two sons, myself and my older brother, Richard M. Bond, a zoologist now living in the Virgin Islands.

Exuberant, temperamental, and indulged at an early age by wealthy parents, Marshall Bond was not destined for success in business. Instead he chose the more hazardous path of high adventure. Although molded by the prejudices of the late Victorian age, he was in his inner life a rebel against conformity and an advocate of the fully experienced life.

In this day of anti-heroes it is interesting to note that he was profoundly influenced by Thomas Carlyle's *Heroes, Hero-Worship and the Heroic in History*. He used to say that no one in his heart really objected to princes and millionaires provided they played their parts with honor and integrity and were neither poseurs on the one hand nor pikers on the other. Among his particular heroes were Warburton Pike, Slatin Pasha, Theodore Roosevelt, J. P. Morgan, and Cecil Rhodes.

He had two spiritual homes, both nurtured by a combination of reality, romanticism, and illusion. One was London, the fulcrum of an empire he greatly admired and the domain of what he considered the highest product of civilization—the English Gentleman. The other lay in the marvelous wilderness of the Far West, where he imagined himself lord of all he surveyed and communed with the ghosts of Ruxton, Bridger, and Kit Carson.

His conversation, especially around the campfire, was highly original, with its blending of humor and philosophy well larded with anecdotes, for which he had a prodigious memory. Full of warmth and zest, he was at least a notable success in human relations and in the breadth and diversity of his experiences. In short, he had a great enthusiasm for the adventure of life and the courage to make his life a great adventure.

I wish to thank numerous friends and institutions for their information and assistance: particularly the Yale University Library; Provincial Archives in Victoria, B.C., and its director, Willard E. Ireland; the Nevada Historical Society; the Huntington Library; Government Archives at Pretoria and its director, Dr. A. Kieser; and the library of the University of California at Santa Barbara. I regret not being able to do full justice to members of my family but wish to acknowledge the help of my aunt, Mrs. Louis W. Bond; her daughter, Mrs. Sidney Warner; my brother, Richard M. Bond; and my cousin Edward L. Bond, who kindly allowed me to use Jack London's letters to his father.

Irving Shepard of Glen Ellen gave me permission to publish the letters of Jack London. Robert N. Mullin provided valuable data on the Lincoln County War. Mildred Couper, a friend of Marshall Bond, did the musical scores. Peggy La Farge Hamill provided her father's Klondike journal. Joseph O. Tobin and two historians, Eric Rosenthal and A. M. Davey of Capetown, supplied valuable information. Among the mining fraternity, I am particularly indebted to Dr. Seeley W. Mudd, Clyde Garrett, Bruce Minard, Martin Engel, Jay C. Stoel, Alan Kempe, and Mrs. Tom Gentry. I also want to thank Sandra L. Hammann for her invaluable help in preparing this manuscript, and Alena Howard for her work on the final version.

M. B., Jr.

Santa Barbara, 1968

Contents

Illustrations

GOLD HUNTER

The Adventures of Marshall Bond

The Judge and His Boys

O N A HOT DAY IN JULY, 1926, a man of schol-
arly appearance, yet rugged in frame and bronzed by the
sun, drove with his younger son into the little town of
Chama, New Mexico, in an old Dodge touring car. Chama
was a nondescript sort of place with a general store, a couple
of gas pumps, and a few hundred houses, mostly shacks. At
the Western Union office he stopped to send a wire to his
wife in Santa Barbara. He signed "Marshall Bond" and
handed the telegram to the operator, who scanned it for a
moment and then asked:

"Are you any relation to the Bonds of the Old Bond
House?"

Obviously startled by this question, the visitor answered:

"My God, I'm one of the Bonds and haven't thought of
the house in over forty years."

The telegraph operator shouted the news to a group of
loafers in front of the store, and as the word spread a crowd
of several hundred excited citizens assembled to see the elusive Bonds who had vanished into thin air so many years before. The Old Bond House had become a legend and had
fortuitously catapulted the family into sudden fame. For

the next two hours the newcomers were besieged by questions and deluged with offers to sit in dilapidated chairs which had come from that venerable mansion.

It seems that Bond's father, Judge Hiram Gilbert Bond, had come to Chama in the summer of 1883 with his two boys, Louis and Marshall, and had bought some mining claims twenty-two miles north of town just over the Colorado state line in Navajo Canyon. The quartz outcropping glittered with gold and appeared to be the answer to a miner's dream. The Judge, who was a millionaire at the time and loved to do things in the grand manner, built a three-storey house near the mine and furnished it with a wagon train of the best Victorian furniture. It was the finest mansion for hundreds of miles, and a fitting residence for a magnate about to win additional millions from a sure-fire mining venture.

But the Judge, although an able lawyer, had not been out west long enough to learn all the tricks of the mining trade. In short, the mine was "salted." The previous owner had loaded a shotgun with gold dust and blasted the quartz so that it looked like a genuine bonanza. After the sale he had hurriedly left for parts unknown.

When Judge Bond discovered the fraud, he closed the house and the mine and returned to his Denver ranch. He was so indignant that he never returned to Chama and never mentioned the affair again.

The Old Bond House stood deserted and neglected for thirty years. Eventually a storm blew off the shutters and most of the shingles. When it became evident that its days were numbered, an enterprising citizen hauled most of the furniture to town and started a hotel. Others quickly followed, and soon not a board of the old mansion was left standing. Perhaps half the shacks in Chama had been constructed from its timbers. The abandoned property was indeed a failure as far as gold mining was concerned, but on a visit to Chama in 1956 the author discovered, too late, that it had just become involved in an oil boom.

Judge Bond was born in Rushford, New York, in 1838, the son of a country doctor. Unhappy at the doctor's second marriage, the boy left home at fourteen and worked for three years as a grocery clerk. He attended Rushford Academy, and while at Hamilton College obtained a franchise to sell a new map of the United States. Within two years he had made $10,000, more than enough to finance himself at Harvard Law School for two years. He had a brilliant record and in 1863, prior to graduation, went to work for the celebrated Wall Street lawyer Chauncey M. Depew, who handled the complex legal affairs of Commodore Vanderbilt.

While in the employ of Depew, the young attorney and a fellow employee were sent to Albany to report on a bill that was of considerable consequence to Commodore Vanderbilt. It was so important that it was debated and voted upon in closed session by the Legislature. Although no outsiders were admitted, the two attorneys managed to sneak into the basement beneath the Assembly floor and station themselves alongside a vent. A legislator in the pay of Vanderbilt was to drop a string down the vent as soon as the vote was counted. If untied, the bill had failed; if knotted, the bill had passed. The moment the knotted string appeared, the two men rushed to the telegraph office and wired the results to New York. Then they monopolized the only line for several hours by sending lengthy Biblical passages, allowing Vanderbilt time to act before anyone else on Wall Street knew what had transpired in Albany.

Young Bond soon achieved a reputation both as a lawyer and as an entrepreneur. By the age of twenty-six he had made $500,000. But the main lesson of Wall Street, which he had to learn the hard way, was that it is just as easy to lose money as it is to make it.

He had completed some complicated legal work for the Erie Railroad. Its treasurer, Daniel Drew, in a pretense of gratitude confided that the line was in deplorable financial condition and advised him to sell the stock short. Flattered by the old scoundrel and unwary from too early success, Bond took the bait and sold five hundred shares of Erie short. In a few days he found to his horror that he could not deliver the stock. Drew owned or controlled every share and had even bought the very stock Bond had sold. To make delivery Drew charged him $1000 a share, which cost him every cent he had. Broke and indignant, he was going to shoot Drew. Fortunately his wife talked him out of it.

Of course Bond was not the only turkey plucked by Drew. In another "Erie raid" Drew fleeced that old pro Commodore Vanderbilt out of $5,000,000. A few years later Drew himself was ruined in a similar squeeze by Jay Gould and Jim Fisk. Ironically, Drew had once scribbled:

> He who sells what isn't his'n,
> Must buy it back or go to prison.

After the Civil War H. G. Bond received a federal judgeship at Orange Court House, Virginia. It was there that Marshall was born in 1867. Also, on the recommendation of Ulysses S. Grant, Judge Bond was appointed United States Commissioner in Richmond, where he processed several thousand bankruptcy suits during the period of Reconstruction.

Life in Virginia was agreeable enough, but too tame for the Judge's restless ambition. When he had recouped sufficiently he returned to New York and made another fortune organizing the Kings County Elevated Railroad Company of Brooklyn. However, as soon as he got one business launched he would sell out and start another. The challenge of new ideas and the risk involved were what really interested him. Throughout his life he made and lost half a dozen fortunes speculating in mines, patents, and real estate. His most profitable venture was an association with Woodward, Stillman, and Platt in the Tennessee Coal and Iron Company of Birmingham, Alabama, of which he was general manager and a large stockholder. Marshall worked there in 1889-90 before his father sold his interest for $4,-000,000. One of his houses was at Decatur, Alabama.

Judge Bond's investments were widespread, requiring extensive travel and numerous residences. He came to Denver as early as 1870 and was admitted to the bar there in August of that year. The *Daily Colorado Tribune* of November 7, 1870, describes his ranch and his elegant new ranch house costing $12,000. The ranch was situated half a mile from the west end of the Larimer Street bridge across the Platte River.

In 1872 he attended the celebrated buffalo hunt near Kit Carson, Colorado, organized by Generals Sheridan and Custer for the Grand Duke Alexis of Russia. In 1874 he was a member of the Republican Convention and the following year was nominated for the Constitutional Convention. He bought into the Concord Mine and the New England Gold and Silver Company in Leadville. He was a director and one-sixth owner of the Virginius Mine near Ouray, Colorado, but unfortunately sold out of that bonanza just before its richest ore shute was discovered. The mine produced $27,000,000. He brought his two boys, Louis and Marshall, to Denver for their summer vacations starting in 1875.

Among Marshall Bond's earliest memories were those of the frontier days in Denver—a roistering community where miners, cattlemen, settlers, and Indians jostled each other in the purchase of eastern goods and in the ever widening opportunities for turning a dollar. He recalled large parties of Cheyenne and Arapaho braves passing through town on their way to hunt buffalo on the plains of Colorado and Nebraska. Occasionally they camped on the ranch, and one day an old chief, brandishing a tomahawk, chased the boy right back into the ranch house. The irate Judge confronted the Indian to find out why his son was screaming with terror. His wrath, however, soon turned to amusement when the chief explained in pretty fair English that the boy was a damned nuisance around the Indian encampment and that the threat of scalping was the only successful way to get rid of him.

In the fall of 1875 the Judge sent his boys to The Gunnery, a boarding school in Washington, Connecticut. Marshall must have been very obstreperous, for Louis wrote the following letter dated January 14, 1876:

My dear Papa.

When Marshall goes skating he thinks he can do as he pleases if I tell him to do what is wright he does what is wrong you know that you told him to mind me after a few days, after you had gone he told me that he was not agone to mind me he said that he did not care what you said about minding me because you was gone and you could not govern him. he comes up and hits me in the face when he gets mad at me and if I slap him he is ready for a fight but if I hit him in the face he will tell Mister Gun and I will half to pump 2 hours. I wish you would tell him to mine me.

Goodbye
Louis W. Bond

At the age of eight Marshall was in the habit of taking frightful chances. Once the Judge was horrified to find him balancing on a log across a ravine at least fifty feet deep.

When asked why he risked his life so recklessly, he calmly replied, "Jesus will save me."

"Who told you that?" roared his father.

"Mother told me," the boy answered.

After that the Judge saw to it that his wife's religious instruction was conducted along more practical lines.

When Marshall and Louis reached the ages of nine and ten, respectively, they decided to go into business. They selected counterfeiting as the line of work most likely to succeed. They obtained a sheet of lead and by carefully pounding a nickel into both sides of the soft metal made a pocketful of tolerably passable nickels. At least they were successful in passing them to a myopic candy store owner. When the latter was informed by the bank that he had been swindled, he indignantly confronted the Judge with the counterfeit nickels. Of course the Judge paid up, but when the boys came home that evening a stern lesson in numismatology was administered with a malacca cane.

As the boys grew older they spent the summers hunting and fishing in the great natural parks of Colorado, or as wranglers with cattle outfits driving bellowing herds of longhorns north from Texas. They loved the vast unfenced plains and the evening campfires where the old-timers told salty stories of Indian fights and bear and buffalo hunts on the old frontier.

On one of these cattle drives along the Goodnight Trail the cook was an ex-slave named Jim who slept under the chuck wagon. Although a good cook, he annoyed the cowboys by continually boasting of how he would fix any "bar" that might venture into camp or raid the chuck wagon. Exasperated after a week of this sort of talk, the Bond brothers decided to have a little fun with Jim. They sneaked a rope under the chuck wagon and, when Jim was asleep, tied one end to a saddle with a buffalo robe thrown over it.

In the dim light of the campfire it looked exactly like a bear. Pulling on the rope from behind the wagon, they suddenly yelled:

"There's a bear in camp! Look out, Jim, it's coming for the chuck wagon."

When Jim saw this menacing apparition charging directly for him, he hightailed it out of camp and didn't return until the early morning hours. For the rest of the trip there was no more talk of "bars."

In 1883 Judge Bond and Charles D. Arms bought a land grant at Socorro, New Mexico, from the Chavez family. It extended for five miles along the Rio Grande and included some 136,000 acres. This may have been a bargain at thirty-five cents an acre, but the terrain was so arid that it took a hundred acres to support one steer.

After the Mexican War these land grants were recognized by the treaty of Guadalupe Hidalgo, provided certain conditions were fulfilled. Under Justice S. B. Axtell a group of unscrupulous politicians known as the Santa Fe Ring began examining titles with a fine-toothed comb. Whenever the slightest question was found, they encouraged squatters to enter the ranch and claim the water holes. A flaw was found in Judge Bond's title, and the usual horde of squatters invaded his ranch. Of course the Judge and Arms brought suit, and fought a losing case all the way to the Supreme Court, which ruled that only an act of Congress could clear the title. Since this was politically impossible, the Ring then bought the land cheaply from the homesteaders. Many ranches bought in good faith were lost in this way. Thus ended the Judge's dream of becoming a cattle baron.

In 1880 the Bond brothers were sent to St. Paul's, an Episcopal boarding school in New Hampshire. Later they attended Yale, where Louis graduated in 1887 and Marshall in 1888. With generous allowances and passes on the railroads, their undergraduate days were gay and carefree. They did what they pleased and were usually pleased by what they did. As students they did well enough, but afterward in business neither seemed to have inherited his father's exceptional ability.

In 1891 Judge Bond disposed of his Denver holdings and moved to Seattle. His first venture there was to organize a syndicate which purchased the Monte Cristo Mine in the mountains back of Everett. The area was so rugged that supplies had to be brought in by pack train. Here was work the Judge's boys could really enjoy. They happily rode off to the mine, where they set up camp, mapped outcroppings of ore, and took extensive samples which ran high in both gold and silver. They also did the bookkeeping.

One day in the following year, while leading a pack train down the trail to Everett, Marshall met his father on the way in.

"No use coming back," said the Judge, "I've sold the mine."

Marshall, who loved this work better than anything he had done so far, was indignant and protested vigorously even though he had known a deal was pending.

"I sold it to John D. Rockefeller for $800,000 and made a good profit," replied the Judge. "Operating expenses are high, and I have a hunch it isn't as good as it looks."

His hunch apparently proved correct. Rockefeller's engineer had based his estimates on the rich surface assays, but further development revealed a considerable shrinkage of values with depth.* Marshall always maintained that Judge Bond achieved the unique distinction of being the only man

---

* The veins were remarkably regular and persistent, but values were spotty. The average value of Monte Cristo ores as a whole was .6 oz. of gold and 7 oz. of silver per ton.

to sell Mr. Rockefeller anything for more than it was worth.

The Judge's journals are fragmentary, making it difficult to reconstruct fully the complex Monte Cristo deal, involving some twenty-three claims. On May 22, 1891, the Wilmans brothers offered him the Pride Mountain group of five claims for $300,000, which he declined. The Judge and Louis then went into the Monte Cristo district with their engineer, George Milliken, and examined all the claims including the Monte Cristo, the Rainy, and the Pride Mountain groups.

A series of intricate negotiations ensued which ended on October 20 in the formation of the Monte Cristo Mining Company, with the Judge as president and Marshall Bond as secretary. J. M. Wilmans, one of the prior owners, retained 223,437 shares; H. G. Bond and Edward Blewett received 196,354 shares each; and Leigh J. S. Hunt of New York, 33,854 shares. The price they paid the Wilmans remains obscure but may have been around $165,000. Marshall, who had spent that spring at Ruby, in the Okanogan mining district, returned in July to help his father.

On October 3, before the organization had actually been completed, Judge Bond sold two claims, The Pride of the Mountains and 89, to Frank Brooks and L. L. Patrick of Leadville for $300,000. Meanwhile on September 16 a mining expert, Alton L. Dickerman, arrived in Seattle to examine the Monte Cristo claims for Colby, Hoyt & Co., representing John D. Rockefeller. An option must have been granted, for the Judge's journal of December 10 reads: "Rec'd $125,000 from Colby, Hoyt & Co. through L. J. S. Hunt for 2nd payment of their purchase of mines in Monte Cristo." The Judge's share of this came to $27,343.75. The amount of the first payment was not recorded.

On January 30, 1892, the journal reads: "Signed contract with Charles Colby, Colgate Hoyt, and John D. Rockefeller for ¼ interest in the stock of the Monte Cristo Co. and also for its treasury stock." The meeting took place at the Union League Club in New York City, of which Judge Bond was a member.

Since there were 3,500,000 shares in the treasury, which had been reserved to pay for a railroad, Rockefeller gained control by a wide margin. He also seems to have acquired the remaining stock outstanding, for the Judge's journal of April 19 records: "Colby, Hoyt & Co. closed the sale of my Monte Cristo stock for $200,000."

One of Judge Bond's many ships came sailing in with the Monte Cristo deal, but unfortunately he missed the boat on a far more momentous development, the astonishing success of which reverberated around the world.

On November 25, 1901, his journal reads: "Deposited in an envelope marked property of H. G. Bond, with H. L. Horton & Co. [his brokers], two certificates of 1000 shares each of the Bingham Copper and Gold Mining Company" of Bingham, Utah. His stock probably represented a substantial interest, as he was elected to the board of directors. Ironically, he finally unloaded these shares with the greatest difficulty late in 1902 for a paltry $10,000.

He knew, of course, that this property was sitting on a mountain of low-grade copper sulphide. He also knew that it was beset by liens and that such luminaries as Senator William A. Clark and John Hays Hammond had rejected it as uneconomical. He did not know that in 1902 Daniel C. Jackling had interested two Cripple Creek operators, Charles MacNeil and Spencer Penrose, in the concept of mining it on so vast a scale as to reduce the cost per ton low enough to insure a profit.

The following year these men formed the Utah Copper Company and by 1907, after the expenditure of $11,000,000, they had organized most of the district and erected a huge mill. The property was later taken over by Kennecott Copper Corporation. The investment began in 1915 and was completed in 1936. During the first sixty years of operation this enormous open pit mine produced nine million tons of copper and paid $1,250,000,000 in dividends.

Marshall Bond formed a real estate partnership in Seattle with Oliver H. P. La Farge.* The latter, a graduate of Columbia University, was the son of the distinguished artist John La Farge of whom Henry James had written: "He was quite the most interesting person we knew." A depression was under way and, in order to survive, these would-be realtors were obliged to camp in the rear of their office and do their cooking on a kerosene stove. In fact, money was so scarce that they would gladly walk a mile to save a five-cent carfare.

La Farge, while scrounging in the real estate business, had been reading *The Simple Life,* by a Frenchman, Charles Wagner, who advocated a return to nature *à la* Rousseau. He soon found the French philosopher a pretentious bore and was so disgusted that he wrote a parody, *The Simply Awful Life,* depicting his own disillusionment with poverty in Seattle.

Many years later, while living in New York, La Farge was persuaded to exhibit for charity his father's paintings and oriental collection. He not only found this tiresome, but one society woman in particular annoyed him by her inane gushing over every picture. He finally got out a fuzzy water color he had painted of a cow pasture in Connecticut and hastily inscribed *Boroloff* in the corner. La Farge was the personification of Gallic wit and culture, but as a painter

* La Farge's nephew, Oliver La Farge, years later achieved fame as an authority on American Indians and author of the bestseller *Laughing Boy*.

he had the least talent of anyone in his family. To the woman he said:

"Madam, you have moved me so deeply by your profound appreciation of art that I want to show you my greatest treasure. It is a pastoral scene of the Ukraine by the celebrated Russian impressionist, Serge Boroloff."

The woman was so overcome by the beauty of this masterpiece that La Farge gallantly presented it to her. He reported that she had had it hanging over her mantelpiece for ten years.

While Bond was in Seattle, four of his Yale friends arrived: Richard M. Hurd, George R. Carter, Billy Goodwin, and A. J. Balliet, all of whom including Bond had been oarsmen at Yale. They brought a secondhand four-oared shell from New Haven and rowed weekends around Lake Washington. Eventually they gave the shell to the newly founded University of Washington and started a fine tradition of rowing which was to bring that university considerable renown. Billy Goodwin coached the first Washington crew, and when the author last visited the campus the venerable shell was still resting in the boathouse.

Balliet enjoyed a modest success in Seattle as a lawyer, but the rest of these men, with the exception of Bond, eventually achieved fame and fortune in the best tradition of Horatio Alger. Carter served as governor of the Hawaiian Islands; Hurd became president of the Lawyers Mortage Company in New York; Goodwin made millions in the Hartford Insurance Company; and La Farge, after years of banking in Seattle and Pasadena, became vice-president of General Motors.

Conditions were discouraging in Seattle in 1894, however, so Judge Bond expanded his operation to San Francisco. The following year he bought a 34.22 acre ranch at Santa Clara called New Park. Arbors of imported French vines produced excellent wines, but prunes were the principal crop. Finding the prune industry unduly chaotic, he organized the growers and developed a marketing program in which the larger prunes were sold in the east and the smaller ones in Germany. He also founded the Santa Clara Valley Bank in 1898. His advice on both business and politics was eagerly sought. In fact, some years later in Washington, D. C., Theodore Roosevelt invited him to lunch at the White House and spent most of the afternoon obtaining his views on the political climate out west.

As result of his experiences in Virginia after Emancipation, the Judge became interested in the education and progress of the Negro population, as revealed in a letter to his son, the only one of his letters to survive:

New York
November 17, 1901

Dear Marshall:

Today I took lunch with Booker T. Washington. He was Milholland's guest. I found him one of the most common sense men I ever saw. He has very broad views and there is not the least evidence of any self-consciousness. His conversation shows great learning without any semblance of pedantry.

He is doing a wonderful work for the Negro. His method of educating them is to make them farmers, carpenters, masons, plumbers, painters, and in fact qualifies them only for industrial employment.

He is being backed by such men as Bishop Potter, Carnegie, Rockefeller, etc. . . .

Yours truly,
H. G. Bond

Judge Bond's houses were overflowing with books, antiques, and art objects of historical interest. In 1899 at an auction in Philadelphia he bought a table* in the style of Louis XVI and a tumbler, both of which had belonged to President Madison. Louis Bond's widow eventually sold the table to the Winterthur Museum. Occasionally it has been on loan to the White House.

The author inherited the tumbler after the death of his mother in 1954. It was a tulip-shaped piece of French cut glass about five inches high and was called a "bottoms up glass," as it was round at the bottom so that a toast had to be entirely consumed before it could be put down. The author, impressed by Mrs. John F. Kennedy's television tour of the White House in 1962, gave it to the White House. Mrs. Kennedy wrote that it was a most welcome contribution to the glass collection and that the detail on it was exquisite.

By 1905 Judge Bond seems to have lost his touch as a financier, for most of his fortune was dissipated in unwise investments, including the mines in Goldfield. In January, 1906, he sold New Park, returned to Seattle, and died there two months later of a stroke. The mansion and ten acres later became a Carmelite nunnery.

In Santa Clara, after taking a course in mining at Stanford, Marshall joined his brother in running the prune ranch and in the social life at Burlingame. There he had a friend named Townsend with whom he often took long walks. One Sunday afternoon, while they were going down a hot, dusty road in the peninsula foothills, they came to a large horse trough full of cool clear water. Since no one was in sight they decided to bathe and tossed a coin to see who would be first. Townsend won, took off his clothes, and stepped in. Just as he began to luxuriate in the delightful

* Described in *Antiques Magazine*, January, 1962.

water, an old lady in a buggy came into sight around the bend. It was too late for Townsend to get out, so he stretched out at full length hoping the old lady would pass him by. However, she turned her horse in for a drink, whereupon Townsend took a deep breath and submerged. The horse was still drinking when Townsend, unable to hold his breath any longer, came to the surface blowing like a whale. With a frenzied snort the frightened animal reared on its hind legs and took off down the road at breakneck speed with the bewildered old lady hanging on for dear life.

Through Richard M. Tobin, leader of the fashionable horsey set, Marshall became friendly with Talbot Clifton, probably the most eccentric and wealthy English sportsman of the day, whose madcap exploits provided a continuous source of laughter and scandal seldom equaled in the annals of San Francisco.

Clifton arrived from Mexico in 1894 accompanied by his dog Roy, a gaunt, sad-looking valet named Betts, and an artist, A. Restori. They stayed at the Palace Hotel, and Clifton, when he had money, kept huge sums in a silver box in his room. He soon became the hero of Monterey by racing a particularly vicious and unmanageable stallion called Guadalupe. After being thrown and breaking his collarbone, he reluctantly sold the horse to another man who was killed by the animal within a week.

At the age of sixteen, Talbot Clifton had come into one of the oldest and largest estates in England. He soon acquired a taste for conspicuous consumption, the sheer extravagance of which would have shamed even the late Aga Khan. By the time he had graduated from Eton and Cambridge he was $3,000,000 in debt. His solicitors insisted that he go abroad for a few years and "rough it" until his debts could be paid off from the normal proceeds of the estate.

"How much are you going to allow me to rough it on?" Clifton wanted to know.

"Five thousand dollars a month, to be paid quarterly, and not a cent more," his solicitors announced firmly.

Clifton thought this a miserly sum, and so it proved. He was unable to make ends meet and, more often than not, continued to wallow in debt. Too proud to accept the charity of friends after his allowance was spent, he and Betts would move out of the Palace and set up housekeeping in a box stall in Burlingame where they slept on the hay. Each morning his valet would kindle a fire in the stable yard and brew his master's tea. When the next check arrived, Clifton would move back to the hotel and throw a champagne dinner for his friends.

Talbot Clifton was a huge, powerful, bearded man who looked and acted exactly like the popular image of a Russian grand duke. Bond laughed at his foibles but envied his prodigious capacity for squandering money on every ridiculous whim. After a drinking spree Clifton would show up at breakfast with a horrible hangover and a temper so sharp that nobody dared talk to him. Betts would gingerly approach the table with a glass of whiskey, which Clifton would pour down with one hand while holding his nose with the other. Then Betts would bring him a plate of ham and eggs and a pint of champagne. After consuming this he would lean back in his chair, stretch out his arms, and exclaim, "Gad, what a glorious day!" After that it was reasonably safe to approach him.

Clifton was a fancier of the fine arts. He commissioned A. Restori to do a full-scale painting of Guadalupe for the music room of the Burlingame Country Club, but it was in music that he yearned to express himself. He decided to take up the flute and hired a pretty young flutist to give him lessons. Blow as he would, however, the sounds that came forth seemed rasping and vulgar. This he attributed to the base metal from which the instrument was wrought. Undaunted, he ordered a special flute made of solid gold, which he was confident would give out the dulcet tones he so eagerly sought. However, the results of this experiment were never made clear; his musical career was cut short by a disastrous love affair with his beautiful teacher.

Clifton enjoyed the gay hospitality of the Burlingame Country Club to such an extent that he ordered a splendid coach from Brewster's, which he intended to present to the club in token of appreciation upon his departure from California. The coach arrived on Sunday, July 29, 1894, and caused a sensation at the club. It had a bugler and was drawn by four perfectly matched black horses. The Clifton crest was on both the carriage and the silver-mounted harness. Its design was a raised gauntleted arm grasping an unsheathed dagger, and the motto read *Mortum Aut Triumphum.* The bill for all this was said to have been $12,000.

Shortly thereafter, at the end of a wild party, Clifton invited his inebriated friends to drive to the club as a fitting conclusion to so momentous an evening. However, when they arrived around 3 A.M., the gates were locked.

"The horses are hunters, we'll take it," cried Clifton, grabbing the reins from the startled coachman.

The first two horses did make it, but the last two and the coach piled up on the gates. The coach was a wreck, but miraculously neither animals nor men were seriously injured. When Betts was told of his master's latest fiasco he was heard to moan, "If he breaks his bloody neck, what's going to become of me?"

In 1962 Joseph O. Tobin, president of the Hibernia Bank of San Francisco, wrote a letter to the author which reads in part:

I had the pleasure of knowing your father and I also knew Talbot Clifton. I have a book written by Clifton's widow which is called *The Book of Talbot*. It is dedicated: "To God for Talbot." She, also, was a little balmy.

I remember one of Clifton's pals here who was a well known race track habitué and quite a character. His name was Dan McCarthy but he was generally known as "White Hat McCarthy" due to the fact that he wore a top hat made of white beaver. In 1887 he won the American Derby and was the sensation of the year in racing! Clifton seemed to be completely fascinated by McCarthy and anything he suggested in the line of horses, wine, women, or song was entirely agreeable to Clifton.

Clifton was a very good whip but was not too good a rider. In those days the Bay District Track was in operation, and he raced there quite often, always in steeple-chase, and generally fell off. However, one day he got a good price from the bookmakers that he wouldn't stay the course and bet them all large sums. He just cantered around the track with no idea of competing in the race and won the bet. He also played polo but very badly.

What really won Marshall Bond's admiration was not Clifton's ludicrous social life but the discovery that he was a remarkable explorer who was as much at home with the Eskimos as he was playing polo with the elite of San Francisco or London. He had a curious compulsion to wander to the ends of the earth, hunting, exploring, and playing his golden flute. Over the next thirty years Bond kept hearing reports of Clifton's adventures and of the commotion his presence always created.

In 1897 Clifton was in Canada hunting musk ox with the Eskimos north of Hudson's Bay. The hardships he endured from cold and hunger would have killed any ordinary man. From 1898 to 1901 he wandered through Equatorial Africa, living and hunting with the natives, and went on safari with

Cecil Rhodes. In 1901 he arrived in St. Petersburg, where he met the Czar, played polo with Prince Orloff, and plunged into a social turmoil even more reckless than that of San Francisco. After seven weeks he grew tired of champagne and caviar, and left for Siberia where he spent the rest of the year along the Arctic Ocean exploring the delta of the Lena River.

He trekked through Australia, explored the jungles of Peru, Bolivia, and Equador, learned to rope steers in Wyoming, and lived like a maharaja while visiting Singapore. Another report had him entertaining the Grand Duke Michael, brother to the Czar, at Lytham Hall, his Lancashire estate. Being head over heels in debt, he had dismissed all the servants but Betts, and the three men were spending the time drinking whiskey and playing whist. He became a legend wherever he went, and he went everywhere, finally dying in Nigeria in 1927 at the age of fifty-nine.

When Clifton abandoned his reckless life in San Francisco, he sailed for Alaska accompanied by his dog and Betts. They crossed the mountains from Dyea to Lake Lindeman, where they built a boat with some prospectors and proceeded down the Yukon River, two and a half years before the great Klondike gold discovery drew thousands, including the Bond brothers, along the same route.

CHAPTER TWO

The Klondike

ALLUVIAL DEPOSITS OF GOLD had been worked along the Yukon River since 1869, but none had been rich enough to attract the attention of the outside world. Then in the late summer of 1896 a prospector named George Carmack wandered up the Klondike, a tributary of the Yukon, and found gold at the juncture of Bonanza and Eldorado creeks. At first the values recovered close to the surface were unimpressive. It was not until the end of the year, when bedrock was reached, that the enormous concentrations of gold stirred the imagination of the entire world.

The news of Carmack's momentous discovery was received at first with considerable scepticism. However, Marshall Bond was in Seattle when the S.S. *Portland* docked from Alaska on July 17, 1897, with the first regular shipment of gold. He saw heavy sacks of nuggets unloaded and transported for safekeeping to the vaults of Wells Fargo. An employee showed him some of the gold and told him the shipment was worth $300,000. Later estimates claimed it weighed over two tons and was valued at more than $1,000,-000. In Seattle, depression immediately gave way to a mad scramble for supplies.

Galvanized into action by the sight of such wealth, the Bond brothers organized an expedition and borrowed enough money from the Judge to buy a year's supply of food and equipment at something like reasonable prices. Marshall sailed aboard the S.S. *Queen* on July 23 with an English friend, Stanley Pearce. Louis left two days later on the S.S. *Mexico*. They arrived in Skagway about a week ahead of the main rush. In 1898 in Dawson they were joined by Oliver H. P. La Farge and Lyman Colt, a rancher from Chelan, Washington, who shared the same cabin.

Marshall's first letter was exuberant.

S.S. Queen
July 25th, 1897

Dear Mother:

Pearce, Collins, Pelly, and two fine fellows from Victoria, Seagrave and Van Millingen, and I have part of the women's steerage partitioned off with a blanket, and we are quite comfortable. During the day we take advantage of our first class privileges and remain aft. We have a good deal of fun and are anything but downcast. The men say the steerage grub is simply awful, but take it as a joke, knowing it will end soon. I heard one fellow grimly remark that if they would serve everything in a trough he wouldn't kick, but that the present manner of service was too much for him.

The tourists are inclined to take us as embryo Stanleys and Livingstones, and it's not at all disagreeable to be so looked up to. One young college youth divides his time between reading Richard Harding Davis' *Soldiers of Fortune* and listening to our talk. I fancy he thinks we are the stripe of Davis' hero, Clay, judging by his open-eyed astonishment. It's very hard to live up to this, for I have no definite notion of how heroes act.

Clifton and his valet took this trip two years ago, going down clear to the mouth of the Yukon. Warburton Pike told the Victoria fellows that he would come in overland from the Cassiar

Country this winter in time to spend Christmas with them. I shall write every time I get a chance. I hope Louis brings the dogs.

Affectionately yours,
Marshall Bond

Two weeks later he wrote:

Embryo City of Skagway, Alaska
6th Aug. 1897

Dear Mother:

We are all wrecks, but the quantity of beans, etc. we stow away is sufficient proof that we still have our health. We had a pleasant trip up, and the *Queen* first put into Dyea Bay. There was a heavy sea and wind and it was impossible to unload her cargo on the rocks—the only landing place.

Capt. Carroll lowered his launch and went to Skagway. He returned with the news that the trail was open, and that two pack trains were running. Calling up the men on the forward deck he put the question, "Skagway and a dock, or Dyea and the rocks?" The crowd shouted "Skagway!" and we pulled up anchor and steamed over—about four miles.

The night before young Kohl, of San Mateo, a friend of mine and an heir to his father's estate of twelve millions, set up a lot of champagne, and Barney Sugrue* made an inimitable speech asking the indulgence of the passengers, saying that "we were putting spirits down to keep our spirits up."

We tied up alongside the dock about 5 p.m. and began unloading. We worked all night without intermission, and at day-

---

* O. H. P. La Farge's journal says: "Sugrue was a popular Irishman with a wonderful gift of oratory, an unusually argumentative disposition, a splendid physique, and two very well trained and ready fists. Although friendly with the Mounted Police, he made rousing speeches against the Dominion Government. Finally to keep him quiet the Government made him Inspector of Claims. I saw him afterwards many times in Seattle when he was in the fruit business. Jack London portrayed his personality in some of his stories under the name of Bellew, but he never quite gave Barney that magnetism that made him so attractive to all of us."

light everything was on the dock. I then undertook to take
Bailey in my canoe, and he got in as he would climb a fence,
and we both upset. We began unloading the things on the dock
into a scow and the first scow was largely laden with my stuff.
A lot of roughs began throwing everything on the shore a few
feet from the rising tide and no wagons near. I remonstrated in
vain and then said I would shoot the first man who tried to take
the scow before the wagons came. Several nice Englishmen said:
"You're right and we'll stand by you."† This settled the rowdies
and they asked permission to pack my things up out of harm's
way. We worked all day in the rain with nothing but a piece of
bread to eat.

Investigation proved that the trail (over White Pass) was not
through at all, and no rush being expected, work on it was pro-
gressing in a leisurely way. To move our impedimenta to Dyea
would be costly and in bad weather, dangerous, and then we
might find no packers. I resolved to go this way or bust. After
a good night's rest we started out with ten horses with 150 lbs.
on each and made the summit about ten that night, very tired—
distance about eighteen miles over a trail like the one from
Silver Lake to Monte Cristo. Here I left Wickman on guard,
as a good deal of stealing was going on.

The next day we returned and the next pulled out again. In
the meantime Louis arrived. It is awfully hard work, and the
horses slip and fall continuously, and we had only bread and
ham to eat. While on the summit I found enough cocoa for two
meals in an old coat I brought from Arizona, and it was greatly
appreciated. My feet gave out the last trip, so Louis went with
the pack train this morning. We have 4300 lbs. on the summit
and 1000 lbs. going forward today. In the meantime I have a
gang of men packing 100 lbs. each on their backs between camps.
One camp is eight miles up, and tonight we shall have another
four miles further to which we shall pack and then move the
rear one four miles ahead and pack to that. From the summit

† Several Americans also stood by him, including Key Pittman, later U.S.
Senator from Nevada.

on, the trail goes over easy grades and through an open country. A chain of little lakes extends within six miles of Lake Bennett which forms the head of the Yukon. Lots of men have become discouraged and have either abandoned their claims or sold out for a song and gone back.

Skagway at the time consisted of but one boarding house where a few dock and trail workers stayed. A man named George ran the place, and his beefy young mistress presided over the kitchen. Since Bond and his party were camped in the timber nearby, they saved both time and food by taking their meals in the boarding house. Competition for space being keen at the table, they adroitly cultivated George and outrageously flattered the cook, even making the absurd suggestion that she accompany them to Dawson.

In the meantime a small pack train had arrived in Skagway, and since George was not without influence they offered to pay him if he could procure its services for the White Pass Trail. After a lengthy silence he asked Marshall to go with him to the edge of the timber, where he said:

"Mr. Bond, I don't want any money, but if I get you this pack train, will you agree not to take my woman away?"

It was none too easy convincing him that they were only joking and wouldn't take a woman over that rough trail under any circumstances. They succeeded, however, and got the pack train. A month later the unfortunate woman agreed to go with another man who really did want her. Blinded by love and jealousy, George killed the offender, the woman, and himself.

The letter continued:

Aug. 10th

The avarice of the owner of the pack train, Mr. Cleveland, has resulted in his being run out of the country and in occasioning us some delay. He was making over $200 a day with his train and wagon team but wanted more. So when a poor fellow from Seattle named Fowler with 100 lbs. on his back fell off a log and was drowned, Cleveland wanted ten dollars for carting his body back to the beach in his empty wagon, that it might be shipped to Seattle for interment. The news spread and in a short time a miner's meeting was called and a Vigilance Committee organized. They closed up Mr. Cleveland's business and gave him until the next day to leave. His tent was cut down and his outfit sold. His partner, Young, was up the trail with our pack train. He was none too nice himself, and the men determined to fine him, too.

Louis and Stanley went down and talked with the Committee, and after three hours talk, during which Louis never drew breath, the Committee agreed to let Young remain but gave him orders to take our entire outfit through without a break. From Pearce's description, Louis' talk must have been most amusing. He made us out as public benefactors and the most unselfish, disinterested people in the world.

Skagway, from a barren beach, has become a booming burg, and some admirer, unknown to me, has named the principal street "Bond St."* We are looked upon with all the veneration we deserve, I assure you. Two saloons, the Klondike and the Packers, have opened up full blast, and in the latter a crap game is going with gold pieces on the table.

Stanley went into the Packers to see the crap game, and a big drunken Irishman came up and banged him on the back and said, "Hello, Tenderfoot!" Stanley at once turned and in a voice loud enough to be heard by everyone, said: "I'm no tenderfoot, and I'll bet you the drinks for everybody present I can fool you in a minute." "I'll go you," says the Irishman, and Stanley immediately pulled out half a dollar and handed it to the man, saying "What is the date on that coin?" "1892," he replied. "Close it in your hand," said Stanley, and upon his doing so, said, "I'll bet you the drinks now for all present it's 1876 and the right man pays." "Agreed," the Irishman replied with the look

* There is no Bond Street in Skagway now.

of a man who had a cinch. "Well," said Stanley, "you are right and the drinks are on you!" The crowd yelled, and the man had to pay, and Stanley, with the remark "I don't even think you're Irish," walked away.

On September 5, 1897, Bond wrote from Lake Bennett:

It has cost us $3100 for packing. I have $3000 left. Thomas McGee, a member of the University Club in San Francisco, and his father brought a lot of burros from California. They have gone down river with part of their outfit, and his partner (whom I have seen often around the Club) is laboring with the swimming donkeys to get the balance of the outfit through.

We hear that the steamer *Cleveland* with 600 aboard and bound for St. Michaels has gone down with all on board. I hope it will prove to be a rumor only. She was an old tub and ran up and down the coast as a tramp ship under several different names.

You would enjoy seeing the picturesque scenery and men around their camps working with might and main building boats or whip-sawing lumber. The dogs are well and enjoy nothing better than jumping into the cold water for sticks. I have a horror of business and like only this life and that which California affords. I take kindly to this sort of existence and feel perfectly at home in a tent. When I walked down to Lake Bennett this morning for my dip, all the men at work on the beach gazed at me in speechless amazement.

We have had a hard time of it packing no less than 100 lbs. on our backs. There are over 1000 horses and 5000 men on the trail and I doubt if 100 get through. The rains and constant travel rendered the trail well nigh impassable. I find myself leading a picturesque though humdrum life, one that is very prosaic, and with no more hardships than I experienced in Connecticut or New Hampshire when I essayed canoeing or mountain climbing. I have never been discouraged a minute and if it wasn't for such an amount of impedimenta, could make it in two days

[Skagway to Lake Bennett]. However, I am more desirous of fame than fortune, and I wish you would not undeceive anyone. Now that I have shown you behind the scenes, do not, I beg, tell the public that my diamonds are paste. I prefer to be regarded as great a man as their imaginations will allow me to be.

Although Marshall regarded the first leg of the trip as no more than vigorous exercise, a mantle of heroism did cloak him and his partners on the second half as revealed in a letter from Dawson.

Dawson City, NWT
October 11th, 1897

Dear Mother:

We arrived several days ago all well, etc. Have bought a cabin with John McGillvray, a New York *Herald* correspondent, and, as our party will not always be together, it will be large enough.*

We are moving in and hope to be comfortably settled in a day or two. Great scarcity of food prevails and we keep ours under lock and key all the time. Flour is $100 a sack. The companies are trying to get poorly outfitted men to go down the river to Fort Yukon where there is plenty of grub to be had.

On our way here, after getting to Stewart River, we were in constant ice floes, and, while somewhat dangerous, we had no accident. Anyone bringing flour, beans, and rice in here by spring will make a fortune. The mines have not started working yet, so it is not as lively as ordinarily. Still gold is everywhere; gold dust is the currency of the country and everyone carries a sack. The tributaries of the Klondike are pretty well located. Many people are discouraged. Louis, Stanley, and I are not. Thomas McGee and his father are going to make an effort to get out of the country before it freezes. They have secured the services of the renowned Jack Dalton to go with them and will probably make it. Dalton says they haven't an hour to lose.

* The cabin cost $750, of which McGillvray paid $250. In the summer of 1898 O. H. P. La Farge bought it for $1,000.

While I believe we shall make money, I don't look for any great amount. Good order obtains here, and last night twenty additional mounted police arrived. There are a number of nice women in town and quite a number of fine fellows. I doubt if the mail service contemplated will get in operation this winter. However, I shall have opportunity of sending letters occasionally over the ice by men going out up the river. We have a splendid cabin, a Catholic hospital is nearby, and Dr. Howe, a friend of mine, is a neighbor. This is a very healthy country, dry and cold. The thermometer has been as low as —10 F., and we were sleeping at the time on the ground in our tents, which was not at all bad.

Dalton brought a lot of cattle over the trail, butchered them at Pelly River, and rafted them down. I have bought a quarter of mutton for $1.25 a pound. Fairbairn has some claims on Eldorado Creek which he thinks he can sell, and is trying to get out. I could sell our coal oil for $50 a gallon and our candles for $1 apiece, but we have none to spare. A railroad over the Dalton River to Pelly River, head of Yukon navigation, would be a bonanza. Sidney Hansard is O.K. and is working for wages. One cannot wear boots in this cold weather. Moccasins are the only things. Our fur rugs would bring from $150 to $300 each. Should father come in the spring, he should do so by the first boat. I do not think that the companies will be able to supply all the crowd that is coming. Only a railroad would make it possible.

The Lakes Bennett, Tagish, Marsh, and La Barge are more or less dangerous. A perfect hurricane blows down their arms without a moment's notice. We tried Windy Arm on Tagish at 4 P.M. when it was calm as a mirror. In ten minutes a gale of wind swept down and drove us ashore. We had to leap into the water up to our waists and unload hastily. How Stanley and I failed to wreck our boats on the rocks is a wonder.

On Lake Marsh so stiff a wind caught us that our canoe trailing behind filled and overturned and made it impossible to handle our boat. We were obliged to cut it loose. I was handling the sail and Stanley the rudder oar. He said he could stand it no longer, as he was exhausted. However, he did and we got ashore.

Then it looked milder and we started again and I took the tiller. Another hurricane caught us: the waves were enormous, so the only thing to do was to keep straight before us. If we should get in the trough of the waves, it would probably mean swamping. Neither of us spoke and by and by I thought I could hold on no longer. My arm was cramped and my strength failing, so I said, "Stanley, if we go down, let's do it like men." He said, "You bet your life," and I knew he was game. So I said, "Sing something for a bracer." He has a good voice and started a rollicking song which was very inspiring:

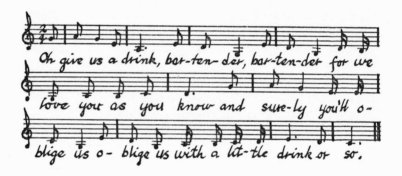

Oh give us a drink, bar-ten-der, bar-ten-der for we love you as you know and sure-ly you'll o-blige us o-blige us with a lit-tle drink or so.

You have no idea what strength is to be derived from a song. It saved us. Our voices reached Louis and Moore and gave them confidence. The mast in Wickman and Bailey's boat snapped off, and they got in the trough of the sea. I thought they were gone, and, though we flew by within 50 feet of them, we could do nothing. I did not dare shout an encouraging word for fear of distracting their attention. We could not look around, and I did not see them again until we had run in behind a point, and then with some glasses we watched their boat on the opposite side of the lake bobbing up and down like a cork. About dusk we saw them land.

The next morning we went to the foot of the lake and waited, for it was impossible to cross over to them. They did not turn up until the day following, for they spent the next day searching for us, believing that we had failed to weather the storm. They were greatly surprised when they found us safe at the foot of the lake. They said they did not expect to get out themselves and had pulled off their boots and had prepared to swim.

Wickman is a character. He never swears, never loses his temper, and is the most considerate, honest man I have ever seen. We have profited by his example and try to restrain our tempers and language. It is easy and more satisfactory, too. We got an expert river man to run our boats through Miles Canyon and White Horse Rapids. Stanley and I went through the Canyon with him and Stanley also went through White Horse. I did not, solely for the reason that I had to help pack our goods around. The three-quarters of a mile takes about two minutes or less to go through. Stewart River was flooded with ice when we reached it and we could not have gone up it if we wished. We have had a long arduous trip and one not devoid of peril. I am glad it is over at last. We are snug as a bug in a rug. Send any mail which may come for us to Dawson. Goodbye.

Affectionately yours,
Marshall

Of his journey through the lakes and down the Yukon, he wrote in a journal:

For the "Chechako," or newcomer, unfamiliar with the country and its conditions, there were many severe and trying tests for his courage all along the inland water route. While we were waiting for more favorable weather, two men with packs on their backs came along following the shore line of the lake on their way back to Skagway. They told us that a Negro they had taken with them had stolen their boat and supplies. We naturally expressed our indignation at a theft of this kind and volunteered to do what we could to bring the culprit to justice when we arrived in Dawson. We were surprised not only to perceive an indifference on their part to their misfortune but to a disinclination to have merited punishment meted out to the author of it. We subsequently learned that the sudden and violent storms at this season of the year had so shaken the nerves of the two white men that they had quit and turned their outfit over to the Negro. They retreated ignominiously and excused their cowardice by insinuating treachery to a man of inferior race who had surpassed them in courage. However, these were the only two men I knew who got as far as the lakes and then threw up the sponge.

The outlet of Lake La Barge is known as Thirty Mile River, and about half way down it we made camp. The country through which we had travelled since leaving Lake Bennett was a primeval wilderness without one white inhabitant, and only a few nomadic Indians. These were living in a condition only two jumps ahead of starvation and many were suffering from tuberculosis. They had brush lean-tos in front of which a fire was kept going as they had scarcely any bedding. There are few experiences more stirring to the emotions than traveling through a vast wilderness.

Early one morning we reached Fort Selkirk where the Pelly River joins the Yukon. Some Indians and a white trader lived there. The latter offered me some silver fox skins for $45.00 each. I have often regretted not buying them as I have since seen this variety selling for $1000.00 a skin.

Fort Selkirk was once a Hudson's Bay Co. trading post, but in 1851 the Chilkats, a warlike tribe from the coast, crossed Chilcoot Pass and descended the 500 miles of lakes and rivers to burn the post, in order to regain their monopoly of trade with the tribes of the interior. The Hudson's Bay Co. never rebuilt it.

Here we found Jack Dalton, the hardy Alaskan pioneer who had discovered an inland route across the mountains known as the Dalton Trail where the presence of bunch grass made it suitable for driving livestock. He was presently engaged in building a raft upon which to float a freshly butchered herd of cattle down stream to Dawson.

On September 30th we passed the mouth of White River. It was pouring a vast quantity of ice into the Yukon. The luxury of gliding along the current came to an end by reason of the ice. It was an interminable job getting ashore to camp in the swift and congested current and even more dangerous getting back into the stream again in the morning. Fallen trees, their roots still holding to the bank, stretched out over the river in many places which with the swiftly flowing ice threatened to fill and crush our boats. Clearing these obstacles from our course was terrifying and sometimes dangerous work and occupied a week before we arrived in Dawson.

The rapids on the Yukon were fast and difficult, especially for the inexperienced. White Horse Rapids was the most celebrated, but Squaw was almost as dangerous. Some men were drowned in these rapids, usually because of poorly constructed boats or overloading. Some curious cargoes, however, went through unscathed, one of the most unusual being a boatload of cats which were sold in Dawson for an ounce of gold apiece. Vermin there had reached alarming proportions.

Near Five Finger Rapids the Bonds met W. P. Gates of Spokane, known as Swiftwater Bill, who had received this nickname because he was deathly afraid of rapids and had portaged around every one of them. However, in the diggings Gates had been lucky enough to stake claim No. 13 on Eldorado Creek and soon made a fortune. On his return to Dawson he started living it up and acquired a dance hall girl, Gussie La More, as his mistress. At length she grew tired of him and went to live with another man. The next morning Swiftwater followed them into a restaurant and immediately bought all the eggs in the place for a dollar apiece. He knew she was crazy about eggs. When she ordered some for breakfast, the waiter told her there were none. Then Swiftwater shouted, "Waiter, bring me a dozen fried eggs!" When the waiter brought them, the girl deserted her lover and went back to Swiftwater Bill.

Of his arrival in Dawson on October 7, Bond wrote:

At 3:30 P.M. we reached "Louse Town," that part of Dawson on the south side of the Klondike River where it flows into the Yukon. Our journey was over and it had taken us seventy-three days from the time we landed in Skagway. Dawson was situated on a flat piece of ground that stretched along the river for half a mile, and back from it about a quarter mile to the hills behind.

The stores and warehouses of the two commercial companies, the saloons and dance halls, and the places of business occupied about two blocks along the river front. This was the center of business and social life of town. A few hundred yards up the river bank were the trim log barracks of the Northwest Mounted Police. Scattered cabins extended from behind the business section to the hills. It is probable that the town and entire surrounding district did not have a population in excess of three or four thousand.

When Louis had arrived in Skagway, he had brought with him two splendid dogs, Jack and Pat, which Marshall had bought in Seattle. The former was to become the hero of Jack London's *The Call of the Wild*. After the huge success of this book in 1903 the various members of the Bond Family always referred to their famous dog as Buck, the name used by Jack London. London changed the dog's name from Jack to Buck, evidently feeling that it would be unsuitable to call his dog hero by the same name as his own.

In a gold rush of such magnitude it was inevitable that the Bond brothers should meet a number of highly original and colorful men who would eventually make their marks in the world—men such as Major Frederick Russell Burnham, the famous scout, Addison Mizner, the architect, and Jack London. They admired London's love of adventure, his keen, inquiring mind, his humor, and his extraordinary warmth of personality. He in turn liked the company of two educated men and was greatly impressed by the stamina of their 140-pound dog.

London remained in the Klondike during the winter of 1897-98, made no money, and left in the spring by way of the lower Yukon, suffering from a bad case of scurvy. He arrived home in Oakland without a cent of cash but with a gold mine of experience upon which to build his literary career. He visited San José frequently and on at least one occasion spent the night at Judge Bond's ranch. He used the Judge's ranch and family as background for *The Call of the Wild*. His only oversight was to refer to Marshall's and Louis' wives as "Alice and Mollie, the Judge's daughters," instead of "Amy and Molly, the Judge's daughters-in-law." Most of the novel, of course, is fictional.

The author has in his library a first edition of London's first book, *The Son of the Wolf*, inscribed:

> Dear Marshall:—With best regards in memory of
> old Klondike days.
> Jack London, Oct. 6th, 1900

To the Yale University Library the author gave a letter[*] from London and a photograph of Marshall Bond, his associates, and their two dogs in front of their cabin in Dawson in 1898. On the picture, which may have been taken by Louis, since he does not appear in it, is written:

> Buck of the Call of the Wild owned by the Bond Brothers
> Dawson N.W.T., May 21, 1908, Jack London

Louis Bond's son, Edward L. Bond, now vice president of

---

[*] Marshall Bond's Klondike diary, photographs, and letters are in the Yale Library.

the First Boston Corporation, has an identical copy. (Obviously the date is that of the inscription and not of the photograph). He also has a copy of *The Call of the Wild* inscribed:

Oakland Calif. April 12th 1907
Dear Louis Bond:
    Here is the book that never would have [been] written if you had not gone to Klondike in 1897 and taken Buck along with you. In fond memories of Sour-Dough days,

Jack London

The letter to Marshall Bond reads:

Jack London
1216 Telegraph Ave.
Oakland, Cal.
Dec. 17 1903
Dear Marshall:
    Lo and behold! I am just reading your letter of Oct. 12th.
    About that time I jammed my unopened mail into a gun case and pulled out on a duck-hunting cruise of six weeks. During this cruise, of course, I opened my gun-case correspondence and answered it. Then I was home for a few days. During which time gun-case remained on the yacht. Last Monday pulled out on another cruise. Am now in lower end of Bay near Alviso. To-day my partner, cleaning guns, discovered your letter, crumpled up at very bottom of case where it had been jammed by the gun. It is a miracle that it was ever found. Might have remained there for years.
    Yes, Buck was based upon your dog at Dawson. And of course Judge Miller's place was Judge Bond's—even to the cement swimming tank and the artesian well. And don't you remember that your father was attending a meeting of the Fruitgrowers Association the night I visited you, and Louis was organizing an athletic club—all of which events figured with Buck if I remember correctly. As you say you expect to be in S.C. [Santa Clara]

for Christmas I'll mail this to you there. Hope to see you soon. Have received a couple of letters from Del Bishop,* and Charley Meyers looked me up recently.

Sincerely yours,
Jack London

P.S. Was it a boy?

The P.S. refers to the author's brother, Richard M. Bond, who was born in New York, November 5, 1903.

E. L. Bond also has a letter to his father which reads:

Papeete, Tahiti, Jan. 16, 1908

Dear Louis:

Do you remember a Sour-Dough by the name of Church who carried a gripsack containing a revolver and some ammunition of yours out of the Klondike and delivered same to you? Well, I've written a story upon that incident. Said story is entitled "Trust." It will be published shortly in the Century Magazine —at least the Century has bought and paid for it.

Sincerely yours,
Jack London

After London's death in 1916, Marshall wrote of how he and London had become friends in Dawson.

Shortly after our arrival in Dawson when Pearce and I stood in front of the Dominion bar to get a drink, our reflections in the mirror resembled a couple of hobos. Two men who looked just as unkempt and forbidding as these reflections of ourselves set up a tent near our cabin until they could arrange for more permanent winter quarters. They asked to be allowed to put their provisions in our cache for the time being, to keep them from the depredations of predatory malamoot dogs, whose un-

---

* Del Bishop worked at the Monte Cristo Mine and later went to the Klondike where he was a close friend of both London and the Bonds.

derfed condition kept them constantly on the lookout for an opportunity for theft, and from light-fingered marauders of our
own breed. This led to an acquantanceship which an occasional
evening in our cabin ripened into friendship.

One of these men was of medium height with very square
broad shoulders. His face was masked by a thick stubbly beard.
A cap pulled down low on the forehead was the one touch necessary to the complete concealment of head and features, so that
that part of the anatomy one looks to for an index of character
was covered with beard and cap. He looked as tough and as un-
inviting to us as we doubtless looked to him.

On a box, out of the circle of light from the lamp, he sat in
silence one night, a confusing blur of cap, mackinaw, and moccasins. Conversation turned to the subject of socialism.* Some
of those present confused it with anarchism. One of our number,
who at least knew more of the subject than the rest of us, clar-
ified it somewhat with his greater knowledge, but this was soon
exhausted. Then from out of the shadow of the lamp, from the
blur of beard and cap, came a quick-speaking, sympathetic
voice. He took up the subject from its earliest history, carried it
on through a rapid survey of its most important points and held
us thrilled by the hypnotic effect which a profound knowledge
of a subject expounded by an exalted believer always exerts.
Intellectually he was incomparably the most alert man in the
room, and we felt it. Some of us had minds as dull as putty, and
some of us had been educated and drilled into a goose step of
conventionalism. Here was a man whose life and thoughts were
his own. He was refreshing. This was my first introduction to
Jack London.

The two dogs we took into the country with us were fine spec-

* Bond's diary of November 17, 1897, refers to a "Long talk with Jack
London on Socialism."

An intimate associate of Jack London in the Socialist movement was Anna
Strunsky. Judge Bond's journal at New Park says: "Aug. 13, 1905. Count A.
M. Lockwitsky and Anna Strunsky came from S.F. to spend Sunday and re-
mained overnight. She has the characteristics of genius. Though only 22 she
has a wide knowledge of literature and great talent for writing and speaking.
She is a radical socialist."

imens. One of them in particular had characteristics of such excellence as to be not improperly called character. He had a courage that, though unaggressive, was unyielding; a kindness and good nature that the most urbane man in the world might have observed with profit, and a willingness to do his work, and an untiring energy in carrying it out.†

I have had too much loyalty and affection from dogs to doubt that they have souls if men have them.

London liked these dogs, and particularly this one which I called Jack. His manner of dealing with dogs was different from anyone I ever knew, and I remarked it at the time with interest. Most people, including myself, pat, caress, and talk in more or less affectionate terms to a dog. London did none of this. He always spoke and acted toward the dog as if he recognized his noble qualities, respected them, but took them as a matter of course. It always seemed to me that he gave more to the dog than we did, for he gave understanding.

He had an appreciative and instant eye for fine traits and honored them in a dog as he would in a man.

During the winter I was busily engaged in mining on Eldorado Creek and saw London only occasionally. He went on several sled trips to locate claims in remoter districts, and observed and drank in the life about him. Prior to the Klondike experience he had two large adventures in life. While still a boy he had been a tramp and hoboed it about the country, gaining the point of view of, and developing great sympathy with, this element.

Then he had served as a seaman on a sailing schooner off Japan and in the Bering Sea. He was still a youth in his early twenties. From a monetary point of view his experience in the Klondike was profitless. Outside of the rare piece of luck which occasionally leads a man to set his stakes on a bonanza piece of ground, mining success calls for knowledge of the subject and a certain, if not a decided, business faculty. London lacked both.

He had the misfortune to develop scurvy, and left on a down

† Presumably Buck was half St. Bernard and half Scotch shepherd.

river boat in the early summer, paying his passage, I believe, by as much work as was possible in his condition.

When I next saw him he was married, had taken up writing as a means of livelihood, and was living in Oakland, California. I spent an interesting day at his house, where I had an opportunity of observing the beginning of a notable career and seeing the methods which brought him success.

His house at that time was but a small affair and scantily furnished. The room in which he worked contained a desk, a typewriter, and behind his chair in easy reach were the works of Herbert Spencer, Huxley, Darwin, and other authors. "I had to first read all these," he explained, "to get a basic knowledge for writing."

"Does writing pay, Jack?" I asked with the frankness of friendship. He answered, "I came out of the Klondike broke, found that my father had died and left some debts. I have paid up everything and am supporting three families.* The first year I never got a thing accepted, and I began to get morbid and believe I was turned down because I was a socialist. I now wonder how the first stuff that was finally accepted ever got by. But it is hard work. He who waits for the Muse to move him will never get anywhere. I write five thousand words a day to discipline and command myself. Much of it has to be torn up, but I make myself write it. Robert Louis Stevenson said that there eventually comes a feeling of great exaltation when a man realizes that he is master of his tools. I hope for that moment."

System and precision characterized his work. Newspaper clippings, articles from magazines and all data he wished to preserve were neatly bound in folders, labelled and filed handy for use. He was a tremendous worker, and an orderly one. He also visited me at our home in Santa Clara, and his description of the place is the beginning of *The Call of the Wild*.

Later when he had become recognized as an author of distinction he was sought after by many people of social prominence in

* He referred to his own family, his mother, and an old nurse.

and around San Francisco. Once I chaffed him at being a social butterfly. He replied:

"That side of life had been denied me, and when I began to be asked to the houses of prominent people I went to broaden my experience, and because I believed it a compliment to my efforts as an author. I was soon disillusioned by the discovery that I was merely being used as an advertising medium or possible feature of interest for other people's social functions. My last hostess held almost no conversation with me, her time being entirely taken up with another woman in mutual recitations of the notables they had met abroad. I think I have learned all that is necessary from such experiences and have cut them out."

During the last years of his life, after he had become a world-wide author, I regret that I never saw him. I should like to have as personal recollections the man in his maturity with all the added wealth to his virile mind that came from work, rich experiences, and notable success.

During his period of development the man was leonine in courage, brilliant in speech, loyal, and independent. The impression lasts over all these years that "Here was a man."

On November 5, 1897, Bond wrote from Dawson:

To begin with, the country is all right. Gold is found everywhere but not always in paying quantities. The only discouraged men are those who expected to find gold as plentiful as gravel. Eldorado is the richest creek. No mining is done on the Klondike, though its name is credited on the outside with it all. Some fellows are proposing to trade on this and have gotten together a number of claims on the Klondike for the purpose of selling to suckers.

There is scarcely what you would term a trained businessman in the country, one of ability and comprehension of the situation. The most prominent figure is Alexander McDonald, a laborer of Scotch extraction. He bought a claim on Eldorado last year for $300 and made a lot of money. He is a terrific plunger and buys right and left, often borrowing money at ten percent a month. He owed $150,000 some time ago, and his creditors thought they had him. In one day he took $30,000 out of the ground and saved himself. It is hard to tell what he is worth, perhaps millions, perhaps nothing.

Do you remember a letter I showed you describing the country from a fellow named Fox? He is a youth of twenty-two but old for his years. He has a claim on Eldorado, a 75 foot piece of ground which is probably very rich. Ten feet above him are two shafts which show $1,000 a running foot, six hundred feet wide. Fox will probably make from $30,000 to $60,000 out of it.

We are all well. It had been —20 F. but is warm again. If you want to read a good book which will give you some idea of life in a cold country, get *The Barren Ground of Northern Canada* by Warburton Pike.

I have broken the dogs to harness, and they are a great help but a great nuisance to cook for. We have 400 lbs. of horsemeat on the cabin roof, and every night I give them a mess of this covered with scraps and grease.

In regard to Alexander McDonald, McGillvray wrote in the *Herald*:

There is in Dawson no newspaper, no bank, no such thing as an insurance office, no shops except those of the two trading companies, where the clerks are to be bowed down to. They are most insolent in their manner of charging 3000 percent profit for a candle. One in Dawson must consider that he is being done a great favor to be allowed to purchase anything, and it is a curious sight to see "Alec" McDonald, worth several millions, endeavoring to be very polite to a puny clerk from whom he wishes to buy a few pounds of nails for one of his hundred cabins.

Of the dog population, McGillvray wrote:

I must tell you about the dogs. It is my honest conviction that no community of this size ever had so many dogs. It is estimated that there are nearly 1,500 of the animals in Dawson City, and as many more in the mines. Most of them are fine appearing fellows, and in the cold season net their owners handsome profits by hauling sleds heavily laden with supplies to the adjacent mining camps. In town they travel in companies ranging from ten to twenty, and the moment they catch sight of another dog away from the company the pack will give chase. Dog fights are so common as not to excite a passing glance.

As winter closed in on the Klondike most of the horses that came in during the summer and fall of 1897 had to be shot, as there was nothing for them to eat. A severe food shortage hit Dawson. Prices were astronomical and men who had not brought in enough for the winter were forced to move out or starve.

A few really did starve. Thirty years later, in London, the author was introduced to Mr. Van Millingen, who showed a photograph of a man who had died of starvation in a Klondike cabin as a result of having been snowbound for six weeks. The flesh had been cut from one of his legs by his ravenous partners and was actually boiling on the stove when help arrived.

Bond was a great admirer of the mounted police, a small group of whom were successful in keeping thousands of hard characters in good order. Only three murders were committed on the Canadian side while he was there. Two of the culprits were caught, convicted, and hung within a month. The third was hanged also, but only after a chase in winter across most of Canada at a huge cost to the government. The certainty of capture and conviction kept crime at a minimum. In Alaska just the opposite was true.

Bond's letters were often repetitious because there was no regular mail service and he could never be sure that a letter entrusted to a friend who was going out by dog sled would ever reach home. Later on in November he wrote from Dawson:

My first letter, which I sent by McGee, will probably never reach you, for he not only thrust it in his pocket in too careless a way, but it is said his party has been held up and his guide, Jack Dalton, killed.* This I hope will reach you through the kind offices of Mr. L. W. Fox, who is going out to try to dispose of some of his properties at the good figures which we hear obtain outside. He will tell you all about us, the country, and conditions of life here.

It has been from 20 to 25 degrees below zero for several days, but until one's breath begins to pop it is considered warm enough. If one is working or walking the dampness inside one's mittens is likely to freeze one's hands. You need not worry about my going around with wet feet.

I have located a claim on Ophir Creek just over the hill from Eldorado. In four days all the land on that creek was staked for a distance of ten miles. A good many men have started sinking, and I shall know something of its value within a month. I shall locate a claim in each district whenever an opportunity occurs. I hope to try for some moose before long, but with —20°, it is no fun camping out.

Our cabin is a good one and is chinked with moss. The roof, which projects in front five or six feet, is of slabs upon which a quantity of earth has been put. We have double windows which are a great luxury. At the end of the cabin we have six bunks like aboard ship, made of our boat lumber, also a table in the middle of the floor. A cache, or storeroom, is behind and joining the cabin. Though only 13 x 16, we have sufficient room for moving around, a light to read by and everything comfortable enough. Kerosene has risen to any price you may ask for it.

---

* Evidently this rumor was false. Bond's diary of October 17, 1907, in Seattle, reads: "Jack Dalton lunched with me and we spent almost all afternoon discussing his [copper] properties."

Kerry's saloon was pilfered the other night, and the thieves took $20,000 which was in a drawer: $8,000 of this belonged to a fellow called "Nigger Jim," and Kerry dreadingly told him of his loss, but that worthy, after comprehending the situation, replied, "Thank God they didn't take the kerosene." Tell Fox that the men who robbed Kerry's saloon have been caught and that Lord, the bartender, was the chief culprit. The money was recovered, and Nigger Jim has been celebrating the event.

While Fox is out I shall take charge of his property, for which he agrees to pay me $15 a day.* I have the privilege of absenting myself whenever I deem my own interests demand it. He has also hired Wickham at my instance, and I have unlimited confidence in his integrity.

The dogs are doing well. Jack is a great worker. I have him pull a sledge load to Eldorado Creek and the next day I ride home. Pat—the bald-faced joker we got from the expressman— is a shirk; he lets the lead dog pull him. They come around every night and make a great fuss for their boiled horse meat, scraps, and grease.

The river is frozen and we shall soon be obliged to stack up a lot of ice in front of the cabin which we will melt whenever we want water. I shall go up to Eldorado in a few days and take up my abode in Fox's cabin and shall use a straw tick he has. I have so little under me that I think of my own bed at home every time I get into mine here. Don't let father talk any unsophisticated youths into coming into this country, for it's a terror.

You would laugh to see the men in their parkas here. Those in which they work are made of drilling and extend below the knees: a hood lined with fur covers the head. Altogether they look like the new woman. Louis and I have moose skin parkas for very cold weather or for sleeping in. With these we look like two cows on their hind legs. While the outside world is talking of politics, poetry, and art, and fancying the subjects worthy of

* Bond drew up the contract between himself and Fox in longhand on half a sheet of paper. It was dated 18th November, 1897. Louis Bond and Jack London signed as witnesses.

much discussion, we find it impossible to get more interesting themes than bacon and beans and their proper cooking in such a temperature.

We asked Fox if he intended carrying a thermometer with him on his trip out. He said, "No, I think I shall carry a little bottle of mercury; when that freezes I shall know it's 40° below, and I can tell by the sound of my breath if it reaches 60° or 70° below." Those who find the winter climate so delightful are those who occupy front seats around saloon stoves and drink hot rum punches for a pastime. As a winter resort for families this country has not been sufficiently advertized. The northern lights at night are often most beautiful, but when I see the electric lights again in Santa Clara I shall make no comparisons unfavorable to the latter. I wish, though, that whenever Jags [Marshall's old dog] waddles up to a plate of food and contemptuously turns his nose up, you'd make him eat it, for it makes me jealous to think he is getting better food than I am.

November 30:

Sam Crawford's brother came to me with the confidential information that a new strike had been made up the Klondike about 25 miles. The next morning Stanley and I were up early and daylight saw us started. We had the sled, the two dogs, our fur robes, and three days rations of bacon, hard tack, and tea for ourselves, and three meals of horsemeat for the dogs. It was 42° below zero and a slight wind blowing downstream made it bitterly cold. I strapped on a bit of fur across my nose and two handkerchiefs over my face. In a short time these wrappings were a mass of ice from the condensation and freezing of the breath, but they afforded a great protection. I wore besides a lynx skin cap, a mackinaw suit, jagers underneath and a sweater, while my feet were encased in a heavy pair of socks, a pair of thick German stockings, a pair of arctic socks, and moose skin moccasins. My hands were protected by moose mittens. I carried also a drill parka with a hood lined with fox tails.

The dogs were cold and anxious to travel fast, and in consequence we had to trot all the way. We made twelve miles in two hours and a half, and, having no tent, were obliged to lay up for the night at a cabin for lodgers. Twelve men and ourselves and six or eight dogs occupied this abode. We slept on the ground and paid a dollar each for the privilege, and took turns cooking on the stove. It was the filthiest place I ever saw. Stanley and I cooked our bacon and tea and turned in and regaled each other for an hour or so with the meals we had eaten in civilization during the last year.

We had hardly gone to sleep when a dog team laden with more prospectors arrived. The new arrivals awakened us to inquire about the news in town: the fact that the dance hall, the opera house, and the Dominion had burned down furnished them food for unending talk and speculation. After getting their own dinner they cooked one for the dogs, the distribution of which caused no end of fighting and whippings. At 2 A.M. they settled down for the night, and I prepared for a rest, but by this time Stanley commenced such a vigorous and aggressive snoring that I was obliged to admit that he was the greater disturber.

We were up early, and after some more bacon, hard tack, and tea started up the river with the sled. It was a steel bluish gray morning, and I have since learned that the thermometer at headquarters in town showed 58° below zero. The sun was never apparent above the horizon, but the tops of the high hills were illuminated with its rays about midday. Everything the breath reached was covered with ice. We eventually arrived at the tributary and ascended to its head. Even though a number of claims had been staked no work had been done, and we regarded it as too unfavorable. Disappointed, we turned back.

Away to the east some 50 miles we beheld the Rocky Mountain Range, its snowy peaks reflecting the sun's rays. Not a sound could be heard nor a living thing seen, and the vastness and awe of solitude was never before so impressed on me. Across that range of mountains lies the valley of the MacKenzie, which pours an enormous volume of water into the Arctic Ocean.

It was dark before we returned to the cabin. The new moon was up, and the North Star almost directly overhead, and the Big Dipper's stars twinkled in the frosty atmosphere like electric lights. The exhilaration we felt immediately vanished as we were once more inside the "Hog Ranch" which we had appropriately named our lodging. Twenty of us cooked, loaned each other plates and cups without even washing them, prepared dog food, and occupied every available foot of the cabin that night. The dogs slept on us or fought, as the spirit moved. Crackling oaths coupled with the Saviour's name interlarded the exchange of ideas and sentiments. Slumber at length settled down on that chaotic crowd, and, after more reminiscences of dinners past and comforts enjoyed between Stanley and myself, Morpheus interrupted my musings on the constitutional clause that all men were born equal. It was dark when we pulled out and reached Dawson by daylight.

Henceforth I live to eat. Much reflection convinces me it's the highest aim of man. Those who dedicate their lives to ambition and think to inscribe their names in the book of fame in letters of gold by making a million are but building in sand and have developed but a low degree of consciousness. I would build pyramids of porterhouse, obelisks of oysters, and punctuate the meter of my poetry with pie.

Bond's craving for good food was temporarily satisfied, for he wrote to his mother on December 6:

Col. Augustus J. Bowie [a wealthy mining engineer] had Louis and me to dinner. We had roast beef, a magnificent boiled ham, succotash, mashed potatoes, stewed tomatoes, chard, yeast bread, peas, and mince pie. I honored my host by numerous helpings and copious consumption. It was a gorge.

To alleviate the monotony of the long dark winter, the men at the diggings took turns visiting Dawson, where saloons and dance halls offered gay but expensive entertainment. In very cold weather the men arriving from the mines would enter a saloon with beard and whiskers so frosted as to be quite unrecognizable. Betting on their identities was a favorite pastime as they began thawing out over the stove.

The Bonds and a group of friends were enjoying the hospitality of the Dominion Saloon* one night when a girl named Mukluk Maud (she always wore waterproof Eskimo mukluk boots) put her foot on the brass rail and said, "Come on, boys, and have a drink," ordering champagne for the crowd. Champagne was selling in the dance hall for $40 a pint, and the bill came to $200, which she paid from a moose-skin sack of gold dust. The miners responded by buying a round, and when that was down the hatch Maud ordered another, and so forth until $3,000 worth of champagne had been consumed, half of which was paid for by the sporty girl. It was her way of showing that her current lover had struck it rich.

Mukluk Maud had come to Dawson on a dog team, three hundred miles up the frozen river from Circle City. She had "lived on the square like a true married pair" with more than one man, but boredom always brought her back to the dance hall. A year later an abandoned lover killed her and then took his own life.

About such entertainment as was afforded by Kerry's and the Dominion, Marshall's journal records:

The saloons and dance halls offered heat and light, companionship, women, liquor, and music. They were the clubs of the community, were well patronized, kept most men from going insane, and demoralized and ruined a few. It is hard to imagine what the dreary winter of 1897-98 would have been

* The bartender of the Dominion was quite a gentleman and a graduate of Oxford.

without them. The comfortable urban moralist is in no position to censure or pass judgment upon either men or women so situated. The Yukon was a world unto itself, an American Siberia where our avarice, ambition, or love of adventure had condemned us to exile.

I can't but recall with pleasure the occasional meetings of genial spirits just down from the creeks, after a freezing walk of from fifteen to thirty miles, as they ran into one another at the bar seeking a drink of Scotch. After a few drinks they would burst into song. What pleasure it used to be if Gordon Bettles added his jovial and magnetic personality and if he were sufficently primed to sing his ever appreciated drinking song:

> Ther's Henry Ward Beecher
> And Sunday-school teachers,
> All drink of the sassafras root;
> But you bet all the same,
> If it had its right name,
> It's the juice of the forbidden fruit.

Most of the dance hall women stood on an equal footing with the men in that they had done their share and played the game on the trail, in running the river or in "mushing over the ice." This common experience was a bond of sympathy and understanding between them. The women offered the lotus of femininity, and the men eagerly ate it up. Most of these women lived openly, and generally faithfully, with men who had won their affections.

These girls were paid a salary of fifty dollars a week for dancing, and etiquette demanded that a man should escort his partner to the bar and set up the drinks after each dance. The bartender handed the fair one a poker chip along with her drink to be cashed in at the end of the evening. Naturally she poured out a drink barely sufficient to wet her lips as this was more profitable to the house and to the dancer's well-being also. A smart girl with a salary and chips would easily average a thousand dollars a month.

On the subject of gambling, McGillvray wrote:

The manner of hazarding money is unique even in a mining camp. The player takes his seat at a faro table, passes over his sack of gold dust to the dealer, who drops it into a small pigeon-hole. The chance of "overplaying his sack" devolves upon the player's honor. He is given full credit and can call for as many chips from the check rack as he desires.

As the checks are passed out a tab is dropped on his sack. At the conclusion of the play the chips on hand are credited to the account of the sack. The dealer hands the player a slip of paper showing the condition of the account, and the latter takes it and his sack of gold to the bar. If he has lost he weighs out his gold dust, or, in the event of winning, the barkeeper does the paying.

About four o'clock one morning a miner known as "Shorty" left his seat at the table where he had been playing all night, saying that he had gone broke. The dealer handed him his bag of dust and his slip, the latter corresponding almost to the grain with the value of the gold. "Shorty" walked over to the bar and invited a couple of other miners to have a drink. Then he was seized with a fatal fit of forgetfulness.

He edged toward the door and was about to push it open when the bartender called to him: "Say, Shorty, haven't you forgot something?"

"Forgot, hell!" exclaimed "Shorty," and the door swung out. When it rebounded it stopped half way, obstructed in its inward passage by the body of a dying man. A flash of flame and the report of a pistol from somewhere in that low ceilinged, smoke laden room, explained the draught of cold air that came in through the half open door. "Shorty" was buried the next day.

On Saturday night, January 1, 1898, the Bonds attended a masquerade ball at the M & M Dance Hall, which was noted for its beautiful girls. Since a substantial prize was being offered for the most original costume, the girls outdid themselves in theatrical effects. Marshall noticed a husky girl with long arms and legs, whom he had never seen before, gliding around the dance floor. She was elegantly gowned but behaved outrageously, whirling her dancing partners right up in the air. When the girls filed past the judges' stand each was asked to explain whom she was dressed up to represent. Most of the queens and great ladies of history put in an appearance that night, but when the big girl was asked who she was, she boomed out, "I'm a whore!" A scuffle ensued in which her wig and make-up were knocked off, revealing the features of Addison Mizner. Many years later Mizner made a fortune designing gaudy Spanish mansions for the ultra-rich at Boca Raton, Florida, and he also did one at 656 Park Lane in Santa Barbara at a cost of $500,000.

Another colorful character was Arizona Charlie Meadows, of whom O. H. P. La Farge wrote:

We were sitting one day in front of our cabin shortly after our arrival when a tall man in a black frock coat, black trousers, and a large black sombrero passed by. His long curly hair hung down sweeping his shoulders. He had narrow piercing eyes, a black mustache, and a small goatee. With him was a rather nice looking dance hall girl. The man was so curious looking and evidently on show that several of us burst out laughing.

Marshall Bond, who was with us, said, "You had better be careful; that's Arizona Charlie Meadows, one of the few dead-shots here and reputed to be dangerous, and that's his girl, Diamond Toothed Gertie."

We were silenced at once but curious about Gertie. It appears that in order to arouse envy or more attention she had had a small diamond set in her front tooth and when she smiled her sparkle was immense.

In December, Marshall Bond wrote to his parents at New Park:

Messrs. Seagrave and Van Millingen, two gentlemen from

Victoria, leave tomorrow up the river and will take this with them. Should they go to California, please do all you can to entertain them, as they are good fellows.

Joaquin Miller, the "Poet of the Sierras," has just returned from Circle City and will probably be here the balance of the winter. The cold has, I fancy, rather frozen his muse and in consequence his effusions have a jerky sort of style so that one might suppose each line represented a thaw. He recited to Newberry, the sketch artist of the N.Y. *Herald,* a recent production of the Klondike which goes after this fashion:

> Say have you been to the Klondike?
> Have you climbed the mountains which beat
> their heads against the sky? etc.

I doubt if it will keep either Miller or the Klondike alive in the minds of man.

Dispatches just in from Fort Yukon tell a tale which makes us proud that the U.S. Army has such officers as Capt. Ray. The improvident and tough element were induced to depart for that point before the river froze as it was generally understood plenty of provisions were to be had there. It seems the men organized a party for the purpose of pillaging the stores at Yukon. Capt. Ray and Lt. Richardson are there for the purpose of establishing a post to quarter troops next year but had none with them. Learning that an attack was to be made, Ray and Richardson put on their uniforms, raised the stars and stripes over the building and took possession. Ray then told the mob to come on if it thought best. He said he would issue rations, but that those who had money would have to pay, while those who did not would have to cut wood in lieu of payment. This singlehanded resistance did the business, and the mob dropped into line and obeyed.

Among the properties for sale are claims No. 24, 25, and 26 on Eldorado. I have no doubt they are immensely rich. The price at which they are held, I fancy, is one million dollars. Jne Erickson, the owner of No. 10 Eldorado, an uninterested observer, tells me he thinks they will have $500,000 on the dumps by June.

Therefore I am of the opinion that a company that would pay the price asked would make money.

A week from tonight is Christmas Eve. I hope Fox will get the little nuggets to you in time. Please give one each to Bertha* and Kate† in the shape of lace pins.

December 30:

A paper, the Seattle *P.I.*, I think, of Oct. 2nd, has reached town and the heavy headlines, "Death, Famine, and Disease in Dawson," have caused us some little amusement. Life in Alaska makes every man a liar, nevertheless we are enjoying the best of health and our larder is still ample. Such a country for rumors I have never seen, and I wish to caution you that no matter if you hear we are hung, drawn, and quartered, there is no occasion for worriment.

Christmas was a most enjoyable day. Stanley and I each got an icicle in our stockings—kind remembrances from one another. In the evening we had a gorge at Col. Bowie's. Sidney Hansard brought up a phonograph which a squaw man has for his inamorata, and we had a musical feast. We sat for hours and listened to Sousa, Robin Hood, and Gilmour's band and appreciated this tinpanny and secondhand music as only those who have none at all can appreciate it. Quite a lot of scurvy in camp. The doctor says it is due largely to wretchedly cooked food and to lack of personal cleanliness. I take my morning bath regularly and feel like a two year old out for an exercise gallop.

Every morning when the temperature was above 50° below zero Bond would soap himself in the cabin, step out of doors with a bucket of warm water which he would pour over himself to rinse off the suds, and quickly jump back indoors before freezing solid. Of course the other miners thought he was crazy.

---

* Bertha Potter, now Mrs. William E. Boeing, widow of the airplane magnate.

† Kate Bond, Louis' daughter, now Mrs. Sidney Warner.

A letter of February 15, 1898, says:

Mayor Wood of Seattle and a Mr. Willis Carr arrived here yesterday with dog teams from the lower river and brought up some mail from Fort Yukon. Louis, Stanley, and Rainey went on a stampede night before last to Swede Gulch—about eight miles up the river—and located claims. There was such a crowd following behind that they had to locate claims by candlelight. It was caused by a Swede bringing in a handkerchief of dirt which panned 85¢.

Again on April 10, at Fox's Eldorado claim:

A squaw man, who has the adjoining lay, and I are going to build a joint flume to conduct the water to our dumps. While we each have sufficient lumber for sluice boxes, we have nothing to construct a flume with; so we are whip-sawing it. He takes the pit end while I saw on top. It is astonishing what fine boards can be made in this way. It is magnificent exercise for the back.

The first of May should see us shovelling into the boxes, and I hope the cleanup will not be disappointing. Am glad you liked Stanley's letters to the paper. I think he writes well, and he writes very rapidly, too. Sometime during the summer I shall start homeward.

Eldorado Creek eventually proved to be the richest in the Klondike, producing $25,000,000 by the end of 1902. One claim alone produced $1,500,000. It was probably the richest single placer deposit ever discovered. The method of mining was to sink holes to bedrock and then tunnel outward. Of course the gravel was completely frozen so that every evening fires had to be built in the tunnels to thaw out enough ground for the next day's work. The gravel was piled up outside to await the spring "cleanup," when water became available. Working in frozen gravel had one great

advantage; it prevented cave-ins. Marshall employed various people as day laborers on Fox's claim, and about one of
them his journal says:

Part of the time I had as workman and cabin mate, Ned Walsh
of New York. He was a graduate of St. Mark's School and Harvard University, was an ex-member of the New York Stock Exchange, and a member of the Union Club. He was a reckless
fellow with great personal courage and a delightful disposition
who, while he worked for me, did a full and fair day's work
each day.

Bond's last Klondike letter was dated June 2, 1898:

We know war has been declared and that the Philippines are
ours. A fellow bringing in a paper of May 3rd with this information made $900 reading it.

Have almost finished sluicing Fox's lay. The water is scarce
and we have to catch it when others are not using it. When I
turned in at 8 A.M. this morning it was the first time in 28 hours.
The men are played out, and I have to fairly drag them out of
bed, and I do all the cooking, too. Stanley has just left for town
to bring us a little grub and to try and sell the dogs. I told him to
ask $500. Alec McDonald,* the lucky man of the country, went
by last night with four pack horses loaded with 200 lbs. of gold
each. I have worked out Fox's lay of 44 x 100 ft. and taken out
$25,000, of which his profit is $6,000.

In round numbers I shall have $3,000, of which Louis and
Stanley get $1,000 each. Deducting father's one-third and ex-
penses out of the country, I shall have less than I could have
made at home playing marbles or shooting craps. The experience has been a bitter one, but instructive, and personally I can
accept the result quite philosophically.

---

* Alec McDonald, "King of the Klondike," eventually lost his fortune in
reckless mining speculations and died broke.

As soon as I can get away from here, I shall go to town and commence converting everything into cash and rustle to dispose of my claims. But my fondest dreams will be realized if I succeed in getting together the $6,000 necessary to repay Father. I shall have some nice nuggets for you. You cannot possibly imagine how I look forward to going home. The merest trifles one fails to observe in civilization become objects of much thought and adoration here. A bath tub, a chair, a woman with a red ribbon around her neck. An orchestra would inebriate me. But food is the thing one's mind constantly dwells on. It appears like a mirage to the sense, ever before the eyes, beautiful to contemplate, but impossible to reach.

Marshall and his brother came home on separate boats. What became of the dogs remains a mystery. Louis tried to take "Buck" aboard his ship, the S.S. *Alice,* but for some reason was not allowed to do so. He left the dog behind after paying for its passage to Seattle on a later boat. When Louis met this boat the dog was not on board and was never heard of again. Presumably it was sold by a dishonest shipping clerk.

In the fall of 1898 when Marshall had returned to Santa Clara, he convinced Judge Bond that great wealth awaited any company willing to go to the expense of bringing hydraulic mining equipment into the Klondike. Consequently they went to London, then the mining center of the world, and persuaded an experienced company to send one of its vice-presidents out to look the situation over. By the time the Englishman arrived in San Francisco boatloads of broke and disillusioned prospectors were arriving from Alaska. Their tales of misery and hardship so unnerved the man from London that he called off the deal. A few years later, after the railroad was completed across White Pass, hydraulic machinery was brought in and proved even more profitable than the Bonds had anticipated.

The total production of gold from the Klondike was $178,000,000. The Bonds' claims contained gold, but not enough to offset the high cost of manual labor, and didn't bring enough when sold to repay Judge Bond's $6,000 loan. To make matters worse, the decision to go into gold mining in the first place cost Marshall a fortune. Judge Bond had been offered the Seattle *Post Intelligencer* for $150,000 and agreed to buy it if his son would settle down and take over the editorship. Marshall, however, was so imbued with dreams of gold and high adventure that he spurned the offer. As things eventually turned out, the *Post Intelligencer* became the only real gold mine in the situation, and Marshall's share in it would have amounted to over a million dollars.

When Marshall Bond returned from London the struggle in the Philippines was still in full swing. Anxious to serve his country and being a lover of horses, he got a job caring for a cargo of assorted livestock aboard the S. S. *Victoria*, bound for the United States Cavalry in Manila. Feeding, watering, and cleaning up after these animals was arduous work, especially in rough seas during the long Pacific voyage. Just before it arrived in Manila the ship was hit by a typhoon. The storm was so violent that half the animals got their legs broken; their suffering was so intense they had to be shot. Marshall's only surviving letter about Manila was written to his fiancée:

Monday, Oct. 9th 1899

Dear Amy:

We sighted Luzon this morning after breakfast. The island from the sea approach presents a mountainous front which continues until Corregidor rock is reached. This bald island stands in the entrance of Manila harbor; a white lighthouse crowns its summit. The harbor is like a huge lake and from the entrance to Manila is thirty miles.

We are dressed in white linen; the jacket buttons up so that it is unnecessary to wear either a shirt or collar. As our voyage down the bay continued we could see Manila in the distance while on the right shore and nearer us was Cavite. It was off this place that Dewey's engagement took place last May. We dropped anchor about three miles from Manila as night settled down on us. Soon to the north a searchlight flashed out a message. From over near Cavite the message was answered by another man-of-war. The heat was oppressive, and every available space on the upper deck was filled with horses hauled up from the sweltering lower deck. They surrounded the smoking room so that it was almost impossible to get in or out. A more sweltering or arduous night I have never spent.

When we arose this morning the cathedrals, palace, monasteries, and typically Spanish buildings were visible from the shore. It is a different looking town than I ever saw before. We soon learned that a hot fight had been going on for two days just outside Cavite, and that the Insurgents had actually attacked within four miles of Manila. We pulled up anchor and steamed nearer shore. As we passed *H.M.S. Endymion* she dipped her flag and her band played "America" and "Hail Columbia." Our officers took off their caps, and the troops cheered.

It is impossible to lay a big ship alongside the Manila wharves, so we had to lower our cattle over the sides onto lighters. I went ashore on the first launch and spent a most interesting day. Crowds of little Filipinos are seen everywhere on our launches, steamers, and among officers. Nevertheless every solitary one of them is supposed to be donating monthly to Aguinaldo's cause. The men look like the pictures you have seen; the women wear a low bodice sort of thing of flimsy material and cut square, leaving the shoulders and chest bare. Many of them allow their long black hair to hang loose.

The launch takes you up a stream walled on both sides. On the right bank is the "Walled City." It contains the palace, the monasteries, and other important buildings, while its moat, wall, and battlements present one of the best preserved examples of the impregnable fortifications of two or three centuries ago. These evidences of Spain's former grandeur and glory bring you face to face with the past. You appreciate how high she was then and you feel how low she has fallen now.

The town is Spanish in every appearance but very much awake now. U. S. Troops are seen everywhere. Officers go dashing by, troopers come and go with dispatches, there is a glorious and exciting feeling in the air, and you realize that the highest tragedy mankind can play is on. Here is the real thing; passions are not pretence, and things are not played but performed. I wish I had enough money to enable me to remain for awhile.

General Lawton is south of the city campaigning; my old acquaintance General Young is forty miles north at San Fernando. Aguinaldo and his main command are in the district. Lawton and Young are both preparing for a reputation, for in all probability the one with the best record will succeed to Shafter's star. The 3rd Cavalry go at once to join Young. It seems probable that I shall be able to go with them and I wouldn't miss the experience for anything. Though I can only be gone a couple of days I hope to see a little of the action.

Among other things I went through the hospital today. It is composed of a series of buildings built around a large plaza or garden. There were several hundred patients undergoing treatment for fever, wounds, and various complaints. I fancied you there and wondered how long you would last in that muggy medicinal atmosphere. I can scarcely wait to see you again. This letter goes by the *St. Paul* which also carries the body of poor Capt. Safford who was killed last evening almost in sight of here.

Affectionately yours,
Marshall

Bond never saw actual combat in the Philippines. In a few days his ship left Manila for Nagasaki, Japan, and then returned to the United States.

The Colorado River

M<small>ARSHALL</small> B<small>OND</small> loved the desert scenery of the lower Colorado basin with its monumental peaks, its abundant bird and animal life, its salubrious climate, and the peaceful river winding for hundreds of miles through a country rich in mines and legends of Spanish explorers.* He spent many winter months during the first two decades of the twentieth century prospecting there and examining numerous claims being offered for sale by other prospectors. In spite of his failure in the Klondike, the mystic vision of sudden wealth illuminated his horizons and impelled him ever onward in its quest.

A lesson he learned to his sorrow at an Arizona mine was not to trust the word of "old-timers" whose remembrance of things past was usually highly colored by dreams of opulence, if not downright dishonesty. An old-timer showed him an abandoned shaft that had filled with water. He said the owner had died and his widow had been unable to con-

---

* In March, 1909, he visited the south rim of the Grand Canyon, where he met the writer John Burroughs and the celebrated author, explorer, and conservationist John Muir, founder of the Sierra Club. He was very sympathetic to all of Muir's ideas except for the latter's dislike of hunting.

tinue development. He claimed he had worked in the shaft himself and that at the bottom, about a hundred feet down, a two-foot vein of high-grade silver ore had been uncovered at the time of the owner's death. He was so convincing and sincere that Bond raised enough money from his friends to pump out and retimber the shaft. Instead of two feet of high-grade silver ore, he found two inches of low-grade zinc.

In 1825 a young British naval officer had set out from Mexico City on a trip through northern Mexico that was to consume the better part of four years. His main objective was the study of the pearl fisheries in Baja California, but he attained lasting recognition when the west branch of the lower Colorado River was named for him. He was Lieutenant R. W. H. Hardy, R.N., and his adventures, including the exploration of the delta of the Colorado and Hardy rivers, are described in his book *Travels in the Interior of Mexico, in 1825, 1826, 1827, and 1828*.

Marshall Bond read this entertaining and informative book and was eager to visit the delta area, still wild and remote, even though three-quarters of a century had passed. In Hardy's day there were thousands of Cocopa Indians living in a most primitive condition along the banks of the river. In fact, their curiosity and numbers gave Hardy no little concern, especially when his small craft lay stranded in the mud for hours between the tidal bores that rolled in and out from the Gulf of California. The Indians told him that his was the first boat to venture up the river.* Some of the descendants of these Indians still inhabited the area and lived in almost the same condition of poverty when Bond and his wife arrived in Yuma on New Year's Day, 1902.

A rowboat was purchased in Yuma and a Cocopa Indian

---

* In 1540 Hernando de Alarcón pushed up the Colorado 100 miles beyond the mouth of the Gila in a vain attempt to bring supplies to Francisco de Coronado.

named Jim hired as a guide. Fifty dollars' worth of provisions furnished their larder, and the storekeeper who had recommended Jim said that they would be less likely to be murdered by a Cocopa than by a white guide. He also explained that, since the lower Colorado was Cocopa country, Mojave Indians were afraid to go there.

Bond's diary for January, 1902, describes the trip as follows:

January 6

Jim proved to be a fine looking specimen. He was a good six feet in height and wore long black hair which hung to his waist. His face was streaked with red and green paint. He wore a pair of blue overalls and a black cotton shirt. Our ability to understand one another lay in his limited knowledge of English and my equally restricted Spanish.

We camped the first night at the Mexican border, for it was a wise precaution to get a pass from the Chief of Line Riders before venturing into Mexico. The next morning after breakfast Amy and I followed an Indian trail which Jim said would lead us to the "Jefe's." For about a mile it paralleled the Imperial Canal where we passed a large dredge at work. We came to the company headquarters around noon and had lunch with the men. Finally the path emerged into a clearing where there were several adobe huts and some tillable land. In front of one were tied two ponies, and on top of it was the sign "Gendarmaria Fiscal." It was the office of an important personage, the Bustamente or head line rider.

At the sound of our approach the occupant came out. He was a stocky man with a black beard but rather light complexion. He was wearing tight trousers, a flannel shirt, and pointed shoes that were much too long. On his head was a peaked sombrero of gray beaver with an enormous brim heavily stitched with gold. At the sight of a woman he bowed, but his surprise was considerable when he learned we were actually contemplating so laborious a trip when in his view there was no need for it. However, without hesitation he said with a shrug and a smile: "The country is yours."

We at once took our departure and started down river at 2 P.M. Saw many quail on the way and killed one duck. We camped on a bank overlooking the river at 4 P.M. Flat country with mountains in the distance. Cottonwood trees border the stream and arrow weed grows everywhere. Cooked our duck in the reflecting oven and it was excellent. The sun set at 5 P.M., and darkness followed almost immediately.

January 7

It was pretty cold last night, and water froze in our buckets. Last night Jim built a good fire, put one of his tiny blankets under him, the other over him, and, lighting a cigarette, prepared for the night. When he awoke this morning he said he was "mucho frio."

We arose at 6 A.M. and, while cooking breakfast, I remarked to Amy that Jim would have little respect for me seeing me do the cooking while she loafed. To this she replid: "I would have less to eat if you didn't." We pulled out at 9 A.M., and a mile downstream discovered Jim had forgotten the axe, and sent him back for it. We passed huge flocks of pelicans and cranes, and smaller ones of geese and ducks. I killed one duck. Saw many deer tracks where we stopped for lunch.

We met a white man in a boat. He informed us that he was trapping beaver; there were lots of them but the smartest he had ever seen being both cunning and wary. He had only caught one so far that day. He said he sold the pelts in Chicago for $6.00 a piece. Before making camp we passed two cowboys and a small bunch of cattle.

Last night Amy and I divided the one duck, and I cooked three big pieces of bacon for Jim. This he refused to touch, though he ate some beans and seemed surly all evening. I believe it was due to his disappointment over not getting any duck. So tonight to show him that in camp all fared alike, I divided the duck between him and Amy and took bacon myself. The effect was as I had anticipated, for Jim fairly beamed the rest of the evening.

After Amy had retired Jim lay by the fire smoking a cigarette. With a knowing smile he said, "Where that man in boat say he was going?"

"To the Hardy River," I replied.

"He no go," said Jim.

"Why not?" I asked in Spanish.

"No tiene papel," answered Jim, meaning he had no permit and would therefore take no chances of going to jail by showing up among the Mexicans below the Indian country. We saw many fish ducks. They were black with long heads, necks, tails, and bodies and were reddish around the eyes.

January 8

Another day through the same flat country. Last night was the coldest yet. Saw great flocks of cranes which made a scolding sort of noise and were very wary of approach. I killed three spoonbills and took a swim at lunch. Jim, who has had his hair done up in mud, took it down, and the effect was like a shampoo. We made a camp in a clump of willows and cottonwoods. Dinner was great with a spoonbill a piece.

January 9

Pulled out at 9:15. Jim has been a most industrious oarsman all the way, but since we have been making rather poor progress, I gave up watching for ducks and rowed diligently. Nevertheless I got two spoonbills during the day. We stopped at noon by some Cocopa ranches but saw only one Indian.

The Cocopa country was higher ground and better adapted to habitation than any we have thus far passed. About 3 P.M. we saw a lot of children scampering up the bank in evident alarm at our approach. They wore nothing but little undershirts, and one was wholly naked. Jim said they were his brother's children. The brother and two squaws appeared and were most desirous for us to land, but we kept on for a mile or two.

Jim's wife lives about half a mile back from the river, and he begged so strenuously to be allowed to see her and gave so many excuses against going on, that we finally camped. Jim returned about dinner time with another blanket, but hearing some shouting down river betook himself in that direction and didn't show up again till morning.

January 10

While we were cooking breakfast, Jim's brother, an ugly mean looking old cuss, showed up. He begged for tobacco. I gave him some Bull Durham, but he seemed to be such an old stinker that I took most of it back. When Jim showed up for breakfast, I gave him a big helping of hot cereal, a chunk of bread and butter, and a cup of coffee with two lumps of sugar and condensed milk. I covered the cereal with a generous coat of sugar. As Jim began to eat, his brother kept up a vigorous powwow in Cocopa. Suddenly Jim arose and with a look of annoyance and resignation started to go away. His brother made a movement to sit down in his stead, looking at me for approval. Upon asking Jim the meaning of this he simply replied that his brother had asked to eat his breakfast. I ordered Jim to eat his own breakfast and promised to give his brother something later. Another buck arrived while Jim's brother was shovelling his food, but there was nothing left but a few lumps of sugar which, however, seemed to give great satisfaction. They were wonderfully impressed with our guns and outfit, and I filled them with amazement palming a coin.

During lunch at the foot of a high mesa I killed three ducks, a mallard drake, and two spoonbills. Passed Colony Landing at 2 P.M. A cleared river bank and a couple of Indian huts were all the evidence we saw of a landing. We camped at 4 P.M., and I made biscuits for the first time.

We think we are about ten miles from the Hardy River. As the tide fills that stream with salt water for a considerable distance beyond its mouth, we shall take a two day supply of fresh water with us in canteens and pails. We are nearing the Cocopa Mts. which appear to be about twenty miles away.

January 11

We pulled out at 8:30. The country became more open, and in the distance could be seen innumerable mountains forming the backbone of the Lower California peninsula. They were all shapes from high table land to sharp cones. A number of cattle and horses were to be seen along the banks, the latter in fine condition.

I saw a wild boar on the bank 150 yds. away and fired but missed him. We landed but could not find him. Rounding a curve, we saw a large flock of snow geese on a sand bar just ahead. When within 200 yds. I fired my rifle and killed one. Though hit squarely in the breast it flopped along for 50 feet or more.

At Adam's camp on the left bank, one mile from the Hardy, we were hailed by an old man who asked us to land and give him the news. I had saved the Los Angeles papers of the 3rd and 4th for just such an occasion and, it being 11:30, we landed for the double purpose of getting information and giving the old man the papers.

He proved to be a German, born in Holstein, but who had been on the river for nearly forty years. He was very polite and considerate of Amy addressing her as "madam" and getting her a plank to step on as the bank was muddy. He had the habit of unconsciously exclaiming "By God" before every sentence. His name was Charlie Tyson and said he had been down to the Gulf on a miserable tub of a sailboat with a man who wanted to examine some soda beds there. Though but 20 miles overland to the Gulf, he said it was 150 miles by river. He also told us there were great numbers of curlew there, and a good many antelope a bit further down the coast on the Lower California side.

While we were preparing lunch, the old man eagerly read the papers getting out an old rusty pair of glasses to do so. He finally discarded the glasses calling our attention to his ability to do without them which he attributed to the superiority of the climate over that of Yuma where, he said, such a feat would be impossible.

The tides are very appreciable at this point, and the water receded considerably while we were at lunch. When the tides are highest great tidal waves called "bores" rush up and overflow the banks of the river. Adams and his vaqueros were away.

A half breed American-Mexican cattleman, who has a ranch above the Cocopa rancherias, rode up. He had a blanket behind his saddle, an old tin can for cooking, and a home made pair of rawhide chaps. He was armed with a Colt 45 sixshooter. I got out my Luger to show him its superiority, but, having put it together wrong, it would not work at all. He was an agreeable fellow and asked us to stop at his ranch on our way up river. I gave each of them a sack of Bull Durham and to the cattleman a small box of figs which he said he would take home to his six children.

Bidding the two men goodbye we rowed down to the mouth of the Hardy and started up that stream. The Hardy is a broad sluggish stream with scarcely any trees along its banks. The current is so slow that the water is too salty from the tides to be agreeable. We pulled upstream for five or six miles and camped at a ranch belonging to Mr. Jenkins but no one was there. A corral and a shack of a barn mark the spot.

As the sun set the fish began to jump. They were numerous and large judging from the noise of their splashes. I got out a large hook and line and, using a plover's leg for bait, attached it to the stern of the boat and left it there for the night. We had the goose for dinner; it was good but a little underdone. While sitting by the fire after dinner Jim began making calculations of the amount of money due him thus far for acting as guide. He finally said, "You lose $5.25 to me now," and grew very complacent at the thought of the wealth I admitted I owed him.

January 12

"What do you want for breakfast?" I asked Amy.

With a yawn she replied, "A good mountain trout."

I went down to the boat and found the fishing line taut with something very heavy pulling at the end. It proved to be a large whitefish having scales and a big mouth.* It must have weighed 15 lbs. I carried it up to Amy and said, "Here's your trout." However, the meat was soft and without much flavor. After breakfast I took my Luger apart and fixed it.

Both the wind and the tide were against us all day, so that Jim and I had to fight every foot of the way. The Hardy averages 100 to 150 ft. in width. It is crooked but is confined within its banks which rise five or six feet on either side. The left bank has considerable rushes. Our direction is away from the Colorado toward the Cocopa Mts. on the west. We camped for the night near Jenkins' white boat about five miles from his ranch. I killed a duck and a crane. We roasted the latter in the reflecting oven, and it proved to be very good not unlike duck or goose.

January 13

When I arose at daybreak, the tide was running upstream at two or three knots an hour. Judging from the volume of water it had been coming in for some time. Both Jim and I felt jubilant at the prospect of a good current with us. However, by the time we had finished breakfast and loaded the boat, the water was still. We headed upstream for the mouth of the Pescador which Jim thinks we shall reach by "media dia." The wind and tide soon turned against us, and it was a dead pull all the way.

At noon we reached the Pescador and found it to be a small stream flowing into the Hardy from the northeast. The Cocopa Mts. do not now appear to be over 8 or 10 miles distant. We entered the Pescador and, it being quite shallow in many places, had much difficulty at times getting our boat forward. Amy prepared quail for dinner which were excellent.

January 14

After breakfast Jim and I went deer hunting leaving Amy in camp. Saw tracks but no deer. Amy has some qualms about be-

* The largest North American minnow, found only in the Colorado River and known as the Colorado salmon or squaw fish (*Ptychocheilus lucius*), which weighs up to 80 pounds.

ing left alone in camp in this desolate country but I have none. She's a good shot and with her double barreled shotgun should be able to discourage unwanted intruders.

January 15

Amy and I went hunting after breakfast. We crossed the Pescador and headed upstream. Soon we came across a covey of quail. Amy fired three or four shots but missed. Later in the day she got three.

January 16

We cooked over a hundred biscuits this morning in order to have a sufficient supply to take us down the Hardy as its water is not fit for cooking. While Amy was cleaning up, I killed four quail near our camp.

We started down the Pescador at 11:30 and had considerable trouble owing to shallow water. When we reached the lowest part of the stream we found it rapidly running dry due to an ebb tide. I had to take off my trousers and jump overboard to get the boat through. The bottom of the Pescador is a clay mud into which I sank very deep but, nevertheless, was able to accomplish more than by staying in the boat. We noticed a great many large turtles dead on the banks of the Hardy with their eyes plucked out by buzzards. Reached our old camp by Jenkins' boat at 3:30. Had a good dinner of quail and canvasback duck.

January 17

Arose at 6 A.M. while still dark. Jim and I pulled out on foot for Jenkins' ranch at 7:45. We struck a gait of at least four miles an hour and maintained it arriving at the ranch at 9:30. The country was bare of everything, save mesquite and brush—no grass at all.

Jenkins' house is all open at the side, with canvas lining being used to wall it in. The summer bedroom is screened, and the roof is made of sticks covered with dirt. Mrs. Jenkins proved to be a buxom good-natured woman. She had a two year old child but was otherwise totally alone. She had some mail for us which Jenkins had forwarded from Yuma by an Indian.

January 18

After an early breakfast I went hunting for coyotes. Although they had been yelping from every direction I saw none. After some rifle practice by both of us we pulled out at 8:30. About three miles above Jenkins' Hardy River ranch we saw lots of hog tracks, and soon saw a pig come down for a drink. However, he returned to the cane brake before we could get close enough for a shot. We landed and soon a big boar came out about 200 yds. away. I fired twice but missed him. We had hardly time to regret our luck when I could hear the brush crackling, and soon a big boar came out about 50 yds. away. I killed him but was disappointed to find that although a large animal, his tusks were worn so far down that as a specimen he was worthless. Killed a curlew and a large snipe. Saw a number of canvasback duck and the largest flock of white geese I have ever seen. Arrived at the Colorado at 4:15 and at Adam's camp half an hour later. In the evening old Tyson, Dominquez, and Andrew V. Adams came down to the fire. Adams is 26, has a herd of 300 cattle here, and has lived all his life in the mountains of Lower California. He sold 18 cattle yesterday right on the ranch for $31.00 per head. The buyer will drive them to Tijuana, a ten day trip by wagon road of 145 miles.

January 19

The grass was wet with dew when I got up. We had a late breakfast as we had invited Adams who had been up most of the night tending herd. Afterwards we inspected his camp which consisted of a wall tent and an arrow weed shack in front of it. He showed me how to adjust a cinch saddle. If it tends to slip forward shorten the back straps of the cinch ring; if backward shorten the front straps.

We pulled out at 10:20. A fierce wind blew up the river. We rowed the boat into a favorable position, hoisted the sail, and made very good headway against the current. Suddenly, however, we were into a wrong channel and got stranded on a sand bar. Down came the sail, and to our consternation Jim began taking off his trousers. We were relieved to discover that he had provided against an unseemly exposure by a loin cloth made of a bandana handkerchief. Back in the channel the wind changed with each curve forcing me to tow the boat with a line from the bank usually called "tracking."

Below our camp that evening lay a long sand bar to which large flocks of cranes flew from every direction with a tremendous din. There must have been thousands of them. After night fall the cranes rose screaming with a mighty roar of wings, doubtless disturbed by a coyote, and then settled down again as soon as the alarm was over.

January 20

Pulled out at 8:15 A.M. We tracked, poled, and rowed as conditions warranted. Jim often poled from the stern of the boat while I rowed. While poling vigorously Jim's pole broke and he fell into the river, but, being a good swimmer, was soon picked up by us.

At Colony Landing a number of Indians gathered to watch us including a squaw with a tiny boy dressed only in a little red undershirt that hung down to his navel. He seemed much afraid of us although I gave him some lumps of sugar. To escape the Indians we poled up the river half a mile to a good camp ground, and Jim was pleased when I gave him permission to spend the night with his friends.

January 21

We had not gone more than a mile when Amy spied a sail boat coming downstream. I suspected it contained the men M. P. Jenkins had written me would have mail for us. Accordingly I went to a good landing place and waited. My surmise was correct as they proved to be J. D. Meadows (a brother of Arizona Charlie), D. L. De Vane, and M. B. Tower. They are bound for the gulf for an outing of two or three months. Meadows wore a beautifully braided buckskin shirt. They had killed a deer up river and generously gave us a quarter. We spent an hour and a half chatting and reading our mail before starting upstream again. Camped at sundown and had a fine dinner of venison, boiled potatoes, chow chow, bread, butter, jelly, and tea. I pointed to the moon which was nearly full and said to Jim:

"I see a woman there."

"No," he replied, "a coyote."

January 22

An Indian house on the river bank which we had noticed going downstream was a smoking heap of ashes. Jim, who was poling in the rear of the boat, regarded the disaster with a dignified but unconcerned satisfaction. When I asked him if the former occupants were "amigos" of his, he said "no" explaining that they were "muy malo" Cocopas and that was why their house had been burned. We met the owner of the ill-fated house, who lay down on his belly on the river bank and conversed with Jim in Cocopa as long as we were within hearing distance.

January 23

At 9 A.M. Amy spied six deer walking along the shore some 600 yds. ahead. Through my field glasses I saw five does and one enormous buck. They drank, and then the buck watched us a moment or two and made off. I landed and, telling Amy to head for the point where we saw them, went into the woods to intercept them. For an hour and a half I wandered through chapparal seeing innumerable tracks but no deer. When I returned to the boat Amy said that when they rowed up the deer were lying down at the edge of the water about 100 yds. away and remained there for some little time. We continued on seeing many tracks on every sand bar but no more deer. We camped under a gorgeous moon.

It took five more days of hard rowing and bucking headwinds to reach the Imperial Canal. Here on January 28

Marshall and his wife camped with some friends in a grove of willows. The next morning they were driven to Yuma, leaving Jim to row the boat up the remaining four miles with the help of another Indian. From Yuma they returned by train to Los Angeles.

Six years later Marshall Bond was again on the lower Colorado. Meanwhile, in 1907 the Bond brothers, having come into part of Judge Bond's estate, decided to indulge themselves with a newfangled gadget that was becoming a national craze, the automobile. Accordingly, on February 23 of that year they bought a White steamer in San Francisco. It was fast, powerful, and thrilling to drive, but quite unsuited for the rough unpaved roads of mining regions where they had hoped to use it profitably. It also proved costly to operate and very difficult to dispose of. Marshall's diary of February 17, 1908, reports: "Figured cost of automobiling for the past year, including the cost of the machine at $8222. If I sell it for $2000 it will have cost us over $500 a month." Finally on May 20, 1908, they sold it in Los Angeles for $1,062.15, suffering a total loss of $7,159.85. Marshall gladly retreated back into the horse-and-buggy age until 1915, when he took a chance with a Model T Ford truck.

In 1908 Marshall went to see the Clip Mine in Lower California. His diary describes the trip:

April 12

Franklin W. Smith and I took the noon train for Yuma. Aboard was one of the Clancey Bros. who have the Picacho Mine in Sonora. Arrived in Yuma 6:15 P.M. and stopped at Hotel Grandolfo. Arizona Charlie Meadows* helped us arrange our departure for tomorrow.

* Bond's Klondike diary of December 18, 1897, says: "Chas. Meadows, celebrated throughout Arizona as 'roper,' called at my cabin. He is a big fine looking man over 6 ft."

April 13

We got our supplies from E. F. Sanguinetti and a tram from Billy Van Horn. Left the Calif. side at 11 A.M. but lost two hours by getting on the wrong road. Arrived at the Colorado River town of Picacho in Sonora at 7 P.M. Put our horses in a corral and slept out. Five men from Ehrenberg arrived at the same time by boat having made 80 miles today. They are going to Los Angeles to see the fleet.

April 14

Left Picacho at 8 A.M. and crossed the Colorado River by ferrying our wagon across on a row boat. This we did by taking off the rear wheels and resting the body of the wagon on the boat's gunwhales with the front wheels on each side of the bow and the tongue tied up in the air. Then we crossed our horses by swimming them over.

At a ranch four miles up river at Norton's Landing we cashed our things and started looking for the Clip Mine. We found the Red Cloud and others but could not locate the Clip so returned to the river and camped.

April 15

About midnight a Mexican, Santiago Lopez, rode up and picketed his horse near where I was sleeping. At breakfast he proved to be a nice old fellow and said he would show us the Clip Mine. We took off at 7:30 A.M. and reached the Clip three hours later. After going through it we decided to drop it as the ore was too low grade to admit of a profit under present conditions. Old Lopez told me much of mining in the early days along the Colorado. He believes the district around Kafa will prove rich.

April 16

Left Norton's Landing at 7:15 A.M. It took longer to cross the river this time as the current carried the boat further downstream. When we had everything across we waited to see some prospectors swim their burros across. The first one fought the lead rope and was in danger of drowning in mid stream when Lopez pulled him alongside his horse and held up his head by his ears.

Later that morning we visited the Picacho Mine and met Willis Lawrence, the superintendent. He proved to be an old Goldfield acquaintance and was in my geology class at Stanford. The mine was not for sale so we returned to Yuma arriving at 4:30 P.M.

In February, 1912, Marshall Bond once again visited the Colorado. On this occasion he took his entire family, including an English nurse and an old lady of sixty-seven, Mrs. William K. Townsend of New York. She was a good sport who, on hearing of the trip, had wired: "Hold everything. Will join you in four days." The party assembled in Needles and began preparations for a 250-mile jaunt down the river to Yuma.

The group embarked in a twenty-foot scow, which held the provisions, and a blue canoe. Bond hired a Chemehueva Indian as a guide and brought along several guns with which to furnish the larder with ducks and quail. To the writer's intense distress, his mother brought a folding rubber tub in which to bathe him whenever enough dirt had accumulated to make the effort worthwhile. He was unhappy with these all-too-frequent baths, as the suds from the caustic laundry soap invariably stung his eyes. The big event of the trip for the author was his fourth birthday on February 10. In celebration a cake was baked in a Dutch oven, and he was allowed to eat all he could hold.

The party camped on sand bars at the edge of the desert, where wood was plentiful, and every night would huddle around a blazing fire to relieve the chill of the cold winter air. Bond was an early riser and would greet the beauty of the first rays of sunshine with a burst of exuberance that was almost religious in its rapture. The crackling of twigs would be heard as he laid the fire, and soon tongues of flame and a column of smoke would ascend on high. When the aroma of coffee and bacon began to permeate the camp, he would arouse the sleepers with a song which meant nothing particular but was for him a paean of praise for the life he loved best:

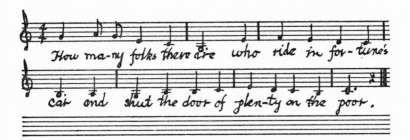

How ma-ny folks there are who ride in for-tune's cat and shut the door of plen-ty on the poor.

This usually inspired a chorus of yelping from numerous coyotes—a melody deeply cherished by men who roam the desert.

Quicksand was an ever-present danger. Once the author stepped into some but his mother hurriedly managed to pull him out before the treacherous stuff had reached his knees. The next day the group came upon a steer bellowing and struggling in abject terror as the quicksand enveloped all but its head and shoulders. Bond got out his rifle and mercifully put an end to its suffering.

In 1912 there were still a good many Indians living along the banks of the river and about the time of the party's departure a blue canoe was reported stolen in Needles. Two sheriffs came into Bond's camp and accused him of stealing the canoe. Just as he was talking himself out of being marched off to jail, two boats manned by Indians came into view, and the sheriff, firing his pistol in the air, ordered them ashore. A cursory inspection revealed that one of their canoes was the stolen one. Bond was released, and the Indians were marched off instead.

When the party eventually arrived in Yuma the old frontiersman, Arizona Charlie Meadows, was so impressed with the exploit that he introduced Bond in every saloon in town as "the only white man who had ever brought three women and two children down the river from Needles without any of them getting drowned." The hero of the occasion got so many free drinks that Arizona Charlie had to help him navigate back to camp, and it took the combined efforts of all three women to get him to bed.

CHAPTER FOUR

The Boers in Mexico

A FEW MONTHS after the conclusion of the 1902 rowboat trip on the lower Colorado, Marshall Bond found himself in Mexico City, involved in a scheme which was bizarre enough to interest the President of the United States.

In the winter of 1902 his father had rented a house in Montclair, New Jersey, and opened a New York office at 40 Wall Street. He had bought the patents to a new cash register and had organized The American Mechanical Cashier Company at Jersey City. On May 31 Marshall joined his father in Salt Lake City for a directors' meeting of the Bingham Copper and Gold Mining Co. The following day they left for New York, where Marshall hoped to find an opening in financial circles. Louis remained in Santa Clara to run the prune ranch.

Early that year a group of Boers from South Africa arrived in New York and sought Judge Bond's advice on politics, aid for their cause, and the possibility of migrating to North America. His journal of July 15 reads: "Was called upon by a dozen Boers, to wit: General A. P. Cronje, Adjutant J. F. Curlewis, General J. B. Wessels, Peter F. Steyn,* J. de Villers, Jubert Reitz, G. A. Frazier, Commandants O. A. S. Davel, Julius Kieser, Snyman, and Captain Hassell.† All lunched with me at the Lawyer's Club."

The Boers were a conservative agrarian people who had emigrated to South Africa from Holland in the seventeenth century. They bitterly resented the gradual intrusion of the British, especially during the Victorian era. The dominating antagonists of that day were the Transvaal president, Paul Kruger, and the millionaire empire builder, Cecil Rhodes. A series of armed clashes finally led to the Boer War in 1899. By 1901, knowing their defeat was inevitable, many disgruntled Boers left South Africa or were looking for a secure place to go. Hostilities were concluded on May 31, 1902, by the Treaty of Vereeniging, whereby the Transvaal and the Orange Free State lost their autonomy.

One of these adventurers was "General"‡ W. D. Snyman, about whom Theodore Roosevelt wrote in a letter§ to his son Theodore Jr., dated Oyster Bay, April 9, 1901:

One of the Boer leaders, Commandant Snyman and his 16-year old boy were out here on Sunday. Snyman was a most interesting man, a great strapping fellow, black-haired, bronzed-face and keen-eyed. He was most interesting about the fighting. Naturally he took a prejudiced view, but he gave me instance

* Steyn was the brother of Martinus T. Steyn, president of the Orange Free State.

† Hassell was an American citizen who fought on the Boer side and was in command of a group known as the American Scouts. He was co-author of *The Mobile Boer*.

‡ Military titles were loosely held among the Boer irregulars and often conferred on a basis of popularity. On his trip to Mexico Snyman evidently promoted himself to the rank of general to impress the Mexicans, and since he looked every inch the part, the title stuck.

§ Reprinted by permission of the publishers from Elting E. Morison, ed., *The Letters of Theodore Roosevelt*, Vol. II, "The Square Deal," Cambridge, Mass.: Harvard University Press, Copyright, 1951, by the President and Fellows of Harvard College.

after instance where the Boers actually captured more English than there were Boers in the fight, and he has an utter contempt for the English fighting. He does not say that they lack courage, but he does say that they are utterly stupid, wholly inefficient and that they get cowed and surrender when they find that they are suffering a heavy loss and seemingly not inflicting any. He was at Stormberg when Gatacre was repulsed. He says there were five hundred Boers and that they took nearly seven hundred prisoners with three guns. He was with De Wet when with nine hundred men he stormed a position held by seven hundred Irish Fusileers. He says that the British actually missed them when they charged in the open against the hill where the British were gathered, and only a single Boer was killed as they rushed up to the lines.

When the war broke out, while I felt a warm sympathy with the Boers, yet I believed the war to be inevitable and felt that civilization demanded the triumph of the English. But I confess that what has gone on has shaken my conviction a good deal. The exposures about Chamberlain's family connections with the government in business matters, and about both Chamberlain and Rhodes in their dealings with the Jameson raid, the domineering folly of Milner and the utter breakdown of the English army, make me feel that the English had no right whatever to go into this task as they did, for their capacity and the justice of their cause taken together did not warrant their position. Moreover, I personally felt very great sympathy with the Outlanders [Boers], regarding them as having been oppressed; but their tame incapacity to stand up for themselves has given me a contempt for them. On the other hand, one cannot help admiring the way the Boers have kept on in the face of the overwhelming material supremacy of the British Empire. It is as gallant a struggle as has ever been made.

Judge Bond saw a good deal of General Snyman in 1902. The latter was a large man in both mind and body. He could visualize problems in a broad frame of reference, and at the

conference table his charm and forthright manner invariably inspired respect and confidence. He had a romantic
vision of a mass migration of Boers to new and sunny lands
in Mexico where they could start life afresh, free from the
tread of imperial armies, and he somehow sold his dream to
the Mexican President, Porfirio Diaz. At that time Mexico
was underpopulated and underdeveloped, and Diaz must
have felt that a vigorous people like the Boers would con-
tribute greatly to the advancement of his country. Furthermore, he was genuinely sympathetic to their struggle against
British imperialism. Snyman's scheme also appealed to
Theodore Roosevelt's flair for adventure, but whatever assistance the latter may have afforded was provided quite
unobtrusively, for he obviously could not offend the British
by openly espousing any Boer cause.*

In the fall of 1902 Marshall Bond was invited by a close
friend, E. Reeve Merritt, to accompany him and Snyman
to Mexico to meet Diaz and discuss the purchase of land.
Mrs. Merritt was a first cousin of Roosevelt, and it seems
highly probable that the President himself suggested the
trip to Merritt. In support of this, Judge Bond's journal
records the fact that on September 18 Merritt conferred
with the President at Oyster Bay.

For the trip Stuyvesant Fish, president of the Illinois
Central Railroad, provided his ornate private car, probably
at the request of Roosevelt. Marshall Bond spent the weekend of October 4 and 5 at Fish's home in New York arrang-
ing the details. On October 7 the three men left on what
Bond described as a "princely pilgrimage of unparalleled
luxury." At every stop after leaving El Paso, Diaz saw to it

* Eric Rosenthal, in his book *Stars and Stripes in Africa*, says that on January 2, 1902, Snyman pleaded with the President for help for the Boers, but
the President refused to intervene. He also says that Snyman saw Roosevelt
again on August 21, 1904, and discussed the plan of settling in Mexico.

Marshall Bond (in wicker chair) at Yale in 1888, a gentleman scholar on a generous allowance.

Judge Hiram Gilbert Bond, Marshall's father. He had successful careers in the East and in Denver, Seattle, and California.

(*Below*) Marshall Bond, Jr., aged exactly four, in a folding rubber bathtub on a Colorado River trip, 1912. The strong laundry soap hurt his eyes.

Dear Louis Bond:—

Here is the book that never would have been written if you had not gone to Klondike in 1897 and taken Buck along with you. In fond memory of Sour dough days,

Jack London

Oakland, Calif.,
April 12, 1907.

Jack London's inscription in Louis Bond's copy of *The Call of the Wild*. London used Bond's dog, Jack as the prototype of London's fictional Buck.

Closeup of Marshall Bond in the Klondike, 1898, with his dog who was later made famous as "Buck" in Jack London's *The Call of the Wild*.

At a cabin in Dawson during the Klondike rush are (L to R) Marshall Bond, Oliver H. P. La Farge, Lyman Colt, and Stanley Pearce.

Boatmen running White Horse Rapids during the Klondike gold rush. Marshall Bond, one of the first men into the Klondike, had gone this route.

Typical miners at Dawson during the Klondike boom. Bond returned with wealth—but only in adventures.

Bond (right) accompanied E. Reese Merritt (left) and Gen. W. D. Snyman, Boer War leader, on a trip to visit Porfirio Diaz in Mexico, 1902, to plan a Boer colony.

The family takes a leisurely boat trip down the Colorado from Needles to Yuma. In 1912, a 20-foot scow was a luxury craft.

Goldfield, Nevada, in 1904. Marshall Bond and his brother Louis sought elusive fortune here.

Marshall (center) and his Klondike millionaire friend, John Erickson (left) examine Goldfield ore worth $10,000 a ton.

Judge Bond (far left) arrives at Godfield, 1904, to inspect prospects reported by son Marshall (far right).

During a 1915 hunting trip along the Mexican border, guide Jesus (left) poses with Count C. Karl Coudenhove and Richard Bond at a boundary marker.

Marshall Bond and Austrian nobleman C. Karl Coudenhove in camp near Ajo, Arizona, 1916. Coudenhove had fled Canada to avoid being made a war prisoner.

Marshall dropped this magnificent mountain sheep at 200 yards on a trip up the Stikine River in 1911. This part of British Columbia was considered "the finest big game country left in North America." (Courtesy Provincial Archives, Victoria, B.C.)

that they were met by brass bands, flag-waving children, and delegations of politicos who plied them with champagne dinners and flowery speeches. It reminded them of some conquering Caesar's triumphal return to Rome. Nothing could have been in sharper contrast to Bond's later trip to Mexico in 1918 when Pancho Villa was on the warpath and shooting every American within gunsight.

To combat the effects of overindulgence, Bond and Merritt, who prided themselves on athletic prowess, would get the engineer to slow down for a couple of miles every morning while they dog-trotted along the tracks behind their private car. The Mexicans must have thought they had been eating locoweed.

In this connection Bond and Merritt had been fascinated with the walking races in Madison Square Garden and became friendly with a good many of the contestants there. A few years later in Walla Walla Marshall recognized one of these men and asked him what he was doing out west.

"Making money hand over fist," said the man.

"How?" Marshall wanted to know.

"Well," said his friend, "I know from experience that a man on foot can always beat a man on horseback, provided the distance is great enough to require the horse to stop to eat. The cowboys, however, don't know this, and I've made a killing betting them five hundred dollars that I can outdistance a horseman in three days."

Bond told of a fiesta given by Don Luis Terrazas, five times governor of Chihuahua, and the foremost *haciendado* in Mexico. Through his ability and the policies of Juarez and Diaz he had acquired immense herds of cattle and extensive ranches amounting in all to some 7,000,000 acres.* In fact the Mormons at Colonia Dublan told a story about

* One account states that Terrazas owned 12,000,000 acres comprising one-fifth of the state of Chihuahua.

Louis Swift, the Chicago meat packer, who, when he ran out of cattle in a drought in Wyoming, wired Terrazas in desperation:

"Can you ship me 100,000 head of cattle?"

Terrazas replied, "What color?"

The fiesta at one of Terrazas' palatial haciendas was the answer to a horse lover's dream. Besides food and drink aplenty, there were ten thousand cowboys assembled in groups of five hundred, each group mounted on five hundred horses of matching color. The cowboys indulged in all sorts of rodeo stunts and contests with amazing skill. One of the most popular was a sport called *el gallo* ("the cock"). A rooster would be buried in sand with only its greased head sticking out. Cowboys would then gallop at full speed past the spot, attempting to grab the bird's head. At such a furious pace it required split-second timing for a man to swing low enough from his saddle to get a grip on so elusive an object. When done successfully it was pretty hard on the rooster.

The Snyman party arrived in Mexico City on October 17, 1902, and put up at the Hotel Iturbide. Marshall wrote his wife:

We arrived yesterday at noon. The entire trip down has been most interesting and has been like seeing the panorama of mediaevalism with a modern mind. Nothing could be more picturesque, and the climate is even better than Arizona.

I have never seen anything like this place. Merritt says it reminds him of Paris. The cathedrals and palaces are immense, and this hotel was built around 1700 by the Marquesa de San Mateo Valparaiso for her palace. Like all houses here, it is built right up to the sidewalk and entrance is obtained through enormous doors which are bolted at night for protection. The building covers a block and surrounds a garden as large as that at New Park with trees just as big.

We called on the American minister yesterday and found him a d——d chump. Then we drove to Limantour's house, the Finance Minister. An English concierge explained that Limantour was at the Palace. We drove there and it is enormous—all courts and corridors inside. Troops everywhere. Three rooms in Limantour's suite of offices were filled with men awaiting audience. We presented cards and were quickly ushered into an inner room. A lot of Mexicans were waiting there too.

The walls were covered with yellow silk, patterned with the Mexican eagle strangling the snake in green. A life-sized painting of Juarez, the Indian peon who rose to be President and who smashed the power of the Catholic Church, hung on the wall. Finally we were all dismissed and told to call on Monday at 4:30 P.M.

Last night I met Mr. Raoul, who explained to us how all revolutions in Mexico in the past had been caused by the Church in Her attempt at power and control. Finally the Liberal Party, of which Diaz is the head, sat on Her for good. Everybody says there is less corruption. While a republic in name, it is really a despotism.

All the peons wear hats shaped like the *Jefe's*. The dudes ride in the Paseo with similar hats covered with gold and silver, short jackets with silver buttons, and trousers with rows of silver buttons all up and down the side, silver spurs, saddles, etc.

October 19

After breakfast we went to the cathedral. I liked it better than Westminster Abbey or St. Paul's. We sat in the plaza and listened to the military band. Then we visited the flower market. I never saw such flowers, nor such artistic arrangements. Do you know that field daisies can be arranged so that you have a combination of white and gold that paralyzes the senses like music?

We drove up the Paseo de la Reforma in a Victoria (35¢ an hour) to Chapultepec Castle where Diaz lives. We passed beautiful saddle horses, their riders covered with silver and gold ornamentation, often a rich sword attached to the saddle underneath the leg.

We lunched with a French mining engineer named Chevriour. He had the Dutch Consul and Senor Macedo, the great lawyer, here as guests. Macedo will prepare Limantour for us tomorrow and will arrange an audience with Diaz. He said Diaz got into power through the common people in spite of the unity of the upper classes. He thinks Diaz a great man.

As we drove back from Chapultepec we had an illustration of the reason Diaz is able to do what he does—three or four hundred thoroughly armed cavalrymen, beautifully mounted, rode up the Paseo. It was a striking picture of force. Diaz also keeps all the artillery here, and most of the ammunition.

October 21

Yesterday we met Limantour. He is a bright man and an able one. He is polished, but I think cold. However, he greeted us cordially and talked for an hour and a half while his anterooms were filled. Snyman made his usual good impression. Limantour is going to consult Diaz. If all goes well they will buy land for the Boers from present owners (there are no public lands in Mexico) wherever Snyman wants and allow the Boers to pay it back over a long period of years. They are anxious for such immigrants.

These people are afraid of American imperialism. Limantour says that their salvation lies in having a government that will be satisfactory in every way. They are very equable to foreigners, but the government is an absolute despotism. Diaz is the whole show. Those who have opposed him have either been shot or have strangely disappeared. Limantour will succeed him.

When we left Limantour we met Porfirio Diaz, Jr. in the corridor of the Palace. He took us through all of Diaz' private apartments, showed us the official gold and silver plate, etc. In a great corridor of a hall were a lot of officers in full dress and swords. They were the President's aides. Capt. Diaz showed me the room in which his father was then closeted with the Governor of Chihuahua. We are promised an audience with Diaz next week. Everyone fears him. Still he is clever enough to fear, or at least see, the U.S. just across the Rio Grande.

Morelia, October 23

We have been to call on the Governor of the State. He proved to be a very presentable old gentleman who told Snyman where the Boers could get land for a song. He said they would be exempt from all taxation for twenty years if they came.

I went around town with Merritt and another fellow. They have an impressive cathedral, numerous old churches, a beautiful park, an old stone aqueduct, and every house patio was blooming with flowers.

Coming back at dusk we saw lots of fires in the streets about the plaza. They were of charcoal in earthen bowls, and women sat around them cooking. When we three sat down, a very fine looking Indian woman with a lovely voice and continual smile laughingly asked us if we would have something to eat. To avoid eating I offered to pay for the use of her chairs. She would not hear of this, saying that we were quite welcome. When I said it was bad business to have her chairs occupied by non-paying customers, she laughingly replied, "Kissing and chatting are always pleasant."

We could not be indifferent after that and there on the sidewalk on tiny plates ate a tortilla rolled about in red peppers, garlic, and God knows what. It was the most gallant act of my life. The charge was five cents, and I gave her ten, which was a lordly extravagance and brought forth all sorts of good wishes.

Morelia is mediaeval, and religion is more important than business. When the Angelus tolled, every man, woman, and child stood with bowed head. A little later a priest drove by in a carriage taking the "blessed sacrament" to a sick person. As he passed every person on the street knelt down. However, in Mexico the priests are not allowed on the streets in clerical garb, the nuns have been expelled, and no church interference is allowed in politics. Two of the leading men in the government told me they were free thinkers. One said he learned English purposely to read Herbert Spencer in the original.

Mexico City, October 25

Last night we met the grandson of the Emperor Iturbide, and he asked us out to his hacienda, saying that he would have a lot of cattle rounded up and would give us an exhibition of roping, throwing by the tail, etc. Unfortunately we could ill-afford the time.

Our experience reminds me of Dumas' description of Louis XIV's court. This afternoon I saw President and Mrs. Diaz driving—he is a very handsome man. When I told young Diaz that Snyman was in a fair way to become a citizen, he said that that was good thing for Mexico.

Today we had a luncheon given us at the Jockey Club*—*the* club of the town. Two Englishmen, the British Consul, and the Austrian Attache were the guests besides ourselves. The British Consul's name is Jerome. He claims to be a direct descendent of Napoleon Bonaparte, and I must say bears a striking resemblance. In himself he is sort of an ass, being in a rut of officialdom. We didn't pay much attention to him. The lunch was superb.

The Jockey Club, a very fine and interesting place, was once the palace of a Spanish Duke. As a club it is purely a gambler's paradise. One of the Englishmen, who had been a member for years, said that he thought $20,000,000 were won or lost at the baccarat table annually. Only the other night Limantour's brother lost $100,000. Be it said to the credit of the Finance Minister, he never plays.

Tomorrow we are off in Mr. Raoul's private Pullman for a few days in Michoacan. When we return, if we don't go to Chi-

---

* Also at the Jockey Club they were lavishly entertained by Martinez del Rio, a member of one of Mexico's oldest families and that country's second largest *haciendado*. Del Rio was a man of great personal charm, and, like many upper-class Mexicans, was educated in England. He was also the father-in-law of the talented and beautiful motion picture star, Dolores del Rio.

huahua to inspect lands (right on the way home), I shall leave at once and let Snyman remain.

Bond's last letter clearly indicates the great enthusiasm that Diaz had engendered for the Boers.

October 27th, 1902
Uruapan, Mexico

Dearest Amy:

We ran down here last evening, having a guard of honor of *Rurales*, and were met at the station by the Jefe Politico, a deputation of citizens, a brass band, mounted escorts, and the entire populace. For a moment we thought we were going to be lynched, when up went a mighty cry of "Viva Boeros!" "Viva General!"

Then the bigwigs climbed up on the platform and to our surprise a man welcomed Snyman in Dutch. Then we were introduced to all the bigwigs, who welcomed us enthusiastically. The crowd yelled and yelled, and Snyman made a speech which was translated by an Italian, and the crowd went wild. Then we had a little champagne with the committee, who told us the best apartments in town had been reserved for us and that we were expected to dine at the house of a leading citizen. We accepted the dinner invitation but signified our desire to sleep in the car. Then they picked up Snyman and hoisted him upon the shoulders of a lot of men, and, amidst screaming and cheering, he was carried to a reserved streetcar to which were hitched four mules.

We followed and when our car was as full of bigwigs as could get in, the band in a car preceding us struck up and our triumphal entry into Uruapan began. Thousands of Indians and peons ran along behind, filling the street, while beside the car rode *Caballeros* dressed in silver and gold embroidered hats and clothes. For the first time in my life I felt the delirium of applause and understood its fascination for politicians and performers, these people to whom it is the breath of life. For a mile we went along in that yelling mob, then got out and walked up a block to the house where our reception was to be held, the *Rurales* with swords clearing the way in front of Snyman. All the time the mob cheering and shouting, "Viva Boeros!"

We entered a very attractive house having the usual patio, and Snyman and the *Jefe Politico* had to appear on the balcony. The *Jefe* made a speech and Snyman shouted, "Viva Mexico!" which made the mob wild with delight. I forgot to say that a little girl presented Snyman with a big bouquet of flowers at the station. When he got out of the streetcar at the end of the procession, a lot of ladies had taken up a position of advantage in another car and waved to Snyman. He took off his hat, shook hands with them, and called for a cheer for them. It being translated, the *Jefe* shouted that the General had said, "Viva Las Senoras de Mexico!" and everybody cheered. They all thought Snyman had paid a very graceful compliment.

Our host brought in several bottles of champagne. When the glasses were filled, his wife, a pretty little woman with a sweet voice, came in and taking up a glass touched it to Snyman's and we all drank. Then she disappeared—as I am beginning to think is the proper thing for a wife—and we had dinner. We had superb imported Rhine wine, French burgundy, and champagne. When dinner was over we again saw our host's wife and bade her good night, and repaired to the plaza where the *Jefe* had ordered the band to play. We took chairs on the sidewalk and watched the people march by, all eager to catch a glimpse of the General. Little boys, girls, women, and men were introduced if their importance demanded it, and we kept two interpreters busy translating and ourselves keyed up in order to answer the demands of Mexican manners.

These people are tremendous Boer sympathizers and still bear in mind their struggle against Maximilian and the French. When we started back our little car was pulled out and all hands accompanied us back to our railroad car.

This morning at 9:30 they came down with saddle boxes and escorted us around town. Tomorrow we start for the cattle country accompanied by a guard of *Rurales*. That is, I am going if I get a wire from you, or find I can get back in good season.

Our hosts have come.

Affectionately,

M.

In November Marshall Bond, who was running low on funds, returned to New York alone, disappointed only in not having had time to meet Porfirio Diaz. He joined the American Mechanical Cashier Company and was made a director, but the tedium of factory life in Jersey City was scarcely calculated to keep him in a state of ecstasy. He resigned on February 14, 1903. Within a year the Judge, who found he had neither liking nor aptitude for merchandising, retreated from the field after sustaining a loss of a quarter of a million dollars.

General Snyman, elated over the extravagant reception provided by Diaz, spent most of the next two years examining ranches, raising money, and enlisting recruits. He might have been more successful in the last category had not the Treaty of Vereeniging been magnanimous in granting individual liberties to the Boers. In fact in some Boer papers he was ridiculed and dubbed "Yankee" Snyman, but this entirely failed to dampen his enthusiasm.

In 1904 Snyman visited the St. Louis World's Fair and even participated in a highly successful "wild west" show called *The Fillis Boer Circus* which included about two hundred Boers and, curiously enough, an equal number of British veterans of the Boer War. On August 21, 1904, he again conferred with Theodore Roosevelt and received considerable encouragement on the Mexican scheme.

The best account of the settlement in Mexico and the eventual collapse of Snyman's dream is contained in an article by C. J. Viljoen in *The Huguenot* of June, 1948, from which the following exerpts are taken:

After the World's Fair ended General Ben Viljoen,* together with Commandant Snyman and a number of Boers, by invitation of President Diaz, settled in the State of Chihuahua in Mexico. They were offered a large estate of 50,000 acres on the River Conchos, of which some 4,000 acres were under irrigation. The ground was excellently suited for the cultivation of lucerne, wheat, maize, ground nuts, etc. There are also some 2,000 head of cattle and about 100 horses on the estate. The conditions on which it was offered to the Boers were very fair; 200,000 Pesos (£20,000) of which the State advanced £15,000 and one of the Banks £5,000, free of interest for a period of 40 years. In return the leaders of the Boer community undertook to bring 50 Boer families as immigrants to Mexico.

The houses on the estate were very simple. They were of mud and brick, and the first task was to make them habitable. The estate was 12 miles from the nearest railway station and 50 miles from the town of Chihuahua. None of the Boer settlers could speak a word of Spanish, and one can imagine what difficulties the language question provided at the start. The sons of Commandant Snyman quickly learnt the most necessary Spanish words so that they managed reasonably well with the workers.

They kept the old Vaqueros (cowboys) and sub-divided the irrigable ground into about 30 pieces of 25 to 60 acres. These pieces of ground were then leased and each lessee was provided with seed as well as with the necessary implements and had to hand over 50% of the harvest. If the lessee himself provided seed and implements he had to hand over only one third.

The Snymans kept about 200 acres to work themselves.

General Ben Viljoen meanwhile stayed on as a member of Fillis Boer Circus in the U.S.A. and only later joined the Sny-

---

* General Ben Viljoen, formerly a member of the Transvaal Parliament (Volkstaad), emigrated to America after his release from a prisoner-of-war camp on St. Helena.

mans. I myself was then still a member of the Fillis Co. and came to Mexico in 1904 together with Haaklas, Malan, and David Spohr. On account of a misunderstanding the Snymans did not know of our coming and because of our ignorance of Spanish we found it most difficult to get from Ortis Station to the Boer Station. All the arrangements had to be made by gestures, but finally the Mexicans also understood what our destination was and placed the necessary means of transport at our disposal.

It was a most surprised Boer family that met us on our arrival. Perhaps I myself had the most pleasant surprise of all for I then met for the first time the attractive 22-year-old Miss Johanna Snyman who, six months later, became my wife. . . .

A whole group of Afrikaaners joined the settlement the following year, amongst others my brother, General Ben Viljoen, another brother, Commandant Wynand Viljoen, my parents, my brother Christiaan and two sisters. Also there were Fritz Coetzee, Van Asweben, Jack Malan, and Hans Van der Westhuizen. . . .

General Ben Vilojen built himself a fine house and for about a year lived in the Boer Colony but the lonely life was too much for him and he returned to the U.S.A. . . .

Commandant Snyman was generally known in Mexico as "General". . . .

After the members of the Boer community had trekked away, General Snyman sold the hacienda in 1908 to a German syndicate and bought himself a similar property across the Conchos River. It was called "La Regina," covered 30,000 acres, of which some 530 acres were intensively worked. The cattle had meanwhile so increased that he was able to sell 350 fat oxen. . . .

I myself moved to Mexico in 1909, where most of the Afrikaaners had meanwhile settled and done well.

During the Mexican Revolution, brother Ben joined Madero, who was a progressive leader and he asked Ben to assist him in an advisory capacity. Madero was in control of the country fairly quickly but unfortunately he was murdered before he could do much and with Ben's Mexican ventures. . . .

General Snyman, however, remained behind. In 1911 the Revolution broke out. Within a year the robbers had stolen all his cattle and devastated his lands. He was forced to escape with his wife and child.

In 1916 Bond received several cordial letters from the genial Boer, who had taken refuge from the revolution in Philadelphia. He reminded Bond of their deep friendship and expressed gratitude for the wise advice he had received from Judge Bond. By this time Snyman had become a staunch supporter of the Allied cause in Europe and urged his friend to do what he could in its' behalf. A few months later Mrs. Snyman wired that the General had died quite unexpectedly. She also sent one of her letters of condolence:

> Sagamore Hill
> Nov. 10th, 1916
>
> My Dear Mrs. Snyman:
> I do not wish to intrude upon your grief, but beg you to let me extend my most sincere sympathy. I greatly admired your gallant and distinguished husband and counted him a friend. I mourn his death. Again expressing my deep sympathy with you in your bereavement, I am
>
> Very respectfully yours,
> Theodore Roosevelt

During Marshall Bond's last visit to New York in the winter of 1930, he and the author were invited to dinner at the Merritts' home, an old brownstone mansion on East 53rd Street sandwiched between two towering skyscrapers. Merritt said he had been offered a million dollars just for the real estate and added plaintively, "Where would I go at my age and what could I do with the money?"

The interior was a red plush museum of the most elegant Victorian decor, reflecting precisely the character, attitudes, and background of its ancient and distinguished inhabitants. Countless knicknacks of ivory, silver, and porcelain crowded the tables and mantelpiece as if competing to evoke memories of former journeys to distant and exotic lands. A delicious meal was served by old François, the French butler, who had been in the family's employ for over half a century. Conversation was largely about Snyman, the Jockey Club, and the running along the railroad tracks which Merritt had enjoyed so much. Mrs. Merritt was nearly blind, and within a few years the house, its occupants, and its memories had vanished, and another skyscraper had been erected in its place.

After the trip to Mexico with Snyman and Merritt, Marshall Bond lingered in New York until he heard the electrifying news of a rich strike at Goldfield, Nevada.

Goldfield

Arriving in Goldfield in August, 1904, Marshall Bond supported himself by writing articles for the San Francisco *Bulletin* and the *Pacific Tribune* of Seattle. After his Klondike experience he was unwilling to speculate with Judge Bond's money, but did urge his father to come to Nevada and invest on his own. He also persuaded Louis that there were more prospects in Goldfield than there were in prunes.

As special correspondent for the *Bulletin*, Bond described his entry into Goldfield in an article published on October 9, 1904:

A six-horse stage carries passengers and express from Tonopah* to Goldfield, twenty-five miles to the south. I secured the box seat beside the driver. The first five miles the road winds along on an upgrade until Gold Mountain is reached. Then in answer to my questions, the driver pulled his team to a standstill and exclaimed: "Now you can get an idea of the mineralization of this country. Back there four miles is Tonopah, a silver

---

* Tonopah was discovered in 1900 and ultimately produced over $150,000,000.

camp; here is Gold Mountain turning out free milling gold ore of shipping value; across there to the west about ten miles is Lone Mountain, producing silver, and away across the valley at the foot of those mountains is Goldfield, a high-grade gold camp. Now, there's the whole layout—silver, gold, silver, gold, just like a marble cake." Starting up his horses, we descended into the valley below at a smart trot, leaving the mountains behind us.

With the leaving of the railroad at Tonopah, the old frontier sights came into evidence. We passed groups of prospectors coming and going, some mounted and driving pack horses before them, others trudging behind burros laden with camp paraphernalia and prospecting outfits. Every now and then great teams of eighteen, twenty, and twenty-two mules dragging three and four heavily laden wagons crept by in a cloud of dust, the driver mounted on the near wheel animal and guiding his mules with a jerk line. Those bound for Tonopah were laden with ore from the Goldfield mines; those going in the direction of Goldfield creaked under the weight of provisions, lumber, and mining material.

Halfway between Tonopah and Goldfield we stopped at Ramsey's Well to water our horses. A signboard stated the charge to be 50¢ per pair. We arrived in Goldfield at noon.

The work of serious mining in this camp may be said to have commenced with the beginning of this year—a period of eight months. In that time over two millions of dollars have been produced. The work for the most part has been done by lessees and men handicapped by scant means, but they have taken out more gold in these eight months than Cripple Creek produced in its first three years of existence.

The area of this mineral bearing formation is at least six miles by four miles. The first considerable work done in the camp which produced large results was on the January and Combination—two claims lying side by side on the eminence of a flat hill. The former is worked by four lessees, the latter by a corporation. In both instances the ore was found practically at the grass roots. For the first six months neither hoisted anything but ore—there was no waste.

On August 17 he wrote to his wife:

I have just been out to the new strike on the Velvet. I honestly believe that I could take a pair of horses and a scraper and in three hours scrape up $10,000. The dirt right in the middle of the road will go $25 a pan. Six inches to a foot below the surface they strike quartz, which will go $90 to $10,000 to the ton. If the vein goes down, and L. L. Patrick thinks it will, it will make a barrel of money.

Now listen to this sad tale. Five days ago I was on that property when they found the first piece of float.* The fellow who found it gave a half interest in it to a man for bringing over a can of water, a mortar, and a pan from a neighboring claim.

I watched them pan up the rock and it showed lots of gold. Had I been in a position to offer a couple of hundred dollars, I could have had a half interest. I had $15.

I have taken a lease (no down payment) on half a claim adjoining, and Patrick has taken the other half. If the vein goes into the ground I may make a killing yet.

Evidently the vein didn't continue, as Bond never made anything in Goldfield except what the papers paid him. Shortly after receiving this letter his wife arrived with their baby, Dick, and moved into a shack. Louis and his family arrived that fall and occupied a shack nearby.

The Goldfield discovery in 1903 was due in part to a temporary stagnation in the silver camp of Tonopah. William Marsh and Harry Stimler obtained a grubstake from Jim Butler and Tom Kendall, and in December, 1902, set out in a buckboard to prospect on their own. In the desert about

* A piece of ore broken from a vein.

twenty-five miles to the south they found some float and located a few claims, among them the Jumbo and the Sandstorm. When they returned to Tonopah for more grub, they had some samples assayed which ran $12 per ton. This was sufficiently encouraging for them to return and do the required location work on their claims. Unfortunately they found no surface values on the Jumbo and let it go. Later it proved to be one of the richest producers. They decided to name the new camp Goldfield.

In the meantime Al Myers and Bob Hart, who could find no work in Tonopah, headed in the same direction and located some claims a little south of Stimler and Marsh. One of these, the Combination, was destined to be the first big producer and one of the best in the new district. The next man to arrive was Charley Taylor, who staked the Florence and relocated the Jumbo. Being broke, Taylor agreed to sell the Jumbo and another claim to Al Myers for $150, but the latter was unable to raise the money. As a result of this, Taylor kept the Jumbo and made a fortune.

L. L. Patrick arrived in July and optioned the Combination from Al Myers for $75,000, which included a down payment of $5,000. Patrick was unable to borrow the $5,000 locally, so he frantically wired his associates in Chicago. He received the money at the last moment, just as a representative of Charles M. Schwab, the steel magnate, was offering Myers $125,000. Within two years the Combination paid over a million dollars in dividends, all from Patrick's initial investment of only $5,000.

The ore deposits of Goldfield were characterized by their great irregularity, their amazing richness even at the surface, and their unusually low content of silver. As in all western mining towns, gambling, prostitution, and saloons throve on the new-found wealth. A unique feature of mining at Goldfield was that one-year leases were made by many of the original claim owners who were too poor to do their own development work. Since these leases ran for only a year three shifts of miners were put on whenever rich ore was uncovered so that the lessees could get the maximum production in the short time allotted. Almost without exception these contracts were verbal and, although involving hundreds of thousands of dollars, were honored in every respect. High-grading, however, was a common practice among the miners, who stole enormous amounts by carrying out pieces of ore assaying $10 a pound in their pockets and lunch boxes. Since the union would not allow the men to be searched, the stolen ore was sold to "fences" posing as assayers. Some of the surface ore was so rich that bull hides were pegged over charges of dynamite so that the values wouldn't be scattered on the desert.

As new strikes were almost a daily occurrence, Bond was kept busy reporting them to the papers.

October 22, 1904, *Bulletin:*

It is no surprise to the old-timers to hear that Claude M. Smith, "Lucky Smith," has struck it again. This gentleman came into the country with a capital of a can of milk and a bag of soda crackers and has done better than many men who were backed with the credit of a national bank. All that "Lucky" has to do is to erect four stakes on a piece of ground, give it a name, and it turns out rich. His latest piece of good fortune bears the name of Rosebush.

The *Bulletin's* special Goldfield-Tonopah number of Oct. 9th was thoroughly appreciated here. In no time every copy was sold, and many who were unfortunate enough to have failed in securing one on the arrival of the first issue offered as high as a dollar apiece for them.

On every side one hears flattering comments of the *Bulletin's* progressive spirit in being the first great daily newspaper to send a representative into the camps to give the outside world the true condition of affairs.

November 2, *Bulletin:*

With the expiration of the leases now ending, a good many men will temporarily be thrown out of employment. It will mark the transition of the camp from the impecunious development under the lease system into one of more efficient production by corporations possessed of abundant capital.

The town itself is growing rapidly. Stone and adobe buildings are breaking the line of wooden structures along the main street, adding both to the appearance and safety of the business section. An imposing array of tents, ever increasing in numbers, stretches out over the desert mesa converting ground of sagebrush and sand into urban property. As fast as lumber can be had the tents go down and houses go up.

From the top of Columbia Mountain one gazes down upon a khaki-colored city, the bare board houses blending with the desert colors, and the whole fringed with the white of tents. A little over a year ago it contained no life save the lizard and heard no cry but the coyote.

November 9, *Bulletin:*

Goldfield has passed through its first election day without mar or mishap. A New England town meeting could not have been quieter or more decorous. In the evening the election returns were read in front of the Palace Saloon. By 9 o'clock it was evident to the most prejudiced that Roosevelt had carried the country. A more dispassionate audience never gathered together to hear the result of a presidential election.

One is constantly getting letters from more conservative brethren, requesting information not only about the camp, but more particularly the character of its citizens, "if there is much shooting and disorder." Suffice it to say to all such that the old West has passed. Neither in Goldfield nor in any other western camp will be found the conditions that existed in the days of Tombstone, the Black Hills, and Leadville excitements. The six-shooter was an indispensable part of one's paraphernalia in the 70's and 80's, or was supposed to be, and a few inches of leather holster peeping out from beneath one's coat was thought to accord protection to the wearer.

But today justice is less halting and uncertain, and public opinion a factor too powerful to be left out of consideration. In the three months the writer has been in Goldfield he has never seen a pistol, and if a search for these were made it is probable they would be found not nearly so numerous as Pasteur water filters.

It was Richard Harding Davis who, in an article some years ago on Creede,* discovered to the world that college men were to be found in mining camps. But with the knowledge of this fact even Mr. Davis might have been surprised had he been on the main street of Goldfield three afternoons ago.

Clusters of men lined both sides of the thoroughfare, and in the general conventionality of costume, khaki trousers, laced boots, and felt hats—to say nothing of the leavening effect of desert and dust—it would have been impossible to tell prince from pauper. Suddenly out of the middle of the street stepped a young man with a football, which he sent soaring by a well placed kick. In an instant a dozen or more men had separated themselves from the crowd, and the leather oval was soon being passed, punted, or deftly caught close to the body with almost as much skill as marks the practice of a university eleven when warming up before a match. There were graduates of Berkeley, Stanford, Yale, Cornell, and other colleges, and one big fellow exhibiting unusual agility proved to be the famous guard on one of Harvard's most famous teams.

* Creede was a gold camp in Colorado.

November 16, *Bulletin:*

Whatever else Nevada may lack, she is not wanting in glorious climatic conditions. This is the best time of year for prospecting, and outfits with camp wagons or burros are striking out in every direction. All sorts of rumors are abroad, and every day some dust-covered prospector mysteriously slips into an assay office and empties his pockets of live looking rock.

Prospectors as a class were incurable optimists and given to gross exaggerations. One old fellow went into a bar and ordered a drink, saying, "By God, I've struck it rich this time!"

When the bartender had poured the drink, he asked, "Is it big?"

"Is it big!" exclaimed the prospector. "If I had the waters of Niagara to mill it, the fires of Hell to smelt it, and the whole state of Nevada as a dumping ground, it would take a million years to work it out!"

Also on November 16:

The rich Velvet claim, which has been the sensation of the camp, together with the Sunflower and Algae, have been taken over by a corporation known as the Velvet Gold Mining Company. Upon the Algae a rich strike has been made on the Fuller-Smith lease, and a large ledge of high-grade ore uncovered. John Erickson,* the Klondike millionaire, has taken the Presidency of the Company, Claude M. Smith is Vice-President, Louis W. Bond† Secretary-Treasurer, and F. H. Lathrop and George A. Kendrick directors.

---

* Erickson had been in London in 1898 trying to sell his Klondike properties with the help of Judge Bond. He may have been a stockholder and even a director of Bingham Copper and Gold Mining Co., for he attended its directors meeting on May 31, 1902, with Marshall and the Judge.

† Louis failed to get rich in Goldfield even though he seems to have started out with a good situation. He died of cancer in 1908.

November 22, *Pacific Tribune:*

Three six horse stage coaches and three forty horse power automobiles carry the incoming argonauts from Tonopah to Goldfield. The former charge $4 a seat and make the 26 miles in six hours. The automobiles charge $5 a seat and cover the distance in three hours. The automobile line is another illustration of the success of a Seattle man, L. L. Patrick, who was one of the first to do development work in the Monte Cristo district in the Cascades. A good many Klondikers are beginning to arrive on the scene. They begin to think there is more gold here than there was on Eldorado and Bonanza Creeks.*

Probably the largest and richest strike yet made in the district was uncovered on the 50 foot level on the St. Ives two days ago. The first assay showed $688 across six feet of ledge, and the walls on either side returned $237. Since then the values have increased until great blocks of ore coming up in the bucket can be seen covered and shot through with gold.

November 24, *Bulletin:*

Two weeks ago a man well past middle life left Goldfield accompanied by his wife to drive through to Los Angeles, there to settle down and enjoy the fruits of their labor. They were Mr. and Mrs. L. V. Lonsway of Seattle and, equipped with a team and a light wagon, they set out for the land of the orange, the olive, and perennial sunshine. But to the surprise of his friends, Mr. Lonsway returned three days since.

It was to be noticed that his step was more firm, his stature more erect, while upon his face shone the smile that won't come off. Why had Lonsway returned, and why that undisguised and undisguishable expression of contentment? Mr. Lonsway was called upon to explain, and in doing so he took from his pocket several pieces of quartz, spattered, ribbed, and shot through with gold.

* The total gold production of the Klondike was $178,000,000 vs. $87,-000,000 for Goldfield.

On the way to Los Angeles he had camped on the Amargosa Road near Beaty's ranch. Being of a curious and inquiring temperament, Mr. Lonsway felt impelled to examine a large ledge nearby which others had passed without notice. With a blow of his prospecting pick he broke off pieces of the outcrop to find the fractured surface glistening with gold. He staked the claim, returned to Goldfield, bonded his discovery to Ohio capitalists for $60,000 with a good down payment, and beatifically awaits the deferred payments. Nearly every available team in town has been hired, and prospectors are scurrying in the direction of the new strike.

November 30, *Pacific Tribune:*

The drift from the 50 foot level in the St. Ives continues to disclose ore of phenomenal richness. Some of the ore being sacked shows assay values from $2,000 to $4,300 per ton. A local wit examining some of the richest ore humorously described it "a sprinkling of rock mixed with gold." Such are the rewards of mining to those who strike it.

December 1, *Bulletin:*

Goldfield is no longer compelled to use condensed milk or take its coffee straight. An enterprising dairyman arrived last week with a herd of cows. The morning after his arrival a milk wagon made its rounds from house to house finding a ready sale at twenty-five cents a quart.

December 7, *Pacific Tribune:*

The extraordinary development taking place in Southern Nevada can best be measured by the railway traffic. It was only a few years ago that the late C. P. Huntington, after a tour of inspection over the railroad that is our connecting link with the outside world, mournfully remarked:

"It is three hundred miles too long or three hundred years too
soon."

Today the road is found to be too short, too narrow, and
utterly incapable of handling the freight consigned over it.
After vainly trying to cope with the situation the railroad officials have notified the public that they will not receive another
pound of freight for the next three weeks. In the meantime they
will endeavor to relieve the congestion which blocks every spur
and side track from Reno to Tonopah. Engineers are making
ready for the spring push by changing the road from a narrow
to a broad gauge. Surveying parties have been in the area for
weeks locating the best route for the extension of the railroad
from Tonopah to Goldfield.

December 28, *Bulletin:*

Sensation-mongers, or people grossly misinformed in regard
to the health and conditions of the camp, have lately been
spreading rumors abroad of sickness, pestilence, and death in
Goldfield. As a matter of fact Goldfield, as yet without any organized sanitation, is a remarkably healthy place. However, it
is nothing uncommon for the thermometer to show a fall of 50°
between sunset and sunrise. Where such sudden changes occur
one must be prepared against them or a chill resulting in pneumonia may follow. But the majority of pneumonia cases can be
traced to inebriety. Goldfield, like every other mining camp, has
attracted to itself a great many men, reckless and roisterous.
These rash spirits too often end up in the frost of night a de-
bauch begun in the heat of the day, only to experience, to borrow from Kipling, that:

> The sickness gets in as the liquor dies out
> And it crumples the young British soldier.

January 8, 1905, *Bulletin:*

San Francisco capitalists, who have been the slowest to take
advantage of the opportunities in the Goldfield district, are be-

coming prominent by reason of their purchases. The Goldfield Exploitation Company, of which Harrison Dibblee of San Francisco is the head, has acquired a considerable area of land and is prospecting it in a systematic manner.

In this connection Bond told of an old prospector who had come to Goldfield early in the rush and staked out a claim. He was a typical minion of the desert, illiterate, bewhiskered, and unwashed, who, like his confreres of that day, wandered throughout the desert with his burro from water hole to water hole searching for the elusive metal. He had no money with which to develop his claim but, by dint of hard work with his pick and shovel, had uncovered enough good ore to attract attention. He received a number of offers but turned them all down, having fixed in his mind a price of $50,000. This was far more than his limited showings warranted, and he was considered a stubborn old fool and impossible to deal with.

Late in 1904 a financier from San Francisco went to look at the old man's claim even though he had been forewarned of its owner's inflexibility. A careful examination of the property convinced him that it had interesting possibilities. Without saying a word to the owner he returned to town and drew up a deed for its purchase at a price of $10,000. Then he went to a bank and deposited a check for that amount, asking the teller to pile it in the front window in stacks of ten dollar gold pieces. The $10,000 made an impressive sight.

The next time he saw the old prospector coming down the street he invited him into a saloon for a couple of drinks. As soon as the old man was in an expansive mood the financier walked arm in arm with him toward the bank. When they came to the window the startled prospector said:

"My God, I ain't never seen so much gold in my life!"

"Would you sell your claim for all the gold in that window?" asked the man from San Francisco.

"You bet I would," said the prospector, "if anybody'd be fool enough to give it to me."

"It's my gold and I'm fool enough," replied the financier. "Just put your X on this dotted line."

January 11, 1905, *Bulletin:*

William J. Shea, one of the lessees on the Velvet, and recently elected surveyor of Nye County, was instantly killed last Friday morning by an explosion of dynamite. He was attempting to thaw it out by a fire when it exploded and blew him to pieces.

The development of the Simmerone shows the wisdom of surrounding the property with a board fence. Three assays across the two-foot ledge return values of $5,292, $7,890, and $13,198 to the ton. Such ore needs to be surrounded by something to protect it. Of all the rich ore found in the camp, that reported from the Simmerone is the richest. This property is said to have ten inches of ore which will average $20,000.

During the first year, until mills could be brought in and erected, ore assaying over $50 per ton was sacked and shipped by team to Tonopah and thence by rail to the Selby Smelter near San Francisco. The lower grade ores were piled up beside the hoists to await the less costly milling treatment. When new strikes occurred in outlying areas, every team was hitched and thousands of eager prospectors sallied forth in wild confusion, their excitement and exuberance seldom equaled.

January 11, *Bulletin:*

Of the new districts, Kawich is the center of excitement. Some enormous specimens glistening with gold are now on exhibition in the Nye and Ormsby Company Bank in Tonopah. Richer

ore has never been seen here, and it is asserted that these phenomenal specimens were broken from a ten-foot ledge, all of
which show gold. A big stampede resulted from the discovery,
claims having been staked in every direction, townsites laid
out, and many lots sold.

January 18, *Bulletin:*

The Combination mill is nearing completion. If the pipe
arrives in time through which its water supply from Alkali
Springs will flow, the stamps will be dropping by March 1st.
With the ability to treat its low-grade ores at a profit, it is highly
probably that the 10% monthly dividend, which the Company
is now paying, will be increased.

February 1, *Bulletin:*

The St. Ives, pending the arrival of its hoist, has begun work
with windlasses. Bodies of shipping ore have been encountered
in two shafts on the main ledge. These shafts will be connected
and mining done through one of them when the hoist is in-
stalled. The drift in the ground on this property, formerly
worked by Richard and Lewis, will also be driven until it con-
nects with the main ledge. Returns just received from the Selby
Smelting Works from three shipments net $214, $269, and $381
per ton. H. G. Bond of Santa Clara and Seattle, who developed
and sold the Monte Cristo Mines in Washington to John D.
Rockefeller, has bought into and taken the Presidency of the
Company.

February 8, *Bulletin:*

Claimholders whose properties are within or adjacent to the
town and who have been plotting the surface ground and selling it in lots, have been experiencing considerable annoyance
of late from jumpers. The latter have been encouraged in this
procedure by a few pettifoggers, whom it is flattery to designate

as attorneys and who for the most part are recent arrivals, hard up and eager to profit through the ignorant and overt acts of their clients.

The trouble came to a crisis when a jumper, emboldened by success and encouraged by an attorney, squatted on a well-located and desirable lot. Unfortunately it belonged to a woman, and one not timid or given to temporizing. She neither begged for justice nor invoked the law, but arming herself with a horse-whip, gave battle to the lot jumper and lashed him over the head, face, and shoulders until he was glad enough to cross the boundaries of her lot and remain outside them.

The attorney who had incited these attempts toward seizure of other peoples property was cited to appear before Judge Bell, where, thinking to override a country Justice, he was promptly fined $100 for contempt of court and being entirely without means with which to pay his fine, was sent to the County Jail at Hawthorne to work it out at $2 per day.

February 15, *Bulletin:*

The contract for extending the railroad from Tonopah to Goldfield has been let. Work is to begin in ten days. By mid-summer it will be possible to take a Pullman car at the Oakland mole and twenty-four hours later, without hardship or inconvenience, arrive in the camps which today command the attention of the mining world—Tonopah, Goldfield, and Amargosa. We are told on excellent authority that on Saturday last 3000 people in Chicago bought tickets for Tonopah. If this is any criterion of the numbers of people that will emanate from other centers, the mining camps will receive a rush that will put Cripple Creek and the Klondike in the category of minor excitements.

March 1, *Bulletin:*

In one week Goldfield has grown so that a mile of territory between the town and Columbia has been changed from sagebrush plain to a city of tents. This section was known as the Penix Addition and was plotted in lots, but the incoming tide of humanity has settled on it like a swarm of locusts and with as little regard for property rights as for the owner's feelings.

When the Penix Addition was occupied, the jumpers began squatting on vacant lots in Columbia. But here a different condition of things existed. Columbia is controlled by a game lot of men. When the lots that these men had paid good money for began to grow white with jumpers tents, Tom Ramsay, Casey McDonnell and a few kindred spirits, who are habituated to suit the action to the word, met and decided that what they had paid for was worth fighting for. They marched from jumper's tent to jumper's tent, cut the guy ropes and threw poles, canvas, and contents into the street, imparting a warning injunction to the owners to trespass again at their peril. Thus far none has seen fit to try. Goldfield property owners have been more decorous and less daring, with the result that the squatters are still in possession.

Two new hotels are in process of construction. The Nevada Exploration Company has just completed a handsome two story office building, and Senator Nixon has let a contract for a three story stone office building which is to cost $80,000. The Goldfield of last summer is fast vanishing and a new Goldfield with urban airs and conveniences is growing in its stead.

The first shipment of ore from the Bullfrog district passed through town a couple of days ago. It was from the original Bullfrog Mine, and the great mule team was proceeded by a band wagon.

Goldfield journalists and newspaper correspondents have organized a press club with a membership of twenty or more. The Bulletin's correspondent has had the honor of being elected the first President.

March 8, *Bulletin:*

Goldfield already outrivals Tonopah in population and she is not out of comparison in point of production. The $3,000,000 which marks her first year's output should be doubled this year, for now capital is not wanting with which to work.

The Blue Bull people are going in for deep work. The Velvet, Mohawk,* Vernal, Jumbo, Extension, Dixie, Tin Horn, Sunnyside, Vindicator, and innumerable other properties are being developed.

March 16, *Bulletin:*

The Florence today is the biggest producer in camp. The ore is not only of remarkable value but the quantity is enormous. This claim produced $600,000 in nine months when worked by lessees. It is sure to do double that this year under the present management.

Around $60,000 was stolen by miners while the Florence was under lease. The lessees were so anxious to get all the ore possible before their lease expired that this high-grading on the part of the miners was scarcely noticed. The same situation occurred in the Combination.

March 23, *Bulletin:*

All the lower lying country to the north of the January, the Combination, and the Jumbo and embraced in the Silver Pick, Mohawk, and Jumbo Extension claims is receiving careful attention. The Mohawk is doing considerable deep work.

The Quartzite is rivaling the Florence in point of production. Since the 20th of January it has shipped 10,000 sacks of high-grade ore. A part of this claim was jumped last week, either without reason or because of a technicality which will probably have no weight in court. One of the men interested in the property apprehended the jumper as he was engaged in solidly bank-

---

* Louis Bond, but not Marshall, was still in Goldfield when the Mohawk turned out to be the richest claim of all. A total of $5,000,000 was taken out in 106 days, and twice that by the end of 1908.

ing his monuments. Quietly walking up to him, he quickly covered him with his pistol and then, disarming him, marched him at pistol point to every monument, making him take them down and finally tear up his location notice.

March 24, *Bulletin:*

Harry Mannon, Deputy Sheriff of Nye County, was shot last evening at Beatty in the Bullfrog district. Mannon attempted to arrest two of the highwaymen who were implicated in the recent hold-up of the wood chopper's camp at Montezuma. Suspecting two men camped on the Amargosa River near Gold Center as the robbers, he drove in a buggy to their camp with Len McGarry. His conversation with the men confirmed his suspicions, and he returned to Beatty with McGarry to get the assistance of Deputy Sheriff McDonald.

When the Deputies returned to the camp and got out of their buggy the shooting began, the highwaymen being the first to open fire. A perfect fusillade followed, and Mannon was shot three times. One bullet passed clear through him, coming out near the backbone. Another entered between the ribs and another pierced the muscles of the right arm. One of the highwaymen surrendered and the other escaped in the darkness, but his capture seems certain. It is feared Mannon's wounds will prove fatal. Sheriff Bradley of Esmeralda and physicians are hurrying to the scene. Lynching is threatened.

April 12, *Bulletin:*

If one man in a settled community where the best possible protection is guaranteed to life, liberty, and property can make $40,000 in a lifetime, how long will it take two men to produce the same amount in a desert? The answer is eight hours. That is the length of time it took two men to take $40,000 out of the Quartzite Mine last week in the winze* on the 15-foot level. Un-

* A steep or vertical passageway connecting two levels in a mine.

fortunately for the men, the gold was not theirs for the getting; it went to their employers, John McKane and Jack Campbell, and associates, and it cost eight hours' time, $8 in wages, and about 80¢ in dynamite, caps, and fuses.

Two of Goldfield's stamp mills started up this week. The Gardener Mill was the first to begin work, followed a day or two later by the Combination Company's mill. The completion of these mills means a great deal to Goldfield.

April 26, *Bulletin:*

That Godliness is an unattainable condition for every mining camp is a widespread belief, and for most camps the next ranking virtue, cleanliness, has been found equally difficult. But for the latter, Goldfield is going to make a grand effort. Her citizens held a mass meeting last Sunday and the question was discussed openly. As a result $2,000 was contributed as a working fund, and Dr. Turner, one of the pioneer physicians of the town, was chosen to take charge of the work. Dr. Turner immediately divided the town into districts and appointed a competent man to take supervision over each. Already the work is well under way and the appearance of the town improved. Not only are the alleys, which have been depositories of filth for a year and over, being systematically cleaned and disinfected, but the very streets are swept and looked after like those of a large city.

May 3, *Bulletin:*

A prairie schooner drew up at the edge of town a few days ago and the two occupants of the wagon descended from the driver's seat and fell to unharnessing and making camp. They had driven all the way from Carson City, camping in the desert, and preparing their meals over sagebrush fires. These men were pushing out into the wilderness to make their fortunes. They were gray-haired, gray-bearded, and one of them was 78 years old.

He was ex-Senator Stewart of Nevada, who had sat in the United States Senate upwards of a quarter of a century, and had returned to the land of his youthful struggles and successes, broken in fortune but brave in spirit—brave enough to commence the battle of life over again at the age of 78. Dressed in flannel shirts and rough clothes, he and his partner wandered about the streets of Goldfield, strangers in a land they had trod when most of the present inhabitants were unborn. His towering stature is no longer erect, but his eye is undimmed, clear, and resolute. The men who have sweated and thirsted in this barren waste wish success unstinted to hoary age which is accompanied by the courage of youth.

Senator William M. Stewart had been a Forty-niner and, like Judge Bond, was a speculator, having made and lost half a dozen fortunes over the course of his long and active life. Unlike Judge Bond, who had lost a senatorial race in the state of Washington, Stewart had little difficulty in being elected senator from Nevada. In Virginia City he had established a reputation as an able and tenacious attorney and had attracted such clients as Wells, Fargo & Co., as well as many large mining companies. He made a million dollars out of a silver mine during the big stampede, and when he went to Washington built a gaudy mansion dubbed Stewart's Castle. By the turn of the century his wealth had been dissipated in various speculations, among them a heavy investment in the silver mines in Panamint City, which was entirely destroyed by a violent cloudburst.

He sold his castle and, undaunted, returned to Nevada to try again. By the time he was eighty he did strike it again, this time in Bullfrog where he opened a law office and won several important mining suits. He built the biggest house in town and became a rich man, on paper at least, by speculating in stocks like the famous Montgomery-Shoshone Mine. A crash in the market, however, again reduced him to penury, and when he died in 1909, he left a law library worth $25, a $200 horse and wagon, and debts of $25,000. While in Goldfield, Marshall Bond counted Senator Stewart among his most admired friends.

Bond often paid visits to the nearby mining camps of Rhyolite, Beatty, and Bullfrog. On July 10 he wrote to the *Bulletin* from Rhyolite:

The main tunnel of the Montgomery-Shoshone is now 225 feet. Part of the way in the tunnel a 90 foot shaft has been sunk which has not only produced a large quantity of ore, but has done much to add to the definite knowledge of this extraordinary property.

This mine belonged to the handsome, debonair prospector extraordinary E. A. "Bob" Montgomery, a Canadian by birth, who had been a farmer in Iowa before going west to try his luck at mining. A kindly and genial man, he befriended the Shoshone Indians. One day in token of gratitude an Indian showed him a rich piece of float and guided him to the spot where he had picked it up. An examination of a nearby ledge led to the discovery of the mine which was to make Montgomery a millionaire. It was said that all the Indian wanted in return for this was a new pair of trousers. Actually Bob gave him $20,000 after the mine was sold.

Bob's wife had left him, having become fed up with tramping the desert. When she heard of the rich strike, she wired: "Hello, Bob, here I come."

For her the desert had suddenly assumed an aura of beauty and romance, and she was determined to help him spend the money. He sold the Montgomery-Shoshone Mine to Charles Schwab for several millions, and with part of the proceeds bought a De Dietrich car in which he roared around the desert at 40 miles an hour wherever the roads were smooth enough.

His next big venture was to buy Ramsey Mason's claims 6,500 feet up in the Panamint Range at Skidoo, overlooking Death Valley. Here he consolidated the claims at Tucki Mountain and developed the Skidoo Mine. He performed the herculean tasks of building a road to the mine through the rugged mountains and laying a twenty-one-mile pipeline to bring in water from Telegraph Peak. He took out over $3,000,000, but with freight at $75 per ton and other expenses proportionately high, dividends amounted to only $365,000.

Bob Montgomery transformed himself from a humble prospector into a great swell. He went to Europe, had his clothes made by a London tailor, and became an enthusiastic authority on vintage wines. However, a few years of this extravagance plus several unfortunate mining speculations found him broke and, like Stewart, he returned to the desert to seek his fortune anew. Back in the mining camps his fancy English clothes and polished ways earned him the nickname of Gentleman Bob.

July 19, 1905, *Bulletin*:

Adjoining the St. Ives, Claude Smith has made a strike on his Gold Horn Company's ground. The ore gives promise of being both extensive and rich.

The recent disastrous fire in Goldfield, and the yet more recent holocaust in Columbia, points a timely warning to the camp's most pressing need—a sure and ample water supply.

Luckily the shacks in which the Bonds lived with their families were on the outskirts of town and escaped destruction from the fire.

Marshall left Goldfield in the summer of 1905, but Louis Bond, who was involved with the Velvet claim, remained there until 1907. Before Louis' departure Marshall paid him a short visit. His diary of November 14, 1906, reads: "Took train to Goldfield. Found town grown and great mining excitement on. Louis was at the Buckskin Mine. Everything in my house was stolen so I sold it for $200 net."

In 1907 Jack London and his wife paid a quick visit to Goldfield and were entertained by Louis and Mrs. Bond. London was greatly impressed by the activity he saw there, but did not remain because of his plans to sail across the Pacific on his yacht, the *Snark*.

The Goldfield *News* quoted London:

I am surprised at the stone buildings going up. This isn't a camp. It's a city and one of the first class. Goldfield is not built on air, as sometimes we are expected to believe. It is built upon mines. Do you mean to tell me that all those dumps out there are all mines—that the money from the sale of treasury stock is going into the ground at this rate in actual developments?

And the ore I have been shown during the first two hours in camp! The Frances-Mohawk with its bands of chemically pure gold, the January-Jones quartz full of gold nuggets, the amazing yellowness of the Little Florence, and the vastness of the deposit.

Mrs. London wrote several bread-and-butter letters to Louis' wife, asking for copies of the flashlight photographs that were taken during the course of the visit. One of these letters reads:

Honolulu, June 3, 1907

Dear Mrs. Bond:

A letter from you was forwarded to me from Glen Ellen, and it's at present down at our headquarters at Pearl Locks, and we are spending a few days in Honolulu, and I cannot get at it; but at any rate, I hope we'll get copies of the flashlights. I am anxious to see them, and to add them to my album of Nevada pictures connected with our eventful trip. It seems only yesterday we were there; and yet, it's some little time ago, and certainly the scene of our good time is a good many miles away.

I want to ask a small favor, which will be a great favor to us, and to someone else. Do you remember Fred J. Church up Klondike way, when you were there? He is very anxious to have one of those pictures of you and Buck, and the cabin, and I am going to ask you to send us one, and Jack will add his signature. We haven't any left. Please send it to Glen Ellen, and it will be forwarded.

Jack is laid up today with very severe case of sunburn, on his arms, and particularly under his knees, from surf-boarding yesterday. He cannot stand up, and I have my hands full keeping cloths on his scorched flesh wet in Hamamelis.

With best wishes from Jack and the Churches.

Sincerely yours,
Charmian K. London

In June, 1937, Marshall and his wife paid a final visit to Goldfield, of which he wrote:

Goldfield is entering the moribund stage, and a few leasers and one company operation mark its final pulsations. We went out to see where we used to live. All the houses were gone except my brother's which still stands and is occupied. The hole that marks my cellar is all that remains of a site where the excitement and pleasures of our youthful experience in a boom gold camp were had.

CHAPTER SIX

The Stikine River

Whenever any extra money turned up, Marshall Bond usually spent it for new camping equipment or an expedition. In 1911 he received a windfall from one of the Judge's former investments and promptly went on a hunting trip up the Stikine River in northern British Columbia, then the finest big-game country left in North America.

July 31 found him waiting in Wrangel, Alaska, for a boat up the Stikine, and he wrote in his diary:

After breakfast I sat in the office of the hotel reading a magazine when a large man in his shirt sleeves, ostentatiously waving paper and pencil, seated himself at the writing desk. In him I recognized the original of a picture hanging on the wall entitled, "Bobby Burns the Dreamy Wrangel Poet." Mr. Burns, in a loud and somewhat inebriated voice, told me that he had a commission to write a poem for a man who wanted to send it to a friend. After scratching off a few words he seemed unable to conjure up the Muse so he went to the bar and had a drink. Then he took up his pencil and wrote a word or two. Then he had another drink. In the course of time his poem was finished and the poet was full. With some difficulty he read:

Dear Friend Jack
I have been in Wrangel for some days
I like the town, the people, and their ways,
But sometime soon I'll be back
And glad to see old Happy Jack.

Had an interesting talk with J. Thompson, the Victoria manager of the Hudson's Bay Co. He is going up the Stikine and at Telegraph Creek will take a pack train of supplies for their post on the Laird River. Part of the trip will be in *bateaux*. On the return he will bring out furs.

On one trip he said Sir Hugo de Bothe and his brother Max were his trail companions as far as Dease Lake. They were so ignorant of camp life that they didn't even know how to light a fire. Sir Hugo had a snake tattoo encircling his body of which he was very proud, and he stripped to the waist repeatedly to exhibit it to the Indians. They were impressed only with doubts as to his sanity. After a fruitless trip as far as shooting was concerned, de Bothe, who was short of cash, wired a rich sister in London for funds. Her reply was "Be a good boy and I'll send you something for Christmas."

Spent the evening with Bronson who is collector of customs. He said that Count Wilcyck* and Count Hoyos saw forty-two bear up the Iskut and bagged eight, five of them black and three grizzlies, one of the latter being very large.

October 6 [1911]
We left Wrangel at 4:45 A.M. aboard the S.S. *Port Simpson*. The river is muddy and is from ¼ to ½ mile wide, but often breaks into two or three channels. A few miles up I observed some salmon jumping; also saw three seals. We passed the mouth of the Iskut at 1 P.M. High snow-capped mountains, rugged peaks, and glaciers formed the background of the scenery, and

* Count Wilcyck was a noted sportsman, arctic explorer, and author of *Gentlemen of Vienna*. He also rebuilt very tastefully a fabulous castle north of Vienna, Burg Kreuzenstein.

cottonwood flats and pine covered hills the foreground. I have never seen anything so fine.

At Telegraph Creek, British Columbia, he joined a pack train of the Hudson's Bay Company which took him to Dease Lake in four and a half days. On August 14 he wrote:

Arrived at Fourteen Mile Camp about a half hour ahead of the pack train. Time six hours; distance fifteen miles from previous camp. Shot six grouse along the trail. Met Indian and white man with three horses going to Telegraph Creek. They had a moose. They said three moose were killed yesterday at Dease Lake, one with an axe as it was swimming the lake.

Found an old fellow named Grif Thomas camped there. He made us some tea and offered us some porcupine stew. He had killed the porcupine the night before with a club.

I caught six graylings in the Tanzilla. Lots of wild strawberries. While I was fishing, Ira returned laden with moose meat, having killed a cow. For supper we had willow and spruce grouse, mallard and butterball ducks, and moose meat.

On August 15 they arrived at Dease Lake about noon.

Hudson's Bay Co. scow awaiting us. The scow was 42 ft. long and 7 ft. wide and was manned by 7 Indians. Each oarsman, after completing his stroke, arose, stepped forward onto the seat in front and then came back on the oar with the full weight of his body and push of his legs and settled back to his seat again. It was effective and something of a spectacular sight.

We had gone about five miles when we saw a cow moose and calf staring at us from the shore in blank amazement. Two of the Indians began shooting, but the distance was too great for accuracy, and both animals hastily betook themselves off. At times the Indians would rest, and I had considerable amusement with them doing sleight-of-hand tricks to their utter astonishment and delight. One old Indian who couldn't fathom these mysteries said I was "too much witch."

We camped that night about eight miles above Pike and reached his camp the next morning. I found Pike* well but Beauclerk on crutches, having cut his ankle with an axe. Beauclerk is quite as charming as ever, humorous, and gracious.

Bond had joined two of his English friends, Warburton Pike, the explorer, and Lord Osborne Beauclerk (pronounced Beauclair), who upon the death of his brother a few years later became the Duke of St. Albans. They were partners in a gold mine near Dease Lake, which Beauclerk financed and Pike worked during the summers. Bond had sent a couple of Indians, Charley and Benny,† to the head of the lake to make preparations for the hunt.

August 17
This morning with the same axe that Beauclerk cut himself—a Hudson's Bay type, sharp as a tomahawk—I cut my wrist clear to the bone. I put a bandage over it as best I could and drew the cut together with plaster. I think it will be all right in a few days. We have talked, read, rowed, and fished. Pike is delightful.

August 23
In the morning the cook tent was taken down and Pike, Beauclerk, Pelkie the cook, and those bound for the mine rowed across to Porter's Landing. After lunch on the beach the men started for the mine, two pack mules taking their outfit. At 2 P.M. Pike and I started for the mine and Beauclerk back to camp to act as cook for the men remaining there. What other mining camp in the annals of the West could boast of having an English Lord for a cook?

* The first mention of Pike in Bond's diary reads: "Seattle, June 26, 1908: Warburton Pike and C. Scott Whiting came up to see me in the morning. They assented to my offering their placer properties for $150,000, to be paid for out of the ground. We all had lunch and a walk to Lake Washington in the afternoon."
† They were Tahltans from the vicinity of Telegraph Creek and were considered expert hunters.

On August 27 he wrote to his wife:

Thompson, the head man of the H. B. Co. with whom I came up from Wrangel, returned to the head of the lake last night from the lower country in a canoe. When Pike and I returned to the lake we found Beauclerk with his ankle worse than ever. He dislikes taking any ailment seriously and so refused to care for his wound as he should have. He did worse and dabbed the wound with some old salve that was given him, bound it with a dirty bandage, and then walked. Consequently infection followed. When I returned he had the leg encased in oatmeal porridge which some half-breed had told him was the best treatment. I boiled some water, washed the porridge off, and washed the wound with permanganate of potash. I painted the whole swollen foot with iodine and bound it with antiseptic bandage. He insisted upon presenting me with his Mannlicher rifle, .256 Model 1903, with a leather case and all the fixings the English have with their guns.

Giving him strict instructions to leave the old-fashioned remedies alone, Pike and I got into a boat and pulled for the head of the lake—28 miles. Pike insisted upon doing the rowing on account of my wrist—which is, by the way, all right. At six we stopped and cooked some bacon and a pot of strong tea (which everybody drinks up here by the gallon and at all times) and topped off with bread and marmalade. Then we rowed on till dark and camped on a shady beach.

Three miles from the head of the lake an Indian came up in a canoe and gave me a note from Charley Quash, my guide. It said, "Mr. Bond, please you come quick other hunter be here tomorrow, I want to be first." Over the still lake we heard the rhythmic smash of oars of a big barge. It was the Hudson's Bay boat with another cargo of grub and supplies. As we drew near, Pike signaled the Indians to stop and we pulled alongside. To our great delight we found Dr. Inglis, the missionary doctor from Telegraph, and he promised to fix Beauclerk's foot.

Pike and Beauclerk are two of the finest fellows I ever met.

Pike is utterly unselfish and too considerate for his own good. Beauclerk is intellect plus culture; he is candor itself, has a happy cynicism and is humorous, and all the while is the most consummately tactful and considerate person imaginable. He is the most gracious man I ever met. You can scarcely conceive of the pleasure I have experienced in the companionship of these two men. They alone justify the trip.

September 2

Moved camp so as to be nearer sheep country and being out of fresh meat kept our eyes open for caribou. Saw a herd of 7. They were about ¼ mile away. Leaving Benny with the horses, Quash and I hurried towards the animals, keeping well out of sight. We were just going up a little knoll, on the other side of which were the caribou, when suddenly the head of one appeared at a distance of 50 or 60 yards. I hurriedly fired at him but drew too coarse a sight and overshot. They began to run now and quickly picking out an animal I took careful aim and fired. A peculiar flick of the body showed he had been hit, and he almost immediately began running in a circle and then dropped. Paced distance 89 yds. It proved to be a young cow. She was shot rather high up back of the shoulder. The bullet struck a rib upon entering and made a hole about the size of a silver dollar and passed out the other side. The shot was thro' the lungs.

With my .22 rifle I had already killed 6 ptarmigan and I later killed a marmot. After lunch I put up my tent and gathered boughs and made my bed. About 3 P.M. Quash and I started out to reconnoiter. He carried my Mannlicher and I my rifle. I soon killed another marmot. Every mountain side Quash examined thro' the glasses with long and painstaking care. After an advance of a short distance he would scan over the same ground again.

At length, to my great joy, he exclaimed, "I see um!" After much difficulty I finally made out 3 sheep at least ¾ of a mile away well up on a steeply sloping mountain which admitted of no cover for stalking. It was then quarter to six, and whatever we did would have to be done expeditiously, as it would be dark by quarter past seven. Leaving the .22 by a rock with a handkerchief tied around the barrel to enable us to better find it later, we hurried stealthily forward. If we could scale the mountain and find decent going on top, we could hasten along the ridge until just above them and probably get near enough for a shot. To accomplish this before dark would require speed.

Crouching on our hands and feet, we proceeded cautiously up a steep rock slide until eventually out of sight of the animals, then up the precipitous slide we climbed with all possible speed. Dripping with sweat and panting for breath, we at last reached the summit. It was impassable. It narrowed to an edge and was pinnacled like a huge saw. Nothing more could be done. We must try tomorrow, if they were there, to approach them some other way, or find them if they had gone. Tired but jubilant we returned to camp about 9:30, ate an enormous meal of ptarmigan and caribou liver and turned in.

Sunday, September 3, 1911, Clear

At 5:30 Quash and I were on our way to the place we had seen the sheep. We discovered them feeding not far from where we had left them but lower down. We finally made out 2 old rams with good horns, and a young ram with horns not good enough. We had approached within ½ mile and no cover was to be had. One ram would generally lie down and watch while the other two fed. Quash said, "The only thing we can do is crawl toward um and take all day if need be. When we get close we get cover. You do as I say and we get 'um."

It was then 6:15 and on our bellies we wriggled forward, pausing now and then to watch the animals with our field glasses to see that they were not alarmed. Quash's eyes snapped and he grinned with joy. Some of the time he would assure me, "They no can see us," and again when the ram on guard seemed looking our way, "He think we porcupine."

The sun was creeping lower and lower down the mountain

side, but as yet we were in the shadow and that was in our favor. On over the frozen ground we wriggled along on our elbows and knees, and our knees felt the frost keenly. Four or five rock slides feathered off into green turf like fingers and it was towards the first of these we made our way. In the green, particularly when the sun reached it, we could be more readily discernible, but against the dark gray rocks we should be less likely to be seen. We wriggled on with great caution, keeping our heads well down. Nearer and nearer we approached until the animals were plain to the naked eye. Quash examined them through the glasses and whispered, "Two fine heads, we get 'um, we get 'um. You do just as I do."

Absolutely flat on our bellies we now pushed along with our toes and elbows. Occasionally I would peep up, and it seemed as though we must be discovered. The wind still kept blowing gently from the sheep to us. Quash finally whispered, "Keep your head down." My nose in the grass, I pushed along and didn't raise my head again. Finally Quash tapped me with his hand and said, "Come quick." We were near enough now for the contour of the ground to offer some protection. The sheep had passed behind a slight ridge, and Quash saw the opportunity of gaining ground. We rose and rushed forward silently and as rapidly as possible. "We shoot from behind that big rock," he whispered as we made a dash for it. I reached it, panting too heavily for accurate shooting, and as I did so saw the three sheep disappear behind another little ridge. Quash with instant strategy saw an opportunity for getting closer still and said, "Come on." But I felt I must have a few breaths, and preferred a longer shot if undiscovered to a closer one at running sheep and my wind gone. Quash was furious because I stopped, but while he started to complain the sheep came into sight again.

It is dreadfully hard to judge distances in such country, but I estimated it at 200 yds. and fired. Apparently it was a miss for all three scattered. I started to aim at one on the right when Quash said, "Shoot left one." I circled my rifle to the left and fired at the blackest of the three sheep as he was bounding away.

He fell, and Quash said, "You got um." The circumference of the sheep's horn at the base was 13 inches, and the length from the base to the point was 33 inches.

Altogether Bond bagged three caribou, two sheep, a moose, four mountain goats, and thirty marmots, to say nothing of a great many grouse, ducks, and ptarmigan.

Charley Quash had several dogs which he used as pack animals for light camping equipment. Whenever they confronted a porcupine the dogs would invariably charge it, getting their muzzles covered with painful quills which Charley would have to pull out. They never seemed to remember these woeful experiences, for each time another porcupine came along they would charge all over again.

Warburton Pike was a hero in Bond's eyes because of his intrepid exploits in the Canadian wilderness and his utterly delightful personality. He was born in Wareham, Dorset, England. After leaving Oxford he came to Canada, and in 1889 made a trip from Great Slave Lake to within a few miles of Bathurst Inlet on the Arctic Ocean. In those days vast areas of the country north of the 60th parallel were still unexplored by white men. His aim was to find musk ox. He started out with several half-breed Yellowknife Indians and their dogs, taking only a few blankets, tea, tobacco, and his rifle, to cross a country infested with mosquitoes in summer and as cold as Siberia in winter. At the head of the Coppermine River on September 27 he found a herd of musk ox and shot a big bull. He was one of the first to bring the skins of these animals back to civilization. One of the finest passages in his book, *The Barren Ground of Northern Canada*, reads:

With the increasing depth of snow there was a noticeable migration of life from the Barren Ground. Ptarmigan came literally in thousands, while the tracks of wolves, wolverines, and arctic foxes made a continuous network in the snow. Scattered bands of caribou were almost always in sight from the top of the ridge behind the camp, and increased in number till the morning of October 20th, when little Baptiste, who had gone for firewood, woke us up before daylight with the cry of La Foule! La Foule! ["the herd"] and even in the lodge we could hear the curious clatter made by the band of travelling caribou. La Foule had really come, and during its passage of six days I was able to realize what an extraordinary number of these animals still roam in the Barren Ground. From the ridge we had a splendid view of the migration; all the south side of Mackay Lake was alive with moving beasts, while the ice seemed to be dotted all over with black islands, and still away on the north shore, with the aid of glasses, we could see them coming like regiments on the march. In every direction we could hear the grunting noise that the caribou always make when travelling; the snow was broken into broad roads, and I found it useless to try to estimate the number that passed within a few miles of our encampment.

This passage of the caribou is the most remarkable thing I have ever seen in the course of many expeditions among the big game of America. The Buffalo were for the most part killed out before my time, but, notwithstanding all the tall stories that are told of their numbers, I cannot believe that the herds on the prairies ever surpassed in size La Foule of the caribou.

In November of that year Pike attempted to cross the Rockies by way of Peace River—the same route Sir Alexander MacKenzie had taken in 1793. He and his four companions were caught in the mountains by heavy snow, lost their way, and nearly starved to death before they got back to the Hudson's Bay post at Vermilion. One night they found a discarded flour sack out of which they scraped half a pound of flour. With this they made gruel and fortified it with slices of a mouse which one of the men had caught and singed over the fire. This was the best meal they had had in days.

In 1892 Pike discovered the Pelly Lakes* above Dease Lake, and following the Pelly River in a canoe down to the Yukon, continued all the way to the Bering Sea. For many months he was cut off entirely from civilization. He described this adventure in *Through the Sub-Arctic Forest*. Pike lived in a shack on an island near Victoria and had a romantic liaison in that city with a lady named Mrs. Elliott.

While hunting up the Stikine River Bond, Pike, and Beauclerk staked out some coal claims in the Cassiar mining district which they called the Ground Hog. They had visions of emulating the success of Robert Dunsmuir, who had made millions out of the Wellington coal deposit a few years before. On their return to Vancouver in the hope of enlisting capital they interested a German friend, Alvo von Alvensleben, in the mine.

Von Alvensleben was a Prussian, the son of Baron von Alvensleben, a close friend of Kaiser Wilhelm II. He was alleged to have become so deeply involved in a society scandal in Berlin that the Kaiser suggested he go abroad for "reasons of health." He arrived in Seattle penniless but got a job picking chickens, at which he soon became expert, explaining that all you had to do was to tie the chicken's legs together, dip the bird in boiling water just long enough to loosen the feathers, hang it on a nail, and then pluck furiously with both hands.

In spite of his skill at this sort of work, von Alvensleben was not without ambition. He decided to go into business for himself and moved to Vancouver, where pastures looked

---

* Provincial Archives offers no evidence to refute Pike's claim of being the first white man to explore the Pelly Lakes, even though they appear on John Arrowsmith's 1854 map. Presumably Arrowsmith heard of them from Robert Campbell, who explored the lower Pelly River in 1840.

greener. There he procured a wagon and delivered vegetables to restaurants and hotels in the downtown area, including the Vancouver Club. After some months of this the Kaiser relented and sent him several million dollars to invest in British Columbia. The humble vegetable man was transformed overnight into a man of wealth and was soon elected to the Vancouver Club. At his first lunch there the waiter looked at him, gasped, and dropped a bowl of soup.

Von Alvensleben said, "Yes, I was delivering vegetables to you a month ago, but now I'm a member, so please continue serving the meal."

For three years continuous correspondence, mining reports, and financial calculations passed back and forth between the four men. Just as things were beginning to look up, World War I started and von Alvensleben's German funds were confiscated by the Canadian government. He himself escaped to Seattle. In 1917 Marshall Bond, who had joined the Secret Service for the duration of the war, reluctantly had him interned on suspicion of espionage.

Von Alvensleben was impressed by the hard work required to bag game in the rugged mountains of British Columbia, in contrast to the easy method of stalking animals with beaters on European estates. His father, the Baron, had a large estate on which he raised rabbits for the Berlin market, but for years had refused to allow hunting on his property. He despised the mock heroics with which the nobility slaughtered huge numbers of animals as "sport." At length, however, he appeared to be persuaded by the pleas of his friends and issued dozens of invitations to an elaborate rabbit hunt.

Early on the appointed day when the elite of Prussia was assembled, guns in hand, a signal was given for opening the warrens. At the very same moment a brass band, which was hidden in a thicket, struck up the national anthem, and the entire assemblage sprang to attention. While the band was playing, a thousand rabbits wearing pink shirts, which the Baron had had sewn on the day before, galloped past the rigid hunters. Not a shot was fired.

In 1914 Bond met another distinguished European whom he described in a letter to the Secret Service:

Recently I spent a few days in Phoenix, Arizona, with my friend, Count C. Karl Coudenhove, an Austrian. He is a man of 31, handsome, worldly, amusing, and splendidly educated, being a graduate of the Universities of Jena and Berlin. At the time war was declared he was in camp with Lord Osborne Beauclerk, now aide-de-camp to Sir Douglas Haig, and Warburton Pike.

An Indian came into their camp and said, "Killing lots of people in Europe!" Other than that he knew nothing. They sent an Indian 100 miles to the Hudson's Bay post at Telegraph Creek and in that way got the particulars. These Englishmen enabled Coudenhove to get out of the country and avoid being taken prisoner. They gave him $100 and a canoe in which he went down the Stikine River to Wrangel, passing the Canadian posts at night. After arriving in Seattle he was advised by Dr. Dumba, the Austrian Ambassador, to stay where he was as it was impossible to get back to Europe.

When Pike and Beauclerk went back to the war they asked me to look up Coudenhove, as he was a good sort. I did so, and we have thereafter been together a great deal hunting and camping.

Shortly after Lord Beauclerk's return to England, Bond received the following letter:

On board H. M. S. Olympic
Lough Swilly, N. Ireland
Oct. 31, 1914, 8 P.M.

My dear Bond:

I know you are anxious for war details, and as we have just

come through an experience that we are unlikely to have again, I write to give you some idea of what one little glimpse of naval warfare has enabled us to see.

We left New York on Wednesday the 21st of October and had an uneventful journey until the following Tuesday, the 27th, when at 10 A.M., when 13 miles from Lough Swilly and three miles from Tory Island, we came suddenly on a wonderful sight. The battleship *Audacious* was sinking. Near her the cruiser *Liverpool* was standing by, while 5 destroyers were constantly circling round, looking just like porpoises. From the land various small ships were hurrying up to help. Imagine a high sea, bright day, and strong south wind. At length only the bow of the *Audacious* was above water, she was listing heavily from side to side, and great waves were breaking over the deck, which carried men away, sometimes washing them back again.

No one knew at the time whether she had been mined or torpedoed by a submarine, and we gradually learned (wild contradictory rumors were constantly flying about) that she had left Lough Swilly for gun practice together with the remainder of the battle squadron, when she had either struck a mine or been torpedoed. She held the record for gunnery in the navy, and was the finest ship of the squadron. It was thought she had been torpedoed.

It was too splendid to see the discipline on board her, and made one proud of one's country. We launched all our boats; three were upset and only two men lost before we appeared. The seamen seemed to take it all most casually and were splendid fellows—mostly only about twenty, and you would have loved to have talked with them and to have seen the way they behaved.

I should have told you that the officers and some of the crew remained on the sinking ship, and we tried twice to tow her, but she wouldn't steer and we had to give it up.

At dusk she was abandoned, and we came in here, where we found the rest of the fleet, which had scuttled back here when it happened, drawn up behind a submarine proof boom.

At 10 P.M. we heard an explosion and saw a great sheet of

flame in the sky. It was the magazine of the *Audacious* exploding, and we thought she had been torpedoed again, but it was probably due to the air-cooling fans in the cordite magazine having stopped, as I believe there had been several lesser explosions previously. One man on the *Liverpool*, which was close by, was killed by a bit of iron, that's all. Directly we got here we had to put out all lights, and we have been held up for four days; and allowed to hold no communication with land; though four government men on board and Charles Schwab (the steel man, who is going to France to supply them with steel cars) were allowed to leave yesterday on giving their word of honor not to talk.

Last night there was an alarm of a Zeppelin attack (although I am the only passenger who knows this) and the crew strewed mats, etc. at 2 A.M. on the upper deck. A picket boat is always circling around us, and one hour ago (7 P.M.) the fleet silently steamed by us out to sea with all lights out.

It appears that two ships ahead of us were sunk by mines Tuesday, and we ran into a mine field and were lucky not to strike one. We were going to Glasgow, but tomorrow we're going to be allowed to leave for Belfast, and a notice has been put up asking passengers "in the interests of the Empire not to mention the events of last Tuesday." I fancy the Admiralty will announce it officially later, but they don't want us to talk yet, as it would give the position of the fleet away.

But fancy expecting an airship attack here! It shows that there have been some elsewhere which we have heard nothing about; indeed, I believe very little of the naval news has been published in the papers. I believe the theory is that the mines have been dropped by neutral ships on their way to or from the U.S.A. Our fleet captured on Tuesday several German trawlers flying the British flag.

Send this letter in to old Pike. I wish I could give you an idea of the drama of the whole scene, and the impression one gets in this Lough (25 miles long) with the fleet two miles away behind their boom. Just now they steamed out to sea quite close to us, and looked like a troop of elephants in single file going to water at night.

Yours sincerely,
Osborne Beauclerk

A few days later a letter from Pike arrived.

Union Club
Victoria, B. C.
Nov. 20th 1914

My dear Bond,

Many thanks for your two letters and the newspaper with Roosevelt's article. It was I thought an excellent article & hits the nail on the head—the Hague Conference is rather rot if there is no power to enforce its terms. I can't see any reason at present why America should be involved unless it should be for the sake of saving the male population of Europe from extinction, which seems to be threatened, and even in that case she would do little good without a good sized army and navy.

I have written home to see if I can get a job as age prevents me from joining any Canadian outfit—but I hate to go home & get nothing to do—it is better here though I feel I can still fire a rifle fairly straight & probably walk as well as many of the younger men.

Many thanks for your kindness to Coudenhove—he is really a capital fellow but talks little English. Tell him that of course we shall be as friendly as ever as soon as the war is over. He knows that England has no cause of quarrel with Austria. Personally I have many good friends among the Austrians & was always treated with the greatest kindness during the six months I spent there. I should like to hear the fate of many of them. I fear there has been an awful slaughter among the aristocracy of all European countries. Do come over and have a couple of days on the island loafing about if you can.

With best wishes to Mrs. Bond and the boys.

Yours sincerely,
Warburton Pike

As soon as Pike was able to wind up his affairs at the mine he returned to England and received an offer from the Admiralty to command a small motor cruiser. Before he could accept, however, the doctor put him in a sanitarium, saying that he was suffering from a brain disease. Confinement and worry over losing his mind resulted in acute depression.

Marshall Bond was greatly saddened by a letter which Coudenhove showed him, written by Beauclerk on December 21, 1915:

Meanwhile he was put in charge of a nurse. He escaped from her and hid in some woods, and his body was found in the sea two days afterwards. He had filled his pockets with stones, walked into the sea and stabbed himself. He was the most unselfish and modest man I've ever known.

Quite unexpectedly the author received a letter dated March 15, 1956, from Fenley Hunter of Garden City, Long Island:

My old field journal reads as follows:

> Foot of Dease Lake,
> Northern British Columbia
> 24 June 1923

We found a monument to Warburton Pike on the trail to Mitchell Mine; it overlooks Dease Lake a short way from the landing. It is a well-built 6-foot concrete pyramid with a bronze plate (facing south), the latter sent over from England by Pike's friends. The bronze plate bears the following inscription:

IN MEMORY OF
WARBURTON PIKE
AUTHOR - SPORTSMAN - EXPLORER
BORN SEPTEMBER 25th 1861
DIED OCTOBER 20th 1915

At that time I was on my way by canoe to Frances Lake in the Yukon to investigate the type and range of mountain sheep in that area at the suggestion of Mr. Sheldon* who was connected with Smithsonian and a great authority on the sheep of North America. It was probably the following year I learned that Mr. Charles Sheldon of Washington, D. C., Lord Osborne Beauclerk of England, and Marshall Bond of Santa Barbara, California, had this monument erected in 1921.

In 1954 the author wrote Beauclerk (who was then eighty-one):

My dear Duke:
I had some recent correspondence with Mr. W. E. Ireland, Curator of Provincial Archives, Victoria, British Columbia, in regard to the late Warburton Pike.
Mr. Ireland told me that his museum had just acquired the original manuscripts of Pike's two books. I told him that I had a file of correspondence between my father, yourself, and Pike which I found among my mother's possessions when she died last March. Mr. Ireland said there is great interest in Pike and his explorations in British Columbia and that he was unaware that any letters of Pike's had survived. I have, therefore, given the file to Provincial Archives, including about thirty letters in Pike's handwriting.
If you have any of his letters or other information, Provincial Archives would be most grateful for them. My father was a great admirer of Pike, and I am sure he would feel that this correspondence would best serve Pike's memory by being placed in Provincial Archives at Victoria.
Incidentally, I asked Mr. Ireland to find out if the Ground Hog coal claims ever amounted to much.† He checked with the

* Charles Sheldon, a friend of Bond's, was the author of *The Wilderness of the North Pacific Coast Islands*; *The Wilderness of Denali*; and *The Wilderness of the Upper Yukon*.
† In 1968 they were under investigation by Japanese interests.

mining authorities and reported that developments there had been disappointing.

Sincerely yours,
Marshall Bond, Jr.

The Duke replied as follows:

Newton Anner
Colonmel
Eire
Aug 7/54

Dear Mr. Bond:

Of course I remember your father well. No one had a higher admiration of Warburton Pike than I had. He really *was* a hero and the best traveller I ever knew. I do possess several letters apropos of a mine, the Boulder Creek, in Cassiar, B. C., which I took a lease of. I went there first as an idle sportsman and worked there with him from 1910-14, after having done a trip with him in a dory down the Colorado River in, I think, 1910. I set up an inscription to him (together with your father) at the foot of Dease Lake, Cassiar, after his death. I always regard W. P. as a great man, of course hopeless in business and rather out of place in civilization.

Yours,
St. Albans

The author advised Mr. Ireland of the existence of a few more of Pike's letters, but the curator wrote some years later that he had been unable to recover any from the duke or his estate.

CHAPTER SEVEN

Pancho Villa

In THE FALL OF 1918 Marshall Bond was hired to examine some silver mines belonging to the Alvarado Mining and Milling Company in the city of Hidalgo Del Parral in the state of Chihuahua, 417 miles south of El Paso. His companion on this adventure was Franklin Wheaton Smith,* an expert mining geologist.

The Mexican Revolution, which had been started in 1910 by Francisco Madero, had, after the murder of Madero, degenerated into a struggle for power between various political and military factions under such leaders as Zapata, Huerta, Obregon, Villa, and Carranza.

By 1916 Carranza, having won control of most of the country, had driven Villa back to his native Chihuahua, where he robbed and pillaged at will in an effort to keep his army together. The Mexicans were engulfed in desperate guerrilla fighting in which no quarter was given and all prisoners were shot.

Pancho Villa was the most celebrated of all Mexican ban-

* Smith's father-in-law, Sir Ernest Craig, came to New Mexico as a young man, made a fortune in the Last Chance gold mine in the Mogollon district, returned to England, and became a member of Parliament.

dits. At one point he had occupied Mexico City, but had lacked the breadth and education to take over the country. When Woodrow Wilson recognized Carranza, Villa expressed his hatred for America by raiding Columbus, New Mexico, and killing sixteen United States citizens there. As a result of this, Wilson in 1916 reluctantly dispatched General Pershing to Mexico with orders to get the bandit dead or alive. However, Villa was more than a match for the Americans on his native soil and easily eluded them. After a few unsuccessful skirmishes Wilson withdrew the troops.

Villa was a bold and resourceful leader, cruel, arbitrary, and unpredictable. He was a rapist and a murderer, and yet when he gave his word it could usually be depended upon. In 1920, after a dozen years of marauding, he was bribed into making peace by the gift of the half-million-acre Canutillo ranch in Durango. However, three years later, while he was driving near Parral in an old Dodge car, his enemies shot him down from ambush.

At the time of Bond's visit in 1918 Villa was very active in Chihuahua, raiding mining towns for supplies and money and fighting Carranza.

From a town near Parral, Bond wrote to his older son:

> Sept 25th, 1918
> Jimenez,
> Chihuahua, Mexico

Dear old Dick:

After all kinds of red tape and examinations of baggage, we crossed the Rio Grande at El Paso and then went through a lot more examinations by the Mexican authorities, and finally got aboard a ramshackle day coach, without upholstering, marked "Primera Clase" and pulled out. A couple of steel ore cars were filled with wild looking, ragged soldiers, having belts of cartridges around the waist and one over each shoulder. Mucho

ammunition. They were Mexicans, not Yaquis, the latter having gone back to Sonora. After crawling through some sand hills
we came out on a level plateau skirted in the distance by mountains on either side.

It was a peach of a cattle country, green grass knee-high as far
as the eye could see. Most of it belongs to old Gov. Terrazas and,
when I went through it 16 years ago, it had hundreds of thousands of cattle and horses. This time all the way down I never
saw a cow except a few milch ones herded around one or two
little towns. The revolutionists had made that equitable distribution of property so many people rant about, not realizing that
property gravitates generally into the hands of those who can
administer it best. Thousands of head were killed for a few
steaks, a dozen men would kill as many animals just for the
tongue. "Put a beggar on horseback and he rides to the devil" is
an old saying. No one now has any cattle, so that much desired
equality is a fact.

I saw a band of ten or fifteen antelope about half a mile from
the train and wished we were camping thereabouts. For 100
miles or more alongside the track are the bent rails of the former
track. They were torn up, heated in fires of burning ties and then
bent so as to be useless, and there they lie, a mute testimony to
the foolish destructiveness of man.

We arrived at Chihuahua after dark but had an hour or so to
look about in the morning. The town was founded in the 16th
Century and has a fine old cathedral and many interesting Spanish houses, severe and forbidding outside, but, through open
doors, disclosed entrancing patios with trees and flowers. At
noon we reached the Conchos River Valley. Here is where my
old Boer friend, General Snyman, had his ranch until he was
run out. Fine crops of corn and vegetables were growing. There
is no danger of starvation in Mexico. Women and children and
old men passed beneath our windows shouting "Leche" (milk in
beer bottles), "Enchiladas," "Tortillas," etc., all through the
gamut of their food possibilities.

We arrived at 8 P.M. and put up at the hotel by the station.

Here also is the *Cuartel** or Military Barracks, and the houses of those employed about the railway. The main town, like so many in Mexico, is about a mile distant.

We learned that Villa had burned the bridge between here and Parral the day before, so we had to stay where we were until it could be repaired. Our hotel is the usual adobe building with patios, wings, and other patios. The part I am in is two stories high, and I get to my room by an outside stairway from the patio. At five the next morning an old Mexican came around, rousing everyone for the southbound train whether you wanted to go or not. I had just begun to go to sleep again when I was startled by heavy rifle fire out in the street. There was a hurrying of feet and shouting of voices as people rushed down into the patio. Then I heard the purr of a machine gun at the *Cuartel* about 50 yards away. I realized that we were being attacked by Villa and rushed into Mr. Smith's room and told him to get dressed and come down into the patio.

When I got there I saw a lot of men and women—one with a little baby at her breast—all looking scared. The scaredest man of all was a slob of a major who had come from the south to pay off troops. I had seen him the night before at supper putting on an awful lot of side before a fair companion. Now he was begging for a suit of civilian clothes, as "the Villistas would kill him if they got in." Someone accommodated the poltroon, and he soon appeared in a suit too small, without hat or collar, and looking the prize scamp he was. He hid his military clothes, hat, pistol, and cartridge belt and was ready to vow himself a "traveller."

Fierce firing was now going on outside in all directions. I looked in vain for some sort of leadership and thought there might be opportunity for at least moderately heroic defense on the part of the civilians. They did nothing. So great is the fear of Villa that the civil population scarcely dared lift a finger.

---

* In an article in the New York *Sun,* April 20, 1919, Bond wrote that this building belonged to a Chinese who had been murdered, and that over the entrance hung a sign saying "New York Hotel."

There was no organization and no cohesion. Everyone was studying his individual problem.

Several men told me they were afraid and asked if I was. I replied, "Certainly not," which was not wholly the truth. I told them if the Carranzistas had courage they could hold them, if they had no courage, they couldn't.

One big black fellow bemoaned his fear, and I joshed him about his size, but it did no good. A little fellow kept following me about, also telling me of the fear he felt. Soon a bullet grazed his stomach and went into his arm. The blood poured out. The poor fellow turned deathly pale, and the perspiration came out on his face. He went away to the doctor.

It was daylight now, and I went out into the street to see what was going on. Behind adobe walls and in trenches, soldiers were firing away. A troop of cavalry dashed out from the *Cuartel* and made for a street crossing the railroad. They were a wild looking bunch with their big sombreros and waving rifles. Before long several riderless horses came back. I saw a captain, dead, carried back to the *Cuartel*. A railway employee was helped by a soldier. A bullet had passed through his stomach. He wore that same dreadful pallor and soon died. A soldier with a gaping wound through his jaw walked solemnly past.

At 8:30 we went out to breakfast. A little peon waitress, all smiles, waited on us and announced beans, eggs, bread, chocolate, and coffee. We took them all but the coffee. Chocolate is fine in Mexico. The bread was pure white flour. Oh Boy! it was good. After breakfast, back to the patio. Soldiers had now mounted the roof above our rooms, piled up a few adobe bricks for shelter along the top and were firing vigorously. Among them was a boy of about your size and age. He constantly stood up to fire and then watched to see if he had scored a hit. Soon a bullet hit him in the temple and he fell dead, his face smeared with blood. Two stretcher bearers got him down off the roof and carried him away to the *Cuartel*.

The attack now became harder, and a lot of Chinamen sought refuge in our patio, very scared looking. The Villistas always kill

Chinamen and Americans. I did my best to make them think everything was all right, though I had inward doubts myself. After nine hours the Villistas withdrew. There were 20 dead within 300 yards of the hotel. A prisoner was taken, being shot through the hips. He was questioned and then summarily shot. Neither side gives quarter.

The next morning I went up to the *Cuartel* and saw the dead loaded on carts and carried away to be burned. I asked permission of a colonel to go into the *Cuartel*. He ordered the guard to let me pass and sent a petty officer ahead, giving a few instructions which I did not understand. The building is a one story affair at least 175 ft. square with a large patio inside.

A covered brick veranda surrounded the patio. Some 8 or 10 dead men lay on the floor, lighted candles burning at their feet, their women folk standing by, occasionally breaking into lamentation. I saw the boy I had seen killed on the roof. The wounded lay on single blankets, some in great pain. Wives of soldiers were preparing meals at little fires in the patio. Armed soldiers were coming and going. It was a weird sight. When I started to go out I was stopped and told I couldn't until I had seen the General. I was a prisoner. That cowardly officer came in, and I tried to make him understand I wanted him to get Mr. Scott, the Company's agent, at the hotel. He couldn't or wouldn't, understand. I showed him my passport and he nearly burst, announcing with indignation the dreadful fact, "You are an American!" I began to think that was the worst thing one could be.

Then in came a crowd, hissing in exhultation, "Uno Villista." I beheld a little boy, between your age and Marshall's, absolutely naked, dried blood on his leg, limping with pain, his face green with fear and agony. He was questioned a few moments, then taken to the pyre and shot.

I tried all possible blandishments to get in to see the General but was told "in just a moment"—always. In his anteroom lay the dead captain in full dress uniform. After being there an hour, the guard suddenly beckoned me to the door and told me

I could go. I found Scott outside. A Mexican had fortunately seen me in there and asked Scott what I was in for. He went directly to the Colonel, gave assurances for me, and got me out.

We walked over to Jimenez. On the way we passed a nice looking house. The doors were open and I stopped to observe the beautiful flowery patio inside. From others we learned that it had been the residence of a widow, her two daughters, and sisters, one of the daughters herself a widow with a year old child. Because the mother of this child had married a Carranzista general—who had been killed months ago—Villa, with his own pistol, yesterday slew the entire family, as well as two maid servants.

When we got to the plaza of the town we sat down under the big trees and with the crowd watched the funeral service in the church opposite for three men Villa had also killed the day before. Suddenly from a side street someone rushed past and shouted, "Villistas!" In a moment everyone fled. We started walking, but ready to run, back to the station. People were fearfully peering from their doors. We looked back and saw a troop of horsemen coming at a walk. We were well ahead. We passed two dead Villista horses, ravenous dogs devouring them. Soon some Carranza cavalry dashed up. They stopped. They recognized the oncoming horsemen as their own men returning.

Yesterday I was taking a nap when I was awakened by voices. Going out on the veranda I learned the Villistas had again returned to Jimenez, and I saw a large body of Carranza cavalry chasing them. Going out in the street, I soon saw a prisoner brought in. He was mounted on a little mule which had been too slow to get away. He refused to answer questions. An officer shot him through the head with his pistol. Eighteen Villistas killed.

A little one mule train car runs between the station and town. The cowardly officer before mentioned, believing the Villistas gone for good after the first day, had resumed his uniform, pistol, and belt, and with a soldier was in the car on his way to town when the Villistas returned for the second attack. Two of them held up the car. The officer threw his pistol and belt under the seat. He was shot dead. The peon soldier killed the assailant and was himself killed by the second Villista.

An Englishmen I met, whose house was searched, had just time to crawl under a blanket on the floor in a corner. A woman sat on him as though the blanket covered a seat or mattress and he escaped detection.

General Murguia arrived this morning with reinforcements. The band played, bugles blared, etc. and this afternoon troops went out as Villa is reported to be but 5 miles from town. Unless he has a much larger force than is thought and is merely trying to decoy the Carranzistas into an ambush, he should be driven off. We shall stay here and go on to our work at Parral when we can get there. If a train goes north tomorrow I will send you this.

> Much love from
> your affectionate Dad

P.S. I should have pointed out the moral there. Had that cowardly officer had the courage to fight, it was an even break and he and his soldier might have killed their opponents.

You may be interested to know that I was writing a letter to your mother during the scrap the first day and had returned this tablet to my room and started down the stairs when a piece of wood hit me in the ear. A bullet had hit the post at the head of the stairs around which I had so shortly turned. Two bullets buried themselves in the wall beside my door. I dug one out and will take it back to Marshall, as he always asks for "curious things."

When they arrived at the railroad station near Jimenez at 8 p.m. the first evening, Bond wanted to go into town, hoping to find better accommodations. However, Smith was very tired and insisted on staying at the hotel near the station. It was lucky for them, for Villa captured the town on his first attack and shot half a dozen Americans there.

When Bond was awakened by gunfire the next morning

Marshall Bond (center, behind girl shading her eyes) joins members of their safari in the Belgian Congo, 1927, to celebrate a kill of lions.

Bond was an admirer of Cecil Rhodes. Here Bond regards the tomb of the empire builder.

On the track of survivors of the Lincoln County War in New Mexico, Bond (seated), his son Marshall Bond, Jr. (far right) and former governor M. A. Otero (next to Bond, Jr.) pose with Miguel Luna and Hijinio (Eugenio) Salazar (standing, second from left) in 1926.

Mr. and Mrs. George Coe at their ranch on the Ruidoso River in 1926 told Bond about old Lincoln County days, when Coe had his trigger finger shot off in the gunfight at Blazer's Mill.

Deluvina "Maxwell" Jaramillo, sunning in front of her home at Fort Sumner, N.M., in 1926 recalled for Marshall Bond the days when she was a sweetheart of Billy the Kid.

Susan E. Barber (in doorway) at White Oaks, N.M., 1926, told Bond of the Lincoln County War episode in which her first husband, Alexander McSween, was killed by gunmen.

Nov 20th 1914

My dear Bond,

Many thanks for your two letters & the newspaper with Roosevelt's article — It was I thought an excellent article & hits the nail on the head — the Hague Conference is rather rot if there is no power to enforce its terms. I can't see any reason at present why America should be involved in —

I have many do among the s & was alw to the greater during the — I spent uld like to ate of man I fear there n ample sla aristocracy of en countries.

Do come on & have a couple of days on the island loafing about if you can.

With best wishes to Mrs B. & the boys Yours sincerely Warburton Pike

Letter from Warburton Pike to Marshall Bond in 1914. The British author-sportsman-explorer saw no reason for the U.S. to join the war unless it was for "saving the male population of Europe from extinction."

(*Above*) Lord Osborne Beauclerk, Duke of St. Albans—a British sportsman and mine owner who was a Canadian camp cook one year and aide-de-camp to Sir Douglas Haig the next. (*Right*) Warburton Pike, noted Canadian explorer, was a partner in Beauclerk's mine and host to Marshall Bond on a Canadian hunting trip.

Beauclerk (left) and Pike at their camp in British Columbia, around 1911. (Courtesy Provincial Archives, Victoria, B.C.)

Gold of the Mojave Desert in California! Walter Trent, associate of Senator Key Pittman, explains his new mine in 1935 to a group including Bond (center).

Mines at Soledad Mountain on the Mojave, showing the immense tailings from the famous Golden Queen mine, lower right.

The last rich strike. Marshall Bond in his camp on the Mojave Desert, 1934. He died in 1941 knowing he had led "a life more interesting than that which falls to most men."

The Middle Buttes mine on the Mojave Desert, showing that not all successful mines require tunnels and shafts.

Bond photographed this six-foot-six prince of the Dinka tribe in Africa, on a trip in 1927. "No king could touch him for dignity, beauty, and grace," wrote Bond.

as the attack began, he said that getting Smith out of bed was one of the most nerve-racking tasks of his life. It was not only dark, but Smith had been stone deaf since childhood. Bond could only communicate with him by sign language. His fingers nearly froze as he spelled out by candlelight:

"V-I-L-L-A A-T-T-A-C-K-I-N-G B-U-L-L-E-T-S F-L-Y-I-N-G G-E-T U-P Q-U-I-C-K."

The world of silence had made Smith a philosopher, for he never betrayed the slightest sign of fear or worry.

Bond later met a Scotch mining engineer who had lived in Mexico many years and enjoyed the trust and confidence of everyone. When General Pershing crossed the border, Mexican government troops as well as Villistas opposed the Americans, and in one of the skirmishes General Francisco Murguia captured a company of Negro troops. The Scotchman heard of this, and, fearing the worst, went to see Murguia. After the usual polite salutations, he asked:

"General, what are you going to do with those American prisoners?"

"Shoot them, of course," replied the general.

"You wouldn't do that," said his caller.

"Why not?" Murguia wanted to know.

"General," said the Scotchman, "the eyes of the world are upon you. Your brilliant tactics and daring exploits are written up by the press in every country, and you are the envy of generals on both sides of the great conflict in Europe. What would the world say if the brave General Murguia were to stoop so low as to shoot his American prisoners?"

"I never thought of that," said the general, and wrote out an order for their release.*

* Ironically, a few years later Murguia himself died before a firing squad.

On September 29, 1918, Bond wrote to his wife from Torreon:

Villa cleaned up 2400 troops three days ago, and a battle was going on about 20 miles out between all forces. Everyone advised us to come down here while there was a chance. No trains have gone north for 6 days and this is the first one south, which left yesterday. Smith and I came on it as did all others who could get away. We brought 2 cars of wounded along. About half way I saw a man hanging to a telegraph post cross-armed. He had evidently been there for weeks, as he looked mummified.

Should Villa happen to defeat Murguia he would kill or rob everyone in Jimenez and then at once attack Torreon. Sacking this city would give considerable money and he would cut off the railways from the south. If Murguia defeats him he will scatter his forces, attack trains, and avoid fighting except where he has the advantage.

We are in a strategic place to make a get away, as well as to get back to Parral. At one of the stations yesterday a Mexican had one of those big land tortoises like you caught. A passenger bought it for 35¢ to make soup of.

On October 2 from Torreon:

We have at last established communications with Parral. Hawkins advises that we remain here until conditions have cleared up a bit. We saw a man this morning who had just arrived from Jimenez. He said General Murguia had gone to Santa Rosalia with his troops and that Villa had slipped in behind him, burned the bridges between Jimenez and Santa Rosalia and destroyed with dynamite a big water tank at one of the stations. His band will divide as soon as pressed too hard, he going in one section and Martin Lopez, his chief lieutenant, in another, only to join forces again later. One aviator could keep tabs on them and direct the federal troops. As it is, this information is dependant upon scouting, which is slow and unreliable.

On October 3 from Torreon:

I received a telegram today from Jimenez saying Villa's whereabouts unknown. I have eaten enough rotten eggs to glut a Chinaman. Anything with a shell is a fresh egg. I begin to suspect Mexican hens lay only after they are dead.

We meet the Mexican refugees in the plaza night and morning and go over the same strategy and guessing as to Villa's whereabouts. It's awfully tiresome. A bunch of Germans are to be seen there also. They look none too prosperous.

Still in Torreon, he wrote on October 9:

We did get away yesterday. We moved our luggage to the train, tipped the porter to retain seats for us, and then arrived to learn the departure of the train had been annulled. No reason given.

The local paper came out with an extra, warning everyone of a plague here, saying 20% of the population had it. Seventy-eight people are said to have died of it yesterday, five of them at the station. Everyone is warned to keep away from public gatherings of every kind. I don't know what it can be unless it is Spanish Influenza.

On October 11 from Jimenez:

After waiting from 7 A.M. to 12:30 yesterday the train pulled out, and we reached Jimenez at 1 A.M. this morning. Our train was packed. We had provided ourselves with a lunch of sardines, crackers, fruit, and a bottle of sherry. We ate it in that crowding and filth, and the sherry buoyed up our spirits amazingly. Such human wreckage as exists in this country is beyond our experience.

Scott was the first off the train and got our rooms. Lots of others had to sit up. I let a little Mexican lawyer who had been our companion for awhile sleep on the floor in my room. I regretted it later for he snored so, I had difficulty in getting to sleep.

October 12

The train for Parral really left this morning. The car was crowded to the very limit and everybody spitting on the floor. It was a disgusting three hour trip, but finally ended.

We came out here in a Ford from town—about two miles. Before we reached town we saw the bodies of two Villistas hanging from telegraph poles. They are said to have been spies and were executed last week.

Our quarters here are fine. Nice sitting rooms, bedrooms, and bath, and a Chinese cook. Mr. Hawkins, the manager, is a very nice fellow. On the outside a barbed wire fence, a high adobe wall within it, and several steel forts protect the mill and living quarters. The mine is about a mile distant, and we shall have a strong guard to and from our work.

Parral, October 15

I am regularly at work now and it is a relief after so much enforced idleness. I have a crew of three men and am sampling down one of the mines. This monotonous job will go on for a long time to come.

One hundred and fifty of the men here at the plant laid off yesterday, having or thinking they have, influenza. They doubtless get scared without much reason, but if they are careful, probably won't get it at all.

The altitude here is over 5000 ft. The days are clear and warm and the nights cool and will soon be cold. It would be a delightful country if it were peaceful.

The Company scouts report small bodies of Villistas fifteen or twenty miles to the north, and beyond that Villa with his main command is moving around, though none seems to know just where. That he will unite his forces sooner or later and attack Parral everyone takes for granted. If he could get the place he could capture both money and loot, but whether he can ever take it remains to be seen.

Our front windows are barred with planks two inches thick and six inches wide and spaced two inches apart to admit light and air. These timbers are nailed at each end to the window sills and further secured by 4 x 4 timbers bolted across them. The doors are two inches thick and secured by two heavy bars. It is thought that this will prevent entrance at the front, which is vulnerable, until ample time is allowed for dressing and escape by the rear into the walled compound and steel forts.

> Parral, Chihuahua, Mexico
> Oct. 16/10

Dear Marshall:

If it were not for the bandits I would love to have you here to ride with everyday. They have the finest lot of ponies. They are of all colors. I think the best one is a grey that a Scotchman named Mr. Millar rides, but I think mine is next. He is a chestnut in color, has the prettiest head and delicate ears imaginable, fine body and legs, and though gentle is as full of life as can be and anxious to run every moment. You would enjoy riding over these hills. A Mexican brings the horses out all saddled in the morning, and when we have mounted we ride away to our work, another Mexican with rifle and pistol accompanying us as guard.

A little Mexican boy about your size sits by my horse all day at the mine or watches him when I am underground. I always call him "Capitan," which is Mexican for "captain," and he grins from ear to ear. The men all call him that now, and he is getting very proud.

Much love to you.

> Your affectionate father,
> Marshall Bond

> Parral, October 27

Dear Dick:

I am anxious to hear whether the influenza has reached St.

Paul's School and whether you and Marshall have escaped it. It is raising havoc here among the Mexicans. It is said over 500 have died in Parral within a week. At the mine I see the Company's saw splitting mine timbers into boards for coffins. The reason these people succumb to it so numerously is that they are undernourished, have scarcely any bedding, and generally only a cotton shirt and pair of overalls as clothing. None of the Americans at the mine has had more than a stuffy cold. The rumor is that the Villistas have it badly also, and it is generally thought Villa is out of business for a time.

Everyday I am underground with a gang of Mexicans taking samples. The work requires one to be very careful, and the concentration leaves little time for other thoughts. Smith, who handles the broad geological details as only he can do it, told me he thought we would be through by Dec. 1st.

My first observation, based on the sight of cornfields and hucksters at the railway station selling produce, that Mexico is in no danger of starvation, proves to be erroneous. The people are dreadfully short of food and clothing. During this epidemic the Company is supplying its employees with a ration of corn to keep them in condition to withstand the influenza. In the mine I am now sampling, only 180 men out of 450 are able to work.

Parral, October 30

The dark cloud on the horizon for me now is the influenza. The mortality here is a fright. I have worked right along with men who had it. They would not return the next day, but thus far I have avoided it. I proceed on the theory of keeping the mouth and nose clean, and this I do with hot water and glycothymolene morning and night. The best advised men here estimate that 15% of the population have died with the flu and resulting pneumonia. Over 1500 out of 8000.

November 4

The peak of the influenza epidemic has passed and the deaths are decreasing daily. There has been a ruction between Gov.

Enriquez of Chihuahua and General Murguia, commander of the Carranzista forces. Many thought it meant another revolution, but we now hear Murguia has been ordered to Monterey —and is going—which does not always follow on order in this country. It is said the Governor, with the ranchmen he has organized, will attempt to get Villa. They go up against the best specialist in that game in this country.

That shrimp of a "captain," who is no larger than Marshall, pulled out a package of cigarettes today. I told him they were bad for him, but he replied: "They are my brothers."

November 14

These people are pitiably poor. The other day while eating lunch at the mine office, I observed a woman outside. She had a fine face but it betrayed great suffering. Finally she came to the superintendent and asked for corn, saying her husband had died ten days previous and that she and her two children were starving. The superintendent is a rough but kindly fellow. He gave her some money and told old Chano, our *mozo*, to get her some corn, and, as she was too weak to carry it, had him carry it for her to her house—a lean-to shed. I had never seen a starving person before.

Yesterday I had our Chinaman buy some beans, sugar, coffee, etc. in town; the Company gave me several pounds of lard, and at lunch today I had old Chano take me to her house. An old woman invited me in to see the children. They were two tiny tots, sick and asleep on the floor without covering. The mother was barefooted and only a cotton dress and ragged blanket covered her. Besides the food, I gave her a 20 peso gold piece ($10 American). She had never seen such wealth and asked its value. When told 20 pesos she nearly fell over. I gave old Chano a peso (50¢) for guiding me and he departed, thinking no doubt like the poor woman that I am a Rockefeller. Tomorrow I shall send her a kilo of meat. There is no work for such a person here now. Men work for 50¢ a day.

The second in command in the Company's guard is Nicanor. He is a tall, lithe Mexican from the mountains, very polite—as they all are—but back of his urbanity is a certain manly defiance. I liked him on sight.

A narrow gauge road—the Parral Durango—runs a weekly train. People from the back country come in for supplies and return on it with them. The night of the 10th Nicanor bade us goodbye, saying he was going home the next day—150 miles distant. As we rode out of the compound one of our scouts arrived and said 50 bandits were attacking the train 3 miles away. We could hear the shooting plainly.

On the way to the mine I told the Scotch engineer with me I could not but feel we were playing a yellow part. He argued we could not afford to mix in their scraps, that it would damage the Company, etc. I told him everywhere I had been all decency was combatted with, "It will hurt business."

They telephoned us at the mine that we had better come back. After our return it was finally decided to go out and lend aid to Nicanor and the besieged women and children. Four Americans and four Mexicans volunteered—others weren't asked or any amount would have gone. I was one of the four Americans, and a heavy load was lifted from my heart as we rode away, but nothing came of it.

On the way we met the engine returning, two Mexicans with rifles on the cowcatcher. They stopped and told us the bandits had been beaten off by 15 armed ranchers on the train. A little boy had been shot through the head and killed, an old man through the stomach, and another through the cheek. Several children were badly shaken up by being dropped by their mothers out of the car windows into an arroyo to get them out of gunfire.

It seems the bandits loosened one of the rails on a bridge over the arroyo expecting to drop the train into it and have easy looting. By some miraculous event the engine stayed on the ties until it stopped. Then a couple of hours fighting followed, the women and children in the arroyo, Nicanor and the men behind rocks.

When it was all over someone produced a bottle of tequila,

and Nicanor got awfully full. When the train got back to Parral he wanted to fight everybody, and the military officials disarmed him and put him in jail. Later one of the Company officials got him out and got back his rifle, but his pistol had disappeared.

I dread the trip out. I am honestly scared. One stands no chance whatever unarmed like a rat in a trap. The coolest man you ever saw is Smith. I do the stewing and planning. He works, reads, and writes, and doesn't worry. He is a downright admirable character—one in a million.

We get the El Paso papers every day and of course know that the war is over and that Wm. Hohenzollern is an exile. I hope to hear of his trial for murder soon. I have always thought him a coward.

This mining district was discovered in 1547. The town of Santa Barbara (16 miles distant) was the center of the district and soon had 7000 inhabitants. It was the capital of northwestern Mexico, California, Arizona, etc. Now it is a very small village.

All the Americans here expect Villa will descend on Parral in the near future, as it is the only place worth looting, and he needs loot. If you read he has taken Parral it does not necessarily mean he has taken us. We are reasonably well prepared for eventualities, so don't worry.

November 16

Scott starts for El Paso day after tomorrow with the mail and two tons of silver. I took up some meat to the mine today and had Chano take it to the poor woman—her name is Soledad Corral. He came back with the information that they were all getting fat. Am glad you ordered that life of Voltaire. I shall enjoy reading it. I have read a little of Whitman's prose, describing his rides on the buses in N. Y., etc., and I have little to add to this other than my love.

Bond had good cause for worry about the trip out, since

trains were frequently attacked by Villa. On one occasion Villa not only stole the silver bullion but shot sixteen American passengers through the head. However, after two months in Mexico Bond and Smith completed their mission and returned to Texas without further mishap.

Marshall Bond made warm friends among the personnel at the mine and received some interesting letters from them afterward. One from George Millar in Parral, January 13, 1919, said:

Just at present you are missing a very interesting time as we are experiencing one more Villista thrill. There are three large bands of about 200 men each and numerous smaller bands within striking distance, and our scouts assure us that they all state their intention of attacking Parral. If we should have to make that trip over the mountains you can be assured that, though you may be missing, you will not be forgotten. All of us will be sorry that you are not riding ahead, loaded down with several sacks of emergency rations.

The favorite evening pastime while Bond was at the mine was to formulate plans for escape in case Villa should attack Parral. Should the Company scouts report an attack imminent, Bond and Smith were to lead a pack train into the Sierra Madre to an agreed rendezvous and await the arrival of the Company personnel who were duty bound to remain at the mine until the last moment. Then the assembled group would make its way across the mountains to Sonora and the Arizona border. In recent years the author has ventured into this country half a dozen times with the Mormons of northern Chihuahua. It is the ruggedest kind of terrain, full of huge barrancas and pine-covered mountains extending several hundred miles to the coastal plain. It would have been a long, hard trip for the mine personnel, but they would have made it eventually, as the country is well watered and abounds in game.

Millar's letter continued:

From the 19th Dec. until Jan. 4th we were without power and accomplished very little. The small band of Villistas, headed by Morena and operating between here and Conchos, finally made good its threat to interrupt the power transmission and blew up two towers. Not content with having destroyed the towers, the band stood guard over them and refused to let the repair men get near, until they were finally driven off.

A letter dated February 9, 1919, from Fred Marston:

I showed your letter to all the boys, and you and reminiscences of the all too short time you spent with us was the subject of a lot of merry conversation, both at the club and the mess room. Whenever we have a Villa scare somebody is sure to say: "Wouldn't Marshall Bond enjoy this!" Last week sixty Villistas captured Minas Nuevas and a village below Presena. They came in at 6:30 A.M., surprised and defeated the socialists and guard. They stayed in possession of the town till 10 A.M. when a special train with soldiers from Parral drove them out. Thy looted the small stores but harmed none of the inhabitants.

George Millar wrote of his capture and ransom:

The country is full of willing disciples of Robin Hood, and no roads nor trails in the vicinity of mining camps are safe by day or night. Highway robberies are a nightly occurrence around Parral. This condition is a logical outcome of ten years of revolution and will be very unpleasant while it lasts. The catching of foreigners and holding them for ransom has reached alarming dimensions.

Just a month before leaving I was captured just half way between the Las Cruces and Refugio mines at midday. I was alone and unarmed, as we had no knowledge of any bandits being so close. Three men held me up, one on each side, and had me covered before I even suspected that anything was wrong. They made me trot on foot up the hill west of Minas Nuevas and kept me there all day. From the hill we could see the front gate of the plant, and my captors promised to shoot me immediately if they saw any mounted men leave the plant to attempt a rescue. They also made me state this in a note sent to the plant with the additional threat that if 10,000 pesos were not delivered to them in cash by five o'clock I would be shot. The bearer of the first note got scared and didn't reach the plant so a second note was sent, and a watchman arrived at the foot of the hill with a sack of money just as it was getting dark.

They halted him at about 300 yards and told him to drop the sack and run or they would open fire. From the sound when he dropped the sack I figured it didn't have more than 1,000 pesos in silver, so thought I had better make a "get away" before they counted it. They were getting nervous anyway, and when I told them I wanted to go now, that they had the money and didn't need me any longer, they agreed but made me start out on foot.

I left at a dog trot, praying for night to come on a little faster, and had covered the first mile before they discovered that there were only 800 pesos in the sack with a draft for the balance, which if necessary I could have made good by signing it, but fortunately I hadn't even thought of investigating the contents. They started after me, but that was the last I saw of them because in the next two miles I beat lots of sprinting records.

It was too much strenuous exercise mixed with nervous strain for me for one day so I asked for a holiday. On the way to El Paso I overheard part of a monologue given by an army colonel to two of his subordinates and I think it will interest you very much. A fairly literal translation is as follows:

"After much study I have discovered why our country is not the greatest in the world. We have the best climate, more timber, more gold, silver, iron, and oil than any other country. We have everything in abundance we need to become great and powerful

with the single exception of *shame*, and if we only had shame
we would undoubtedly be the greatest country in the world
today."

What do you think of his philosophy?

Fred Marston's last letter described the capture of Parral.

Long Beach, Cal.
June 27th, 1919

Dear Mr. Bond:

Your letter from F. N. Worth with clipping from New York
Sun duly received and most glad to hear from you I was, and
the article was most entertaining and appreciated. Mr. Hawkins,
who is now living just one block from me, at the Virginia Hotel,
tells me that your article has appeared also in the *Literary Di-
gest*. You are sure some journalist! You never even mentioned
those glorious sunsets at Parral! Well, that also marks you for a
success in that line for the public wants facts and not sentiment
and that is just what we Americans interested in Mexico want
put before the public. D . . . watchful waiting etc. . . . !

After you left, and right up to the night of the real attack on
Parral, we had rumors and alarms galore, every day and night
and with our meals, that's what the conversation and interest
centered on. Thirty poorly mounted and armed bandits went
into San Francisco Del Oro camp about 6 P.M. when all the staff
was seated at supper. They arrived in real Wild West style, yelling and shooting off their pistols, surrounded the mess hall, two
of their leaders going in and commanding all to throw their
hands up, then marched them out and lined them up with their
hands still in the air. They relieved them of all their pockets
contained, then, while two men kept them covered, the rest of
the gang looted all the rooms. They stayed till 1 A.M. eating,
drinking, playing the phonograph and altogether greatly enjoying their "stay in town." Then they told Harrison, the manager,
that he must pay 5,000 pesos. He told them he only had 3,000
pesos in the office in Parral. They then told him to give them

one of his employees as security that he would bring out the 2,000 the next day to their camp. His choice fell on a new recruit, fresh from the States, and the bandits departed, leading the hostage with them. Harrison sent out the money next day and the American was liberated.

This happened at least a month before Villa's attack on Parral. Villa told Harrison that when he heard of the bandits' raid he immediately rounded up that gang and personally shot the leaders with his own pistol, and we believe he did, as we now know they couldn't have been his men.

Well, finally our scouts reported that all the Villistas in Mexico were converging toward Parral, and a woman in Parral sent out word that she had received a letter from her husband who was with Villa, telling her to go to the mountains, as they were coming in Friday night. It was straight dope!

At 1 A.M. Saturday, 25 men opened fire on the town from the protection of the big cemetery on opposite side of town from where we were. At daylight others had arrived, estimated to be 300 whom we concluded were balance of Martin Lopez' gang. About 9 A.M. they gained possession of a block of houses on edge of town and then started a systematic series of tunnels through connecting houses, right to center of town. Our runners kept us posted as to how the fight was going, and at 2 P.M. it was reported that the Villistas had the main plaza and the big cathedral, and Mr. Hawkins told us all to pack up, as we would move into the Palmilla mine. Our new Ford was kept busy all afternoon taking over our belongings and a big stock of provisions.

At 5 P.M. we were all in the mine, everybody except the night crew of Mexicans running the mill. All the native women and children, all the horses, a herd of goats, a big stock of corn and beans, all the Chinamen, the Ford, in fact everything and anything that anybody had any idea would be useful or that they wanted to save. There was plenty of good water in the mine and everybody was quite jolly and confident that no force could take us out of the mine.

As the gringo staff had been increased to 18 or 19 men and

there was only 12 mounts including the mules, all thought of flight had been abandoned several weeks before. The San Francisco del Oro crowd and the Veta Colorado Mining Co. had their offices in town, the staff motoring out to the mine and back everyday. All Saturday night *socialista* deserters and the entire staff of regular garrison kept passing the mouth of the tunnel "beating it" to the mountains. Sunday morning the only defense in town was about 30 *socialistas* and 25 regular soldiers, with no officers, isolated on the little mountain fortress in center of town, the spot that was always considered impregnable. Villa sent an autographed letter and one of his personal guards, offering them good treatment if they would surrender, and after several ballots they accepted, and the town was totally in Villa's hands at 11 A.M. Easter Sunday.

Of all the prisoners taken, Villa immediately executed 4 men, viz. old Louis Herrera and his two nephews and an Italian merchant who had been fighting with the *socialistas*. All *socialistas* and Carranza soldiers were disarmed and given their liberty unconditionally.

Sunday evening about 5 P.M. Villa sent Harrison and Macfarland of the San Francisco Co. out to us in their car, with a message from Villa to the effect that there was no reason for us to hide in the mine, that all Americans and foreigners were guaranteed protection and full liberty to remain in his territory or depart for the U.S.A.—that Mr. Hawkins must arrange to pay $50,000 gold to Villa's agent in El Paso or the works would be destroyed. Whether the Company paid or not, all employees were guaranteed protection. As Harrison and Macfarland said all foreigners captured in Parral had utmost faith in General Angeles* who was associated with Villa, we came out Monday at noon, after Hawkins had been into Parral, met General Angeles and sent out word to us to return to the plant and start up the mill which had shut down Sunday noon.

* General Filipe Angeles was an artillery expert, a man of the highest character, who had joined Villa purely for ideological reasons. Later he was captured by government forces and died before a firing squad, bravely scorning the cloth to cover his eyes.

Mr. Hawkins, together with a representative of the other two companies, left Tuesday for El Paso, via auto to Chihuahua, to arrange to pay the indemnity. I stayed 3 weeks longer, had two personal interviews with Villa in his private sitting room at Cuartel General, and he gave me a passport which he signed personally with an indelible lead pencil in my presence, and I came out with Mr. Clun in his car as far as Chihuahua where we caught a train for Juarez. We found Chihuahua City in a big panic, all outlying garrisons were concentrated in the city, barbed wire entanglements were being strung completely around the town, and no admission after 10 P.M., no lights, and other signs of a besieged city everywhere.

We left Parral at 5 A.M. and arrived at Chihuahua 11:30 the same day. Changed tires 25 times. Left Chihuahua next morning at 8 A.M., arrived Juarez 6 P.M. That's better than railroad time in normal times!

Mr. Morris was discharged by Mr. Hawkins by letter and telegram, so he never came back. When I left, Mr. Millar was put in charge of everything. When Villa was driven away from Juarez, the Company got word to Millar, who is a British subject, and all Americans were sent to Jimenez for security till Villa shows what his policy is going to be toward American mining companies. That left only Millar and Webb now running the entire plant with Mexican foreman and labor.

I believe all the mining companies paid Villa the "forced loan" which he assessed them, though I am in no position to say so positively. All people of means in Parral district also had to "come through." Our agent in Parral paid 12,000 pesos, all Chinamen, Spaniards, merchants also, according to their ability. We understood and believe that Villa got 1,000,000 pesos out of Parral in gold and silver currency.

Before starting for Juarez he abandoned Parral district entirely after destroying the R.R. beyond repair. So now there is nobody there except inhabitants who are continually becoming fewer in number and poorer.

As I told you before, I resigned as soon as I hit El Paso and am now sporting in the surf here everyday with my family, and will probably be able to do so all summer unless things pick up in my old stamping grounds in the copper fields of Arizona or Russia. I expect to return to Mexico someday and clean up a fortune and have many delightful days in that fine country doing it.

P.S. In the mine when I brought out your emergency rations in their original packages, many remarked that all we lacked was your cheery self to complete the party and general hilarity.

F. M.

Billy the Kid

W HEN THE AUTHOR was a teenager the heroes of the "Wild West" who appealed to him most were the gun-toting, fast-shooting men of action like Wild Bill Hickok, Clay Allison, and Billy the Kid. A family friend, former Governor Miguel A. Otero of New Mexico, had known them all. It brought boundless delight when in July, 1926, he agreed to accompany Marshall Bond and the writer on a trip to Lincoln, New Mexico, to interview the survivors of the Lincoln County War in which Billy the Kid had played so prominent a part.*

Miguel A. Otero, a descendant of an old and distinguished Spanish family, had had a long and successful career in the mercantile business with the firm of Otero, Sellar & Co., which had been founded by his father. The headquarters of the firm kept moving west across Kansas and into New Mexico, paralleling the construction of the Santa Fe Railroad. For this reason Otero, in his younger days, always found himself on the threshold of the frontier and knew all the characters connected with this westward expansion.

---

* Later Otero wrote a book, *The Real Billy the Kid*, which he dedicated to Maurice Garland Fulton and Marshall Bond. Except for several early portraits, he used Bond's photographs as illustrations.

In 1897 Otero was appointed governor of the New Mexico Territory by President McKinley and served two successive terms under Theodore Roosevelt.* He was a rotund little man with a keen sense of humor and a true politician's ability to remember nearly everyone by his first name. Being popular, energetic, and bilingual, he found all doors open to him; thus as a guide he was without peer.

On the way to Lincoln he regaled the Bonds with stories of the old frontier. He said Wild Bill Hickok was the fastest man on the draw he had ever seen. In Hays City he was walking down the street with Wild Bill when a drunk desperado named Bill Mulvey suddenly confronted Hickok with a rifle and threatened to shoot him. Otero was standing only twenty-five feet from the scene and fully expected to see the end of Wild Bill at any moment. However, the latter calmly waved his hand to an imaginary person behind Mulvey and called out:

"Don't shoot him from behind. He's drunk!"

In the split second in which Mulvey whirled around to see who was threatening his rear, Hickok drew a pistol and shot him through the head.

Otero knew Clay Allison very well, as the latter frequently traded with Otero, Sellar & Co. He said Allison was the only man Bat Masterson was afraid of, and he went on to tell the story of the most celebrated duel in the annals of the West. It took place between Clay Allison and another desperado named Johnson in the Texas Panhandle. Allison had a flair for the macabre and proposed that the two of them dig a grave six feet deep, six and a half feet long, and two feet wide. They were to strip themselves to the waist and sit down at the two ends of the grave, each with a bowie knife in his hand. At a given signal they were to start fight-

---

* Otero was also the author of *My Nine Years as Governor* and a two-volume work called *My Life on the Frontier*.

ing and were not to stop until one or the other was dead. The survivor was to shovel the dirt back over the victim. Although Allison won, he was so badly cut up that he had great difficulty in shoveling the dirt into the grave and was lame for the rest of his life.*

The author had read about the polite form of dueling in Dumas's novels, and had learned in school how Alexander Hamilton had been done in by Aaron Burr, but he now felt that the D'Artagnans and the Burrs had been permanently eclipsed by this grisly performance of Clay Allison. Allison's stock rose enormously in the author's estimation, and the governor was asked for more.

Otero replied that during a holiday in the town of El Morro, Colorado, he and four friends were playing poker in a room above Harrington's Saloon. It was a cold day and a fire was burning in a large Charter Oak cooking stove. Just as the game was getting interesting, Clay Allison came roaring into the saloon quite drunk and began shooting his pistols through the ceiling. The poker players, finding themselves in the line of fire, had only one safe place to go. They remained on top of the stove for three quarters of an hour with arms clasped around each other and dancing a lively jig to keep their feet from burning until Allison ran out of ammunition.

The governor also told about a crusty old justice of the peace, Hoodoo Brown, who presided in Las Vegas, New Mexico. He was not only said to be crooked but was particularly notorious for his fiery and picturesque speech. Otero said he once attended a murder trial in Las Vegas at the end of which the jury rendered a verdict of guilty. Hoodoo Brown put on his black cap and pointing his finger at the accused, shouted:

* Some authorities consider this story a myth. Otero told it for what it was worth and did not say he had heard it from Allison.

"Stand up, you syphilitic son of a bitch, while I throw the harpoon of justice into you!"

At dinner on the first evening of the trip, Governor Otero described his impressions of Billy the Kid. He said that he had had a long talk with the Kid on a train going from Las Vegas to Santa Fe; Billy was in the custody of Sheriff Pat Garrett and was on his way to Mesilla to be tried for murder. He liked the boy, found him charming, intelligent, and a born leader.

He said that Billy, while intensely loyal to his friends, seldom forgave his enemies and couldn't bear to admit defeat in a fight or in any other undertaking. He was of the opinion that the boy might have amounted to something had he had a more normal upbringing and a better education.

Billy the Kid, also known as Henry McCarthy, Henry Antrim, and William Bonney, did have a normal life until he was fifteen, when he was jailed for the theft of some laundry from a Chinese. He escaped by going up the chimney and seems to have spent the ensuing two years working as a cowboy in Arizona. It was near Camp Grant that Billy killed his first man, Frank P. ("Windy") Cahill, a hulking bully of a blacksmith. He escaped again and made his way to Ruidoso Creek in New Mexico, and after working on several ranches, took employment at the ranch of John H. Tunstall in Lincoln.

The "war" was caused by the business rivalry between two groups in Lincoln. On the one side were James Dolan, Lawrence Murphy, and John H. Riley,* all veterans of the Union Army, who had a store dealing in general merchandise, horses, and cattle. These men were completely unscrupulous. They had one of their crowd appointed sheriff,

* The men were partners, but Murphy and Riley spent most of the time at their ranches during the Lincoln County War.

and through their Army connections were able to hood-
wink the officers of nearby Fort Stanton sufficiently to cheat
the government on large cattle contracts with the Indian
reservations. Most of their cattle were stolen from the extensive ranches of John Chisum. Hovering in the background of the Murphy-Dolan-Riley crowd were S. B. Axtell
and the Santa Fe Ring.

On the other side were John H. Tunstall and Alexander
A. McSween. The latter, with his attractive wife, Susan, had
settled in Lincoln in 1875 and started practicing law. He
was honest, well educated, and deeply religious. He fell
afoul of the Dolan crowd when he agreed to represent John
Chisum in a case involving the above-mentioned firm in
cattle rustling.

Tunstall was a splendid young Englishman of means and
education who came west to go into the cattle business. He
bought his equipment from Otero, Sellar & Co., and was
given a letter by them to McSween. The two men at once
became close friends and formed a partnership in the merchandising business in competition with the Dolan store.
Tunstall also acquired a cattle ranch and founded the Lincoln County Bank. Billy the Kid worked as a cowboy on
Tunstall's cattle ranch and developed a deep affection for
this kindly, generous employer, and according to eyewit-
nesses who were interviewed the feeling was mutual.

This kind of competition was more than the Dolan group
could stomach. Consequently in February, 1878, Dolan
sent his stooge, Sheriff Billy Mathews, to get Tunstall on a
trumped-up charge. Most of the posse, including Morton
and Baker, found him fifteen miles from Lincoln herding a
bunch of horses. They shot him down in cold blood.

Billy the Kid, even though he still was a minor figure so
far in the war, swore he would kill all of Tunstall's mur-

derers and very nearly succeeded in doing so. Within a few days Morton and Baker met death, and on April 1 a fusillade from behind an adobe wall in Lincoln mowed down Sheriff Brady and his deputy George Hindman.

The most impressive survivor of the Lincoln County War was the charming and gracious Mrs. Alexander McSween.* The Bond-Otero party found her living alone in what appeared to be near destitution in a shack in the ghost town of White Oaks, New Mexico. With dignity and humor she showed the meager furnishings of her home and said it was as good a place as any in which to relive the memories of her tragic past. Her home in Lincoln had once been the only cultural center in town and had contained the first piano brought into Lincoln County. It was a moving experience as this gallant old lady sat on the porch and without rancor unfolded her story.

She said that she had formed a warm friendship with Billy the Kid while he was in the employ of her husband's partner. She said he was a great favorite with women in general, being both polite and considerate, neat in appearance, and an accomplished dancer. He was trusted by both McSween and Tunstall and well liked by everyone, especially the native Mexicans, for whom he never refused to do a favor. In her opinion his murders were necessary for self-preservation, and to that extent justifiable. It was interesting to discover that everyone who had known Billy the Kid was loud in praise of his many virtues and sought to excuse his faults on the grounds of necessity and misfortune. It seemed that the aura of romance and publicity with which the Kid's exploits had been endowed over the years had to some degree affected the judgment of these people; for without him they

---

* She had become Mrs. Barber, but had been separated from her second husband for some years.

would have been nonentities. It was also clear that he had had gifts of leadership far in excess of the ordinary outlaw.

With tears in her eyes Mrs. McSween related her version of the most famous fight of the Lincoln County War, in which her husband was killed and her house ravaged by fire. An old native, Hijinio (Eugenio) Salazar, also gave a first-hand account, taking off his shirt to show the wounds he got in the fight, saying that one bullet still remained in his body. The fight was a three-day affair, and the main scene of action was in McSween's house in Lincoln. In the house were eleven men and three women, including the Mc-Sweens, Salazar, and Billy the Kid.

The Dolan forces were strongly entrenched in their store and hotel, and their hireling, Sheriff Peppin, posted a ring of sharpshooters at strategic points around town so as to block escape from McSween's house. For the first two days a lively exchange between sharpshooters occurred, during which one of Peppin's right-hand men, Charlie Crawford, was killed at nine hundred yards by Fernando Herrera. After that Peppin and Dolan decided to send to Fort Stanton for troops to dislodge the people from McSween's home.

Colonel Dudley, the commandant at Fort Stanton, was a drinking companion of Dolan's and quite obviously in the latter's control. He arrived in front of Dolan's headquarters to confer with Sheriff Peppin accompanied by a troop of cavalry and a squad of artillery with a twelve-pounder and a Gatling gun. He then passed McSween's house without stopping, returned to camp where he had a talk with a Dr. Ealy, and finally retired to his tent.

Mrs. McSween explained that she and the others in the house, including those guarding the rear, congregated in the front room on the assumption that Colonel Dudley would use his troops and his good offices to effect a truce and work out a peaceful settlement. He refused to intercede, however, thereby giving moral support to the Dolan faction.*

With the guards no longer on the alert, Dolan and three of his men sneaked up to the rear of the house with pitch pine and coal oil and set the place on fire. Mrs. McSween was the first to detect the smoke. The house was a twelve-room adobe and burned slowly. But as the roof timbers in each room began to collapse, the inmates had to move to another. It was only a matter of hours before they would have to make a desperate rush for freedom.

While McSween was praying and reading his Bible, Mrs. McSween decided to do what she could to persuade Dudley to employ his troops to save her husband's life. As she left the house several bullets whizzed by her, but firing ceased when it was realized that she was a woman. Twice she made the trip to beg and plead with Colonel Dudley, but he was drinking and insisted that he had no authority to interfere. Then, with the other two women, she left her husband and the house for the last time.

As night fell only one room was left unburned. It was clear to the eleven men inside that their moment of decision had arrived. If they could only get across the first thirty feet, which was lit up by the flames, they would have a chance of evading death or capture under cover of darkness. The Kid offered McSween a gun, but he stuck to his Bible, saying; "I would much rather die than spill one drop of blood."

Failing to persuade McSween to defend himself, Billy shouted to the others; "We have one chance in a million—let's take it!"

Hijinio Salazar said that the first men to leave were Harvey Morris, Jim French, Vicente Romero, and Billy the Kid, who ran out toward the gate in the fence on the east side of

* Colonel Dudley, instead of being cashiered from the Army, was cleared by a military court and in 1899 received an honorable discharge.

the yard. Young Morris was killed, but the rest got away in the darkness. McSween and those remaining, who were supposed to make a dash for the north gate as soon as the attackers' attention was focused on Billy and his group, hesitated too long. When they started across the yard they were mowed down by a hail of bullets.

Salazar, who had dashed out with McSween, was wounded and dropped to the ground, feigning death. After the fight one of Dolan's men, Andy Boyle, kicked him and jumped on his body several times. The agony was almost unbearable. Then Boyle cocked his rifle, aimed at Salazar's heart, and was about to fire when someone said; "Don't waste another shot on that damned greaser. He's already dead."

Hours later Salazar, who was crazy with thirst, crawled to the creek for a drink, and after fainting several times from loss of blood, found refuge in his sister-in-law's house. Dr. Appel, of Fort Stanton, who was in Lincoln, was summoned to dress his wounds. Just after the doctor arrived four of Dolan's men, who had followed the trail of blood, burst into the room and threatened to shoot the wounded man. Salazar said he owed his life to Dr. Appel, who bravely confronted the men, saying; "If you kill this man, I will personally see that all four of you are hanged."

Six months after the death of McSween, Sheriff Peppin resigned, and Dolan was forced to seek refuge in Fort Stanton. The Lincoln County War slowly came to an end.

After photographing and interviewing Mrs. McSween and the other survivors, the Bond-Otero party drove eight miles to George W. Coe's adobe ranch house on Ruidoso Creek. Mr. and Mrs. Coe gave them a warm welcome, and after posing for their camera, entertained them for several hours with stories of the Lincoln County War and Billy the Kid. George Coe and his cousin, Frank Coe, had participated in many fights along with Billy.

During the battle at McSween's house, Coe said, he and two other men were in a warehouse about thirty yards away. Just as the three women were leaving the burning house one of Dolan's men, Jack Long, came running with a can of coal oil, intent on setting fire to the warehouse. The three women pleaded with him not to go through with it.

"I was holding my gun cocked on him," said Coe, "but dared not fire for fear of hitting Mrs. McSween, who was standing between us. Finally she stepped aside and I fired but missed because Long had leaned over to pick up the oil can. An outhouse stood nearby, and he ran into it to take cover. For the rest of the afternoon, when we had nothing better to do, we riddled the outhouse full of holes. To save his life, Long was forced to crawl down into the pit. Afterwards he remarked that it was a gruesome experience but certainly preferable to death."

The author noticed that George Coe was missing his trigger finger and asked him how it happened. Coe looked ruefully at his mangled hand and said:

"A gunman named Buckshot Bill Roberts shot it off in a fight at Blazer's Mill in March, 1878, about four months before McSween was killed."

Buckshot Bill, who had received this nickname from his numerous gun fights, had heard that there was a $100 reward offered by the Dolan faction for the capture, dead or alive, of the killer of Sheriff Brady and George Hindman. He came to Lincoln and offered his services. Being a professional in this sort of thing, and utterly fearless, he decided to tackle the job alone. It was not long before he discovered Billy and his friends at the mill.

Dick Brewer, Charlie Bowdre, George and Frank Coe, John Middleton, and Billy the Kid were having dinner in Blazer's house. They watched Roberts get off his mule, armed with two six-shooters, a rifle, and a belt full of cartridges. They had no idea of what he was up to. Frank Coe, who had known Roberts, walked with him to an open doorway on the other side of the house for a conference. Roberts was in a dangerous mood and refused Coe's suggestion that he give himself up.

Dick Brewer, captain of the group at that time, quickly concluded that it would be wise to take Roberts, regardless of consequences. Charlie Bowdre, followed by Brewer and Billy the Kid, started around the other side of the house with their guns cocked. As Bowdre turned the corner he drew a bead on Roberts and yelled:

"Throw up your hands!"

"Not much, Mary Ann!" replied Buckshot Bill.

The two men fired simultaneously, Bowdre's bullet smacking into Roberts' stomach, wounding him fatally. Roberts' shot glanced off Bowdre's cartridge belt and hit George Coe, who reflected:

"With my usual luck, I got there just in time to stop the bullet with my right hand. It knocked the gun out of my hand and took off my trigger finger."

Roberts retreated into the room, dragged a feather bed onto the floor, and lay there dying but still determined to shoot it out. Brewer found a spot, behind some logs, affording him a view into the room through the doorway. He started firing, but as he raised his head for a second to look, was killed instantly by a shot from Roberts. Buckshot Bill died the following day.

Marshall Bond asked George Coe for his opinion of Billy the Kid's character. Coe said that one night around the campfire the gang was boasting outrageously about how many of the Dolan crowd they were going to get, and of the daring ways this was to be accomplished. Suddenly a series of pistol shots went off. Every man except Billy the Kid dove for the brush. The Kid, who had said nothing while the boasting was going on, yelled for them to come back to the fire and scolded them for acting in a way so contrary to their brave words. To teach them a lesson he had slipped some cartridges out of his ammunition belt and dropped them into the fire.

George Coe went on to say that Billy the Kid, Charlie Bowdre, and Tom O'Folliard were the bravest and most effective fighters in the gang. They had steady nerves, were moderate in drinking and smoking, and were not the type of men who killed just for the sake of killing.

When General Lew Wallace, the author of *Ben Hur,* was appointed governor of the Territory of New Mexico, he offered an amnesty to all participants in the Lincoln County War who would lay down their arms. He even made a special trip to persuade Billy the Kid to testify in court against the murderers of Tunstall and McSween. On the promise of amnesty the Kid allowed himself to be "captured," but afterwards resumed his old ways. George Coe said he himself accepted the offer and became a rancher, but that Billy the Kid knew that the hatred and bitterness engendered by the war had made it impossible for him to settle down. He would simply become a target for his old enemies if he tried it. Bowdre and O'Folliard decided to stick with him.

At Christmastime in 1880 O'Folliard was killed after dark in ambush by Sheriff Pat Garrett's posse in Fort Sumner, but the others managed to escape. Then in April, 1881, Bowdre was killed at Stinking Springs, and Billy the Kid was captured there. He was taken to Las Vegas by Garrett and thence to Mesilla, where he was tried and convicted of murder. He was returned to Lincoln for execution. While in Lincoln the Bond-Otero party had visited the building in which he had been jailed and they talked to Miguel Luna, who saw him escape after killing his two guards.

On the night of July 13, 1881, the Kid paid a midnight

visit to the home of his friend Pete Maxwell* in Fort Sumner. Garrett, who had been waiting for the Kid in that vicinity, happened that very night to be sitting in Maxwell's unlighted bedroom. The Kid entered quietly in his stocking feet and began talking to Maxwell. Suddenly realizing that someone else was there, he said *"Quien es?"* Maxwell whispered to Garrett, "That's the Kid." As Billy started backing away, Garrett drew his pistol and killed him with the first shot.

After visiting Frank Coe, whose story was much the same as his cousin's, the Bond-Otero party drove to Fort Sumner. Pete Maxwell was no longer living, and his house where the Kid was killed had burned to the ground some years before. They did meet an elderly Navajo woman, Deluvina "Maxwell," who had once loved Billy and who had been there the night he died. In spite of her rheumatism she graciously led the party to the unmarked grave. They also met Jesus Silva, who had buried Billy. The Kid had stopped for a late supper with Silva the night he was killed. Silva said that he had had no meat in his house and had therefore suggested that the Kid get some from Pete Maxwell. It was while trying to get meat that Billy the Kid met his death.

Upon returning to Santa Barbara, Bond wrote Mrs. McSween and sent copies of some photographs. She replied as follows:

White Oaks, N.M. 11/7/26

Mr. Marshall Bond
Santa Barbara, Calif.
My Dear Sir:

I beg your pardon many times for not having answered your very kind letter before this. The letter has been misplaced for

* Pete's father, Lucien B. Maxwell, formerly owned the huge Maxwell Land Grant in Colfax County, New Mexico.

a long time and just yesterday was very happily surprised in discovering it among some others my niece had taken from my desk in ridding up things.

I take pleasure in thanking you for the photographs and also for the kind invitation to visit you in your home, of which pleasure I shall avail myself should I ever go to California, and take pleasure in returning the compliments and invite you with your good wife to visit me in my home humble as it is, also your son to whom I took great favor and wonder has he gone to the Far East again.*

The photos are very good and afford me great pleasure to view all of you, and reflect upon the interesting hours we spent together. Am sorry the photographs of Mr. McSween and myself were failures, come and take them again.†

I have not heard a word of Mr. & Mrs. Otero and wonder did they go to Panama. Their son was elected Auditor.

We are having quite cold weather here and makes me wish I could be in a warmer clime but circumstances compel me to remain here.

With kindest regard to you and Mrs. Bond also son
I remain

Yours very truly
Susan E. Barber

---

* Gone east to school, that is.
† Refers to old photographs Bond had attempted to copy.

CHAPTER NINE

Cairo to Capetown

W ITHIN A YEAR of the trip to Lincoln County with Otero, Bond was asked by an old friend, John H. Denison of Santa Barbara, to join an expedition through the entire length of Africa. Denison, a retired minister, had become a keen student of archaeology and especially of Egyptian history. Also in the party were Charis Denison, Margaret Davison, Hugo Goodhue, son of the famous architect Bertram Goodhue, and an inept white hunter named Barnes.

Bond expected to find himself engulfed in the vast tropical wilderness of equatorial Africa where the skills he had learned in the mountains of the West would be necessary to his survival. Instead, to his considerable disgust, he discovered that colonialism had penetrated everywhere, and that the "white man's burden" consisted of complete domination of the native population. Gone were the vicissitudes and perils that had confronted Stanley. Instead the white traveler was deluged with luxury, servants, and champagne.

From Cairo on February 28, 1927, Bond wrote of his arrival in Egypt:

The sea was a beautiful blue, the climate brilliant like Arizona, the buildings odd and interesting. The landing in Alexandria yesterday was picturesque and pandemonium. Blacks, Egyptians, and Sudanese all wearing red fezzes lined the quay waiting to devour us. All our stuff was turned over to them, and I was sure we would never see it again. We sat in a deluxe Pullman, and a polite French steward served an excellent dinner with delicious Turkish coffee. The Nile Valley is green with cultivation like the Imperial Valley. The river is interesting by reason of the feluccas and the many tall date palms that border it.

We rode camels on the desert near the Pyramids. The British have a lot of troops here too. No American can understand their extraordinary ability as rulers till he gets into a country like this.

The things from King Tut's tomb are wonderful. The sarcophagus his body rests in is of gold and weighs 1,000 pounds and is inlaid with turquoise, lapis lazuli, and red carnelian. The gold is beautifully carved and looks brilliant and fresh. This inner gold casket is in a larger one of gold inlaid with stones. All sorts of beautiful gold ornaments and even his canes are there. Also his throne, bed, and chariots are all covered with gold. I gazed for a long time at my great prototype, Rameses II. You may not believe it but he was more mummified than I.

Because of Bond's prominent nose he was often accused by his friends of looking like Al Smith or the mummy of Rameses II. He resented the comparison to Smith but was flattered by his remarkable resemblance to the great Egyptian Pharaoh.

Luxor, March 4
This morning we went through the temples of Karnak and Thebes. They are colossal and the sculpture with its symbolism most attractive. Leading between them was once an avenue of sphinxes a mile long. This place had a million people centuries before Christ and the greatest religious buildings the world had

ever seen: 20,000 war chariots were kept in the city constantly ready for attack.

This afternoon we went to see a snake charmer. We got into a small Nile sailboat and went up the river about a mile to a garden. The snake charmer walked about shouting in Arabic. Soon he "smelt" a snake and reached into the bamboo, pulling out a cobra. After teasing it until it raised part way up flattening its head and neck, he made it lay its head in his hand and then put it in a basket. Next he picked up a big scorpion and handled it but didn't get stung. Later he pulled a horned puff adder out of some dry bamboo. It was pretty belligerent, but he finally handled it all right. This snake charmer is famous throughout Egypt, has never been detected in any trickery, and the people of Luxor accept his miraculous powers with implicit faith. To-morrow we are going to the Valley of the Kings.

March 5

From the terrace of the Luxor Winter Palace Hotel you look across the Nile and five miles of green bottom lands to a high range of pinkish hills where the Kings were buried. Every artifice was employed to conceal the mouths of the tombs, probably to prevent robbery. A little mound marked King Tut's tomb, and we entered it first. The one room we saw in there was full of crated treasure so we didn't see a great deal. Nearby was the tomb of Rameses VI. We went over 200 feet down a huge gallery about 10 feet square before coming to the treasure chamber and other ceremonial rooms. One of these was 40 feet long, 20 feet wide, and 20 feet high with carved walls and beautifully decorated ceiling in gold and black. In this had rested his sarcophagus until it was removed to the Cairo Museum. The smooth walls of the corridor were covered with splendid carved bas-reliefs and thousands of small hieroglyphics telling of his life and of various symbolic events, such as the God of Death presenting Rameses with the Key of Life.

One is surrounded by myriads of cringing, whining people constantly seeking to render some useless, unsought, and unwanted service. They want to act as guides or sell you scarabs, necklaces, cigarettes, fly brushes, and curiosities of every kind and condition. No one will take no for an answer but seeks to overcome your resistance with argument. They are thick as flies and more irritating. As salesmen they are the world's worst, as they incur the hatred of their customers before they have inspected their wares. I am determined to buy nothing in Egypt.

There is something about hotel life and its crowds of standardized dumbbells that bores me to death, and I get tired of being personally conducted, as everyone is in this country. I would like to ship a canoe to the head of the Nile via Mombassa and come down to Cairo camping out.

The party stopped to inspect the dam at Aswan and to visit a 40,000-acre tract of land which Sir Ernest Cassell, the builder of the dam, had acquired for $1 per acre when it was sandy desert. With irrigation it was producing an annual income of $1,600,000, and had been inherited by Sir Ernest's niece, Lady Mountbatten.

March 10

We took a boat from above the dam yesterday afternoon and started for Wadi Halfa. We each have a comfortable stateroom on the upper deck. There were two Englishmen and two Austrians besides ourselves. The latter knew Coudenhove. One is Count Sigismund Szechenyi, nephew of the Austrian Minister to Washington, and the other is Count Edward Almasy, who was with King Charles when he attempted his coup d'etat of taking the Hungarian throne at Budapest. They were going up the Blue Nile shooting. We sat up till 11:30 talking. They told me much about European politics and asked me to come and see them in Vienna.*

We had a champagne dinner tonight in honor of my birthday,

* The only travelers they encountered were mostly Austrian aristocrats. A few days later they met another expedition on the Nile led by Baron Louis Rothschild and Count Khevenhuller.

and Denison had the cook bake a cake. At 9:30 P.M. we went ashore to see the most remarkable temple in Egypt, Abu Simbel, built by Rameses II. It is carved out of solid rock in a high cliff. Four huge chambers extend back into the rock 181 feet where four statues sit which are lighted only at dawn by the rays of the sun as they shine through the portal. This temple is one of the most superb and moving sights in the world and the bas-reliefs, carvings, and great rooms are indescribable. The Nubian Desert of golden sand stretches away on the right bank.

March 11

We arrived at Wadi Halfa this morning and, as soon as we had passed customs, boarded the train and were soon crossing the Nubian Desert on our way to Khartoum. It is a real desert without a spear of grass or vegetation for hundreds of miles. We were delightfully comfortable, as the cars are painted white to absorb the minimum heat and protected from glare by screens and lightly colored windows.

Khartoum, Sudan, March 13

Dear Marshall:

This city is situated on a flat plain between the Blue and White Niles. The Governor-General's Palace is huge but not beautiful and its spacious halls are hung with clusters of native weapons. Black Nubians in turbans and linen shorts and jackets are on guard, and smartly dressed Tommies are everywhere. The Palace garden is large and beautiful. In front of it is a bronze statue of General Gordon mounted on a camel and in front of the War Office is one of Kitchener on a horse.

In the afternoon we were invited to the Palace for tea by the Governor-General, Sir John, and Lady Maffey. We sat at small tables in the garden under the trees and were waited on by Sudanese servants in oriental costumes. Sir John is a very tall man of considerable personality and charm. Later he took us into the Palace and pointed out the spot where Gordon fell in 1885. In 1898 Kitchener revenged the deed across the river when he killed ten or fifteen thousand Dervishes in the battle of Omdurman. For eleven years the Mahdi and his successor, the Khalifa, kept Slatin Pasha a prisoner. You will find his experiences in a book entitled *Fire and Sword in the Sudan* by Slatin and Wingate.

The author not only read Slatin's exciting book but had several long talks with this celebrated and delightful man in 1931 when he was living at Merano, Italy, just below the Brenner Pass. One rainy morning, after presenting a letter of introduction from Coudenhove, the author received the following note:

Saturday

Dear Marshall Bond:

I am sorry for you that you have such bad weather—If you have nothing to do, come and have tea with me this afternoon at 4:30.

Yours sincerely,
R. Slatin

Slatin Pasha was an engaging little man with a mustache, a keen sense of humor, and a wealth of anecdotes. He was endowed with the kindly, gracious manners of an Austrian gentleman of the old school. In 1878, while he was serving as a lieutenant in Crown Prince Rudolph's regiment in Bosnia, he received a letter from General Gordon offering him a position in the Egyptian army in the Sudan. He obtained a leave of absence and said good-bye to his parents, little dreaming that it would be seventeen years before he would see them again.

In 1883-84 while Slatin was in command of the province of Darfur, a Moslem revolt took place under a religious fanatic, Mohammed Ahmed, known as the Mahdi. So great was the zeal and magnetism of the Mahdi that he swept everything before him and became the undisputed ruler of the Sudan. Slatin was forced to surrender, and about a year later at Khartoum the entire Anglo-Egyptian army was slaughtered. Gordon was stabbed to death; his head was cut off and presented to Slatin as the latter stood in chains.

"My heart seemed to stop beating as I gazed silently at this ghastly spectacle," wrote Slatin later.

For eleven years Slatin endured slavery under two of the cruelest men in the bloody history of Africa. He was starved, beaten, tortured, and spared execution only because he had become a Mohammedan and was considered valuable as a hostage. However, during the first year of his captivity, he was allowed to write occasionally to Gordon while the latter was still holding out in Khartoum.

When Slatin heard that Gordon took a dim view of his surrender and his change of religion, he wrote that he had fought twenty-seven battles against the Mahdi and that toward the end his Egyptian troops, who were Moslems, blamed his defeats on the fact that he was a Christian. He changed his religion solely to bolster their morale, and when his position became hopeless he surrendered to avoid unnecessary bloodshed. Gordon, a Christian fanatic, could not forgive him on either count.

Slatin said that he acquired a harem of horrible women while he was imprisoned. Whenever one was found so fat, ugly, and pock-marked that nobody else wanted her, she was invariably presented to him as a new bride or concubine and he dared not refuse. He painted a dreadful but amusing picture of life amid this gang of waddling monsters.

During his long years of captivity Slatin's name became famous throughout the Christian world, and all sorts of plots were hatched to rescue him. It was not until 1895, however, that his plans for escape finally succeeded. He managed to flee one night on a camel and made the long and hazardous journey back to Egypt in twenty-three days.

A tumultuous welcome awaited his return to Europe. He

was knighted by Queen Victoria, made a baron by the Emperor of Austria, and a pasha by the Khedive of Egypt. He returned triumphantly to Khartoum in 1898 with Lord Kitchener and Winston Churchill. From 1900 to 1914 he served in the Anglo-Egyptian army as Inspector General of the Sudan. When World War I began he returned to Vienna and was put in charge of that section of the Red Cross dealing with prisoners of war. His humane efforts on their behalf won him such respect that, as soon as the war was over, the British restored his army pension.

When the writer met Slatin Pasha he had mellowed, at seventy-four, and was able to discuss the events of the past with a great deal of humor. He had the same boyish enthusiasm and kindly twinkle as old Reeve Merritt. His house was full of ivory, swords, African weapons, and autographed photographs of dozens of potentates, including Franz Joseph and King George V. He exhibited some beautifully carved Egyptian jewelry which he said was three thousand years old.

One Sunday Slatin gave a small luncheon and seated the author next to a Frau Burg, formerly Berta Czuber, the daughter of a mathematics professor in Prague. She had been a great beauty in her youth, and the Archduke Ferdinand Karl had fallen in love with her. When his uncle, the old Emperor of Austria, opposed their marriage, the Archduke renounced his titles and rights of succession, shortened his name from Hapsburg to Burg, and married her anyway. The author thought she was well worth it.

Slatin said that when he came to England in 1895 he was summoned by Queen Victoria to appear at Balmoral in Scotland. He got into trouble by remarking to Sir James Reid, the court physician, that the castle seemed too small for the Queen of England. Sir James repeated the remark to the Queen, and during dinner she said:

"So, Slatin Pasha, you do not think Balmoral a big enough place for the Queen of England?"

"I was frightfully embarrassed," Slatin recounted, "and could only mutter incoherently, for nobody dared talk back to that formidable old lady. For a moment I found myself wishing I were back in Khartoum."

Several years later he was again summoned by Queen Victoria, this time to Windsor. An aide was assigned to escort him through every room in the huge building until he was completely exhausted. He finally got to his room just in time to change for dinner. When the guests were seated, Queen Victoria leaned across the table and asked:

"Slatin Pasha, do you think Windsor Castle is big enough for the Queen of England?"

Slatin showed the author a letter from King George V inviting him and his young daughter, Anne-Marie, to lunch at Buckingham Palace during his forthcoming visit to England in the summer of 1932. After reading it aloud, the old general said:

"Bond, my shabby frock coat is in rags and tatters and I can't afford a new one to wear to the Palace, so I wrote to my old friend in London, General Wingate, and asked to borrow his. He is about my size and has an elegant wardrobe. However, Wingate double-crossed me and showed my letter to King George."

Then Slatin produced another letter from his desk and handed it over with a broad smile. It was from the king's private secretary and read:

I have been instructed to inform your Excellency that His Majesty, King George V, is quite sure that General Slatin will be absolutely magnificent when he arrives at Buckingham Palace in General Wingate's frock coat.

In spite of his long years of service and many staunch admirers, there were some who could never quite forgive his surrender and his denial of Christianity. Apparently one of these was Lord Herbert Kitchener. Sir Ronald Storrs, in his *Memoirs,** says of Kitchener while he was ruling Egypt:

He was quick at disposing of unpalatable issues as we had the pleasure of noting one day when the most variously betitled servant of the Egyptian Government—Al-Ferik General Baron Sir Rudolph von Slatin Pasha—arrived for luncheon. He had come primed to discuss his pension, and it was immediately clear he was leading up to something. "Well, Lord Kitchener, I am afraid I've not made a great financial success of my life." "No one who knew you, my dear Slatin, ever thought you would." "Here I am for twelve years prisoner of the Mahdi, naked, often in chains, captured on active service—and yet not one piastre of pay throughout." "Well, Slatin, you can't say your out-of-pocket expenses over the period amounted to much," and the party suddenly found itself discussing aviation and the cotton crop.

Unlike Gordon and Kitchener, however, Sir Winston Churchill, in his *Frontiers and Wars*, explained Slatin's military predicament, his pretended conversion, and his ultimate surrender in kindly and sympathetic terms.

After his retirement Slatin paid a last visit to Khartoum in 1927. Marshall Bond, who greatly admired him, only missed meeting him by a few days. While in Khartoum Slatin happened to fall in with a group of British and American tourists who were being shown the historical sights by a pompous Arab guide. At one place the guide said:

"Ladies and gentlemen, this is the exact spot where Slatin Pasha stood when they brought him the head of General Gordon."

* *The Memoirs of Sir Ronald Storrs*, G. P. Putnam and Sons, 1937.

"I beg your pardon," Slatin said, "but I'm standing on the exact spot where Slatin Pasha stood."

The guide drew himself up and replied:

"I'm the official guide here and know what I'm talking about. Who do you think you are, anyway?"

"I'm terribly sorry to disagree with you," answered Slatin, "but I just happen to be Slatin Pasha."

On March 17 Bond and his friends left Khartoum on a quaint little river steamer, the *Fateh*, and continued up the Nile to El Dueim, Kosti, Renk, and Malakal. In this region bird life was especially impressive. They saw

. . . egrets, crested cranes, herons, sheldrake, widgeon, teal, thousands of spur-winged and Egyptian geese, marabout and European storks, snake birds and cormorants whitewashing the trees with their guano, and white-headed fish eagles whose eerie scream has been taken by many writers as embodying the wild untrammeled spirit of Africa.

At Renk they were honored by the visit of a Dinka prince:

And then there came down on the dock the most wonderful creature we had ever seen. He looked about six foot six in height and 21 years old. His sooty black figure was splendidly proportioned and he walked with the calm insolence of a prince. His brow was bound with a diadem of four strands of beads. His head was shaved to a ridge which was cut to the form of a cock's comb. Around his arms were gauntlets of tightly woven brass wire and blue beads. He wore anklets and sandals and flourished a short spear with a banneret with the gesture of a courtier of Louis XIV. No king could touch him for dignity, beauty, and grace. We presented him with a string of beads which he took negligently, and a mouth organ which seemed to interest him, as he went off playing it.

Malakal, March 24

We have progressed 511 miles up the White Nile and have 578 more to go to reach Rejaf. We daily see numerous huge hippos rise to the surface, look at us in amazement, go under and come up for another look. Along the shores crocodiles sun themselves and slide into the water if we come too near. They mostly sleep with their mouths open, so I imagine they have adenoids.

We finally came to the country of the Dinkas and Shilluks. Here was real savagery, and I liked it. These people were nearly all over six feet, straight and slender. They do not go in for agriculture or labor, but hunt, fish, and keep flocks. Consequently they were much more interesting to Denison and me than the other peoples. From the boat we constantly saw bunches of naked children carrying spears and thrusting them into the bull rushes, often bringing up huge fish. When they would stand and look at us they had a way of resting one foot on the other leg above the knee like a figure four.

I have had the greatest fun with all the natives ashore doing my few palming tricks. They would rush off to bring friends to witness these wonders. Then I would take one of their spears, pretend to squeeze my wrist, open my spear hand, and there it remained against the open palm. They tried it and their spears fell to the ground. They went wild with excitement.

The British Colonial Civil Servants are a fine lot of men and complete autocrats in the large areas they control. Just this little group of Englishmen who, in the name of the King, stand here to administer justice, enforce law and order, and good health, and who, by the prestige of that magic word, hold all the wild savage forces of this continent in order and save it from the chaos, misery, and despair of thirty years ago.

Denison, while rather reticent about his own philosophy and beliefs, is really a great despiser of comfort-loving people and with his large intellectual interests complains about nothing.* How much the girls get out of a trip like this I can't fathom.

* Denison wrote *Emotion as the Basis of Civilization,* Charles Scribner's Sons, 1928.

They seem fairly interested in a civilization that is today as it was thousands of years ago, but the introduction of a young Englishman into our midst seems to them much more exciting than past, present, or future. I feel the trip has been a great thing for me. It is hard to understand ancient civilizations without having seen them. Also it is impossible to understand "The White Man's Burden" unless one sees how the English handle it.

Soon they were engulfed in a vast gloomy marshland, the famous Sudd, covering an area as large as England in which vegetation runs riot and which is dominated by endless floating islands of graceful papyrus. Here they visited small villages of stark-naked Dinkas, saw crocodiles, hippos, and on one day more than 150 elephants. It was the Sudd and malaria which had prevented men since the dawn of history from discovering the source of the Nile by way of Egypt and the Sudan until Sir Samuel Baker, in a terrible ordeal, hacked his way through in 1870.

March 28

We have been four days in the Sudd. It is dreary beyond words. We all sleep in chairs periodically during the day. The odor of cooking and of the native in the hot dining room kills the appetite in spite of the fact that the food is really excellent. I still have dysentery and have to eat slops or go without and consequently have lost pounds. As soon as the sun goes down we don our mosquito boots. They are lined canvas, like a hip rubber boot, and are supposed to keep one from mosquito bites, as the mosquito is supposed to fly low. However, we all get a few bites on arms and neck by the mosquito doing what he is supposed not to do. If the bites are from a mosquito who has bitten a malarial Negro we are due to have it, and it takes ten days to find out.

As a permanent place of residence, I would never choose the tropics. The white man is only about 40% alive and has nothing to live for. But for a trip of great interest, with no thought of permanent residence, it is hard to beat the Nile. The great disappointment to me is to find that the "wild" country is pretty thickly populated. There are 6,000,000 people in the Sudan. Game exists, I suppose, because the only weapons allowed are spears.

On April 1 after a sixteen-day voyage of 1,100 miles, the *Fateh* arrived at Rejaf, the junction of the Nile-Uganda route. That night Bond and Hugo Goodhue decided to try the food at the hotel. While enjoying cool drinks on the verandah after dusk, Goodhue mentioned that his father had built the town of Tyrone, New Mexico, for Walter Douglas, president of the Phelps-Dodge Corporation, and was proceeding to give his estimate of the renowned mining tycoon when a figure arose in the darkness and said:

"Before you go any further, let me state that I am Walter Douglas."

To casually mention a friend from America and suddenly have him appear from the gloom of central Africa gave Goodhue quite a start. Mrs. Douglas and their three daughters were also along, and the two parties merged for a whole day to exchange information and experiences. Douglas had come up from Capetown primarily to see the great Katanga copper mines in the southern Belgian Congo. He said he was astonished by their wealth but thought that in some ways native labor was wastefully employed.

Kampala, Uganda, April 12

From Rejaf we motored into the northern Belgian Congo and were shown about the country by one of the officials, Baron Van Zuylen. He took us to the village of a chief, Ikibondo, where we spent the night in a rest house maintained by the chief for white guests only. His menage consisted of a beautiful park of native trees and palms. The chief's conical thatched roof house was beside a brook across which, hidden in the foliage, were the houses of his favorite wives. Everything was neat, clean, and lovely.

The women of this tribe [the Mangbettu] had elongated heads due to the tight binding of the heads of infants. This custom originated from a ruse to prevent the physical attractions of women from engaging unwelcome attentions of the Arab slave traders.

The Baron told us of some of their customs:

"They are brave fighters but as their intertribal wars are no longer permitted they have much time to sit around, and their thinking seems to be largely of sex. Immorality and perversion are the prevailing order rather than the exception and occasion a market for boys. They are adept at birth control, and wives bear but few children.

"Poisoning has attained such perfection among them as to become an art.

"They believe in the 'Evil Eye,' and, where a member dies, a means of ferreting out the offender is to poison a chicken and then ask the bird if the person suspected is guilty. The death of the chicken is conclusive proof that he is."

The chief gave a dance for us that night. He sat on a portable throne and behind him sat his forty wives, each on a little stool. They were naked except for a bit of cloth that hung from a girdle in front and a small oblong mat behind. The chief wore a headdress of white and magenta feathers, a giraffe's tail behind, and a leopard's tail hanging in front. He danced several times and was vociferously applauded by his wives. Women who own only one-fortieth of a husband appreciate him. The music consisted of five drums of different tones and was not unpleasant. A fire was built and the dances continued around it. The sexes danced separately. Ikibondo sent for native beer during the dance and an attendant dropped the jar. He immediately had him put in jail and sent another man for more.

Van Zuylen took the party to an experimental elephant farm where the Belgians were training African elephants. It had always been assumed that only Indian elephants could be tamed and trained. At first the Belgians' efforts were in vain: they couldn't catch mature elephants and found that young ones died of fright or shock. At length a young one survived and was used to capture others. These they succeeded in training, and a large amount of heavy work was being done by them.

At Gombari a message was sent into the jungle offering money to buy salt if the Pygmies would come to town. A long line of these tiny people marched up in front of the rest house, led by two old men with beards. They wore nothing but small breech clouts and only carried bows and arrows. They were light brown in color, and some of the younger ones were very good looking. They were indifferent and even contemptuous of gifts such as necklaces. They had no religion, cultivated no fields, and lived on raw meat. They were completely independent of civilization except for their passion for salt.

From the Pygmy country the party drove back to Uganda and visited Kampala and Entebbe. They were received by Sir Daudi Chwa, King of Uganda. Somewhat to their surprise, the king lived in a modern bungalow, wore European clothes, spoke good English, was a member of the Church of England, and had only one wife.

April 20
Entebbe, the capital of Uganda, is a beautiful place with rolling fields dotted with trees—as smooth as an English park and overlooking Lake Victoria Nyanza. Our shooting trip is now planned and will be a long drawn out safari to Tabora by way of the Lualaba River back in the Belgian Congo. We have champagne and whisky galore, but I am awfully sick of it, though it is astonishing how warm champagne bucks you up in this rotten climate.

From Entebbe they drove to Mvarara, where the culture of the natives was based solidly on cow worship:

When the first cow faced us with her gigantic spread of horns, we could hardly believe our eyes. These cows beat anything ever invented in the bovine line, and it is not surprising that here one should find the real adoration of the cow. It is surprising to find a race which boasts that all its vigor and warlike courage is based on milk. The men are tall of stature, slender, and athletic with fine features and straight noses. With women another ideal has been at work. Their beauty and charm increases with their girth. They are fed constantly on milk and allowed to do no work save cleanse the milk jars. To please his cows a man is careful to keep his daughter fat, beautiful, and chaste. The result of such diligent cherishing is that they acquire such a mass of fat they can only walk a few steps without stopping to rest. Their whole life centers around cows. When a man dies his body is wrapped and he must wait for burial until his cows come home. Then in the presence of his beloved cattle he is buried in a heap of dung at one side of the corral.

Bukoba, Tanganyika, April 26

We arrived here yesterday and leave by steamer at midnight for Mwanza on the south end of Lake Victoria Nyanza and from there go in safari out into what the British call the "Blue." This was a German settlement before the British took Tanganyika and is one of the most beautiful spots I ever saw. There are fine roads, shade trees, tropical shrubbery, and a wooded island stands near the shore. In the distance lay a chain of islands, and of course the opposite shore was invisible, for next to Superior this is the largest lake in the world.

Barnes had preceded us and had tents erected in a garden. His idea of camping is luxury which most people while camping seek to avoid. We had an army of blacks dancing about and getting everything wrong. I asked them to keep away from my tent but they didn't understand. Dinner was served in the garden. We had soup, fish, chicken, cold ham, and tongue, potatoes, vegetable marrow, huge avocados, deserts of fruit salad and trifles, then a savory of macaroni and cheese, champagne, port, and coffee. *That* is being "Out in the Blue." Unless we strike something different, I should say "Out in the Blue" could be closely approximated by motoring from New York to Philadelphia, camping and shooting over the intervening spaces between settlements. One should have about five Negroes to get in the way and mix up and take away your things every time you turn your head. If I were to do this trip on my own, I'd do it just as we do in Arizona but with one good boy to get wood and clean up. Everything beyond this is a nuisance.

Lake Victoria Nyanza was crossed on the *Winifred*, whose captain was a serious little Englishman gravely concerned with the moral reputation of his ship. When Bond visited him on the bridge, he confided plaintively that all was not as it should be:

"I try to keep my ship, sir, like Caesar's wife, above suspicion, but it is not always possible. Do you recall the beautiful lady occupying stateroom A and the distinguished-looking gentleman in stateroom F? Well, sir, they both got on at Entebbe and from the way they were carrying on I suspected the worst from the very start of the trip."

When Bond, who was doing his best to keep from exploding with laughter, asked the captain if he had any proof of this, the latter replied:

"Sir, I have a little fox terrier on board and when my suspicions were sufficiently aroused, I gathered up a handful of his bones and put them between the sheets of the gentleman's bed. Well, sir, there have been no complaints, no complaints at all."

Tabora, Tanganyika, May 5

We left Mwanza for the end of the railway at Tabora, 120 miles distant, in two Ford cars and a Chevrolet truck. It took four days on account of the softness of the ground and we were mired constantly. We had a chief get us 81 Negroes and these we took along to get us out of the sticky places. When the road was good we dashed forward, the Negroes running as fast as they could behind. They would catch up when we got stuck, and then with forty or fifty of them pulling on a rope and the rest pushing, we usually got out and on to the next big hole. I enjoyed it more than I would have had it been perfect going.

The Negroes are virtual slaves, but interesting and amusing. I rode with the driver of the truck, a young Frenchman. Life must have been a struggle for him as he had no sympathy or softness either for himself or the Negroes. Some of them at times would be dilatory in walking up to the rope, or they would do something stupid, and he would jump out and smack them good. This man was awfully polite and considerate but never smiled. Life was a scrap for him, and he worked like a dog and made the blacks do likewise.

Zebras, giraffes, and wildebeests were plentiful along the way, and Bond shot several Thompson's gazelles for the Negroes to roast over their campfires. The inefficient Barnes brought mountains of food for the party but no drinking water. They had to filter water from a mud hole. At the railhead Denison, who became ill with what he thought might be the dread blackwater fever, ordered a special train ($600) to take them to Kigoma on Lake Tanganyika.

While in the Tabora district they paid a visit to Saidi, sultan of the huge Wanyamezi tribe. He was part Arab, highly intelligent, and a good administrator of 6,000 square miles of territory. The British paid him $10,000 per year on which he supported seventy-five wives, forty-five children, and two motor cars. This tribe was so strong in the days before the advent of the white man that none of its members was ever enslaved by Arabs. On the contrary, it used its power to capture Negroes from weaker tribes which it sold to the Arabs. Bond often mentioned this horrible aspect of African history in which a main objective of intertribal warfare was for one group of Africans to capture another and sell its members to outsiders as slaves. At least the white man had put a stop to this.

An amusing feature of the Tabora district was the trouble the British were having in maintaining two thousand miles of telegraph lines. The natives loved to adorn themselves with copper wire and were constantly stealing the wire for jewelry. The commissioner said that in the previous year five miles of wire had been stolen. When the culprits were caught, however, they were acquitted in court because no one could prove that the wire they had in possession was actually that from the telegraph line. Everyone knew it was, but no witnesses could be found to testify.

Kigoma, Tanganyika, May 10

When the special train arrived at Tabora where we boarded it, Major Müller, Chief of Staff to General Von Lettow who conducted the German East African campaign, got off. He is going through the country paying off the Negro soldiers the Germans had during the war. Müller had a brilliant record and is the most impressive man I've seen so far. He is tall and thin like Alvensleben, with light blue eyes that smile but look dangerous, a large expressive mouth, a sensitive pleasant face, but behind outward affability the trained ruthless warrior. The British all think highly of him.

In the afternoon we went out to Ujiji, six miles distant. A long straight street runs through the town deeply shaded by Kasuarina trees. It is the second largest native city in central Africa and has a fine view of Lake Tanganyika. Native houses and Indian bazaars line either side of the main street. It is full of atmosphere. Down one of the side streets, we came to the tree under which Livingstone and Stanley met. The tree is fenced in and a stone monument records:

LIVINGSTONE
STANLEY
1871

Back in Kigoma that night Hugo Goodhue came down with malaria and amoebic dysentery, forcing a delay of several days.

Hugo has recovered although still taking injections of emetine. The Governor came yesterday for the christening of the German ship the government raised and rehabilitated. It was interesting to see the natives who assembled to witness the ceremony. The better class of Negroes were dolled up in white cotton garments, and the wild Bushmen in leopard skins carried spears. Along the road to Ujiji big husky blacks, naked except for a little goat skin suspended from the shoulders, came along with enormous loads on their heads, their bodies glistening with perspiration, and a little mosquito of a Hindoo who owned the cargo marched along in front with a cane. Africa has the numbers and the brawn to exterminate the Europeans and Hindoos overnight, but it hasn't the brains.

After watching these natives, I have come to the conclusion that disaster will never develop them. They have always had disasters. Slave raids, wars of aggression, and sickness have been put upon them but they have simply bowed to them and never organized. Vanity, I think, is their only salvation. Inculcate in them the greatest possible number of wants, and the industry necessary to fulfill them will develop the brainiest and most energetic as nothing else will.

I saw two slimy Hindoos returning home from their shops being carried in hammocks by sweating Herculean blacks who could have swallowed them whole, but the Hindoo has a higher type of mind and so was carried. Africa is a land of shuffling feet —bare feet. There are no beasts of burden—the tsetse fly sees to that. So from sunrise to dark hordes of men and women trudge along with burdens on their heads. Human muscle is the machinery of Africa. The white man's rule is the world's biggest confidence game. Prestige alone does it. Among ourselves we talk of tribal ceremonies and customs continually, but it has become sort of a professional life and lacks novelty. I shall appreciate the Negro a lot more when I have bidden him goodbye. Denison is taking the Scottish Dr. Sanderson and his wife along to the Congo.

Elizabethville, Belgian Congo, June 1

We crossed Lake Tanganyika and spent a night at Albertville. Then all day by rail through uninteresting brush country to the Lualaba (the southern fork of the Congo River). Two days later twelve Negroes paddled four or five miles up a tributary with our camp outfit. We camped under a large group of shady palms 200 yards from a native village. The Sultan came out to greet us, and we told him to have his men sweep up the ground. The prestige of the white man is such that he can order as many natives as he wishes at any time for any purpose.

The Sultan took off his hat, which he wore for swank in our honor, went to his village and returned with a gang of men, himself armed with a rhinocerous hide whip. He bawled his men out, and the ground was soon immaculate. Then tents were set up, and our Negro servants made their cook fire a little way off. This was Barnes' "great game country" and it was rotten. I shot an antelope, the Doctor and Barnes four buffalo, and Hugo a wart hog. My two gun bearers were skillful trackers and it was a pleasure to see them maneuver, but the shooting was terrible.

Bond was disgusted at missing the great herds of game which abounded in British territories that Barnes had purposely by-passed. It was evident that he was *persona non grata* to the British authorities for some misdeed in the past, and as a guide and white hunter he was one of the worst. Furthermore, he had picked a time for the hunt when the grass was too high to see the game properly and when the mosquitoes were rampant.

The other Sultan from across the river came over and camped under some trees seventy-five feet away. He had a mosquito netting, 15 or 20 wives, children, and attendants who slept close by him. Some of the buffalo meat was brought in although it already stank from exposure to the tropical sun.

I awakened at 3:00 A.M. and heard an animal's teeth crunching bones. "A hyena has Hugo's wart hog," I said to myself. The Sultan's people must have heard the sound too for they sat up and started moving around. The moment they did so, two lions eating the buffalo meat not twenty feet from them let out hoarse threatening roars. The men, women, and children screamed in terror and ran to our camp in the inky darkness, crouching close to the girls' tent.

I got out of bed, lit a lantern, got my rifle and then had our scared boys light other lanterns. I put one in front of the girls' tent, one in front of Denison's and two out in the path between our camp and the lions. Lights generally keep them off. None of us was scared, and all Charis could think of was to ask for a cigarette. It was so dark we couldn't see ten feet. We had the boys make some tea, smoked, and listened to the lions chewing their meat and cracking bones. Just before dawn we heard them slipping off through the high grass. Hugo and I went out for an hour but saw nothing of them. We knew they would return again at night.

The only way I could see to get them was to build a platform in a tree and shoot as best we could by flashlight. The girls wanted in on it, so we had the Negroes construct two platforms of poles about fifteen feet up in a tree fifty feet from the meat. We took wraps and our rifles and went up about 8:00 P.M. Dr. Sanderson, Hugo, and I sat cramped and crowded on one little platform, and the girls on a somewhat larger one.

At 10:00 P.M. we heard the lions and slowly and quietly got ready to shoot. I pressed my flashlight. It wasn't much good but revealed a lion side on. Dr. Sanderson saw two, but from my position I saw but one. We fired simultaneously. I saw the flash of a tawny body and heard them retreat in the high grass. We couldn't see our sight at all so a miss was to be expected.

Ten minutes later we heard the meat being dragged away

(two big buffalo legs lashed together and staked to the ground). We were ready, and I pressed the flashlight. The lions' eyes gleamed like emeralds. Again we fired simultaneously. Not a sound. We waited and waited, and then we heard a smack on the earth and a choking growl about 200 feet away. It sounded like a dying lion, but we couldn't be sure. We fought mosquitoes, fell asleep, awakened cramped, smoked, and fell asleep again.

As dawn came I went to the meat. There was the first lion, one bullet in his brain, the other in his heart. Out in the grass 200 feet away lay the second, with two bullets through his body in vital spots. We couldn't have shot better in broad daylight, but of course it was mere luck. Each of us could truthfully say he had killed two lions but neither of us could say he had killed one. That sort of shooting from a tree is no sport at all, just murder of a courageous beast.

Soon the old Sultan came along. I told him we had killed a simba (lion) but he wouldn't believe it. I led him over to his camp site of the night before and he saw the huge beast. His eyes popped out and all he could say was a shrill, throaty "ugh" over and over again. Then I took him to the second lion and he nearly blew up with "ughs." He ran to his relative's village and soon both Sultans returned with a mob of men, women, and children. They "ughed" and "ughed" and then fell to chattering like a million magpies. Their great enemies were dead.

The next day we took the *Prince Leopold* up the Lualaba and three days later reached the railhead and came through to Elizabethville last night. The food and water were awful. I have long since given up drinking anything but wine or beer. I have lost seventeen pounds. We stay here till Wednesday to see the copper mines and then leave for Victoria Falls, Bulawayo, Johannesburg, Kimberly, and Capetown where we should arrive about the end of June.

Since the above was the last of Marshall Bond's letters, the concluding extracts are from the daily journal written consecutively by the six members of the Denison party.

June 6, Lualaba, River

The first thing that strikes the traveller in the Belgian Congo is its wonderful system of waterways. Transport is the primary difficulty of all colonies, but here in the Congo with its thousands of miles of navigable rivers stretching out to all points of the compass like a vast cobweb from the central channel, the problem is already half solved. The Congo basin has the most remarkable river system in the world, of which the Belgians have not been slow to take advantage.

The natives of this riverine country are the Balubas, a poor lot compared with their brothers of the highlands. When the steamer puts in at the numerous wooding stations, a shouting mob of black humanity collects to bargain fish, fruit, eggs, and other food stuffs. They are a happy laughing lot with "money to burn," more than they know what to do with, for the mines, railways, and oil refineries in the Congo have brought comparative wealth to the laziest scallywag in this vast territory. All do a bit of trading up and down the river, rear fowl and duck, collect palm oil, or catch and dry fish.

Greeks and other white traders usually have stores in the larger villages. The mines dominate all life here. The inevitable *askaris*, the native policemen who really run the Congo, as far too much authority is given them, were much in evidence. On board with us were the inevitable Greeks, found everywhere these days, who gambled at poker and faro, drinking beer in the intervals. There was a doctor from Ruanda who had been a member of the Belgian mission to that country to arrange the recruiting of laborers for the mine. There was also a Plymouth Brother who read his Bible and said his prayers in the early morning and kept aloof from us all.

June 7

As an implement for the generation of noise, we are prepared to back the *Prince Leopold* against all comers. It's iron decks are marvelous sounding boards for the vocal efforts of the hundreds of natives who live below in a constant state of exhilaration. After rushing several times to see if murder was being committed, we have accepted their wild shrieks and howls as the normal state of affairs. Loading wood is an inspiring process, for each native throws each separate stick with all his might on the iron deck where it reverberates like a clap of thunder and rouses sleepers to profane activity.

There is one native with a voice that would wake the dead who seems to know everyone along the river and shouts his salutations which are vociferously echoed by enthusiastic little cannibals who caper about madly and yell. Our friend is apparently conveying all the latest quotations of the stock market to the riparian town—"buffalo steak ten centimes the kilo, lion shoulders at one franc, wart hog kidneys down to fifty centimes, wooden gods ten francs apiece." It seemed to be the same message repeated over and over till our ears ached.

The two girls of our party wandered disconsolately around the decks whence all the young Belgians and Frenchmen had fled and in the pitchy blackness entered the first stateroom at hand, which happened to be that of the tall cadaverous misogynistic missionary of the Plymouth Brethren who had long ago lost all faith in the virtue and character of young women in Africa and who was earnestly endeavoring to avoid their persistent seductions. Seating themselves genially on the bed and missing the head of this unfortunate minister only by inches, they opened up one of those gay little midnight conversations for which they are deservedly famous. He endured for some time in silence but at last felt he must protest. "Ladies," he said in his deep solemn voice, "I think you must have made a mistake in the cabin. I am a missionary." They departed silent and crestfallen.

June 8, Lualaba River

A Belgian official who has been a passenger on the boat disembarked at Kyabo. He is completing his thirtieth year of service and is due to retire on a pension. Accompanying him was a five year old Negro son, chocolate in color and having a wooly head. According to the steward, this official intends to arrange for the training of his bastard son so that he may get a job as a mechanic on the government railway. A French doctor aboard assured me that this is a common experience in Belgian official-dom. There are those who feel that the prestige of the white man in the Congo is beginning to be undermined. Some tell us, however, that the more or less permanent alliance of a Belgian official with a native woman does not offend the natives as much as the temporary alliances to which Englishmen are prone.

The Belgian Congo, despite its 12,000,000 native population, is said to suffer from a labor shortage. In years past the laborers were largely recruited from Rhodesia, but the British have put a stop to this. As the streams abound with fish and bananas can be raised with a minimum of effort, the native prefers the free and independent living nature affords to enforced hard labor. The country around Katanga has been decimated by sleeping sickness and many thousands have died. Organized recruiting is necessary to get the numbers required for work in the mines and the conivance of chiefs is enlisted. In the mining compounds liberal food and amusements are furnished as well as physicians and hospitals. This, of course, is wise philanthropic selfishness.

June 10, aboard the train to Elizabethville

After breakfasting royally on steaks and gazing out of the windows at miles of dusty forest with tall trees and tangled underbrush, we pulled up through yards that reminded us more of Chicago than Africa at the station of Elizabethville, capital of Katanga Province. The station platform, marvelous to re-late, was crowded with women in smart felt hats and costumes obviously from Paris, escorted by very fat and uncouth Belgian men wearing breeches and puttees, and in the majority of cases large diaphanous beards.

Elizabethville was quite a large town—for Africa at any rate —boasting 2,000 white inhabitants, mixed Belgian and British. Motors, motorcycles, and bicycles dashed about at what appeared to us a mighty dangerous speed, which enveloped the choking passer-by in clouds of dust. There were two rival hotels, the Metropole, famous for its bar and biweekly movies, and the Bruxelles, noted for its excellent cuisine. We were extremely surprised by the shop windows, many of which had a decided Parisian touch. We had not seen such a display since Cairo.

June 11, Elizabethville

After breakfast we paid a visit to the smelter of the Union Minière Company which is situated at the edge of town. We climbed through the coal dust to the top of the furnaces and looked through the open doors on the raging smelter of flame in which all the colors of the rainbow seemed blended, glowing red and deep blue and above them all great tongues of luminous green that roared and leapt up in sheets of colored fire. The party watched fascinated for a long time and saw the little cars of ore pushed by natives, who for once seemed active and energetic, approach the lip of the flame. At noon when a huge negro struck the furnace with his crowbar, a stream of molten copper burst forth, fell with a splash into car after car, and in a few minutes was transformed from liquid fire to a dull coppery slab.

June 12, Elizabethville

The Katanga highlands are eminently suited to permanent occupation by white people, with high elevation and a well defined rainless period of six months when the weather becomes cool and bracing. They are unbelievably rich minerally—gold, silver, tin, copper, lead, chrome, coal, diamonds, and radium—nowhere else has nature distributed such a galaxy of wealth. Agriculturally too, now that the tsetse fly is being dispersed by closer settlement, they are attractive. They are a well timbered and well watered country, open and park-like in places and of considerable beauty. Nothing can stop Katanga from reaching a high pinnacle of fame second to none in the world of mines and minerals. If Belgium had opened her colony generously to foreign enterprise, Katanga would by this time be bringing into Belgium ten times the riches it does now. But truth to tell Katanga and the Congo are too big a proposition for a young and small nation like Belgium to handle.

Amongst the many mines, each with its separate management, housing, and hospital buildings, the big mine of Kambove stands out as one of the largest and oldest and seems inexhaustible in the richness and quantity of its copper deposits. Then, not far from Kambove, are the radium mines which have now ceased operation because the world has been overstocked already from this mine.*

In two touring cars we visited the landing ground of the Sabena Company to have a look at the big airplane that had arrived from the lower Congo yesterday evening and designed to carry ten passengers. This enterprising company subsidized by the Belgian Government has only recently inaugurated this airline and now Leopoldville can be reached from here in two days.

One extraordinary feature of Elizabethville is the ant hills. All around the town rise these huge hillocks, usually with a tree ornamenting their summit. The golf course especially is decorated with them, and the ants are always supplying new bunkers.

The party left Elizabethville by train on June 15, but not before Bond had recovered somewhat from a bad attack of malaria.

June 17, Rhodesia

We woke up in the Livingstone station and knew that real civilization had us in her clutches once more. We were no longer explorers of central Africa, but simple tourists at a popular resort and fair game for the hordes of native boys selling walking sticks, bead necklaces, and baskets. In fact we might have been in California if it hadn't been for the farm wagon drawn

* These mines were extensively worked for uranium when the atom bomb was invented.

by eighteen oxen and the natives in their bright calico clothes.

No words can describe the majesty and beauty of Victoria Falls on the Zambesi River which hurls itself over the rim, a white and foaming torrent, with a deafening roar into the ravine four hundred feet below. The spray is everywhere and great clouds of it rise out of the ravine and dissolve in mist that soaks both rims and may be seen for miles. These falls are a mile and a quarter in width and fall into four main cataracts and were discovered by Livingstone in 1855. We climbed out onto the eastern rim to view the rainbows and could distinguish three shining in the mist.

June 20, Bulawayo, Southern Rhodesia

We pulled into the station at Bulawayo at 10 A.M. and immediately stepped into two Dodge cars and started for Cecil Rhodes' grave at "World's View" in the Matoppo Hills thirty miles away. The country we passed through was the same bush veldt we had from Victoria Falls and was well grassed. The Matoppo Hills are round-topped granite mountains covered with huge isolated boulders. At the foot of one on which Rhodes is buried we parked our cars and walked up a gently rising path to the top. The grave had been excavated in solid rock with a large bronze tablet embedded in a granite slab on which was the inscription:

HERE LIE THE REMAINS OF
CECIL JOHN RHODES

It was a beautiful view and a fitting resting place for South Africa's great empire builder. Below the brow of the hill has been carved into the granite:

THIS GROUND HAS BEEN CONSECRATED AND
DEDICATED AS A BURIAL PLACE TO ALL WHO
HAVE DESERVED WELL OF THIS COUNTRY

A little further off a large granite tomb holds the remains of Major Allen Wilson and his companions in arms, all of whom died at the hands of King Lobengula and his Matabele warriors in 1893. A bronze frieze of life-sized figures extends around four sides of the tomb depicting the brave men who died in that fight.

Actually half a dozen scouts survived this famous fight, having been ordered by Wilson to charge through the hordes in a futile attempt to get enough reinforcements to prevent the massacre. One of these was the American scout, Major Frederick Russell Burnham.* He was nimble, dynamic, resourceful and seemed to look right through you with a pair of sharp blue eyes that conveyed the impression of intelligence and determination.

Burnham learned the art of scouting from an old frontiersman named Holmes who had served with Kit Carson and gained practical experience in the Tonto Basin War against the Apaches. In 1893, captivated by the immense reputation of Cecil Rhodes, he went to South Africa and distinguished himself in the first Matabele war against King Lobengula and his 80,000 warriors.

With the elimination of Lobengula, things quieted down until 1896 when the Matabele rose again under a fanatical high priest, the M'Limo. A massive uprising was planned in which all the whites were to be killed. Fortunately an extraordinary piece of intelligence was discovered by a scout named Armstrong—the exact location of the M'Limo's secret ceremonial cave. Armstrong and Burnham, in a feat of unparalleled bravery, hid in the shadows of the portal, and Burnham shot the high priest as he was leading thousands of his followers into the cave. The procession was so stunned that the two scouts had just enough time to make their escape.

Burnham was in the Klondike when the Boer War began, but returned to South Africa to become chief of scouts on the staff of Lord Roberts. After a brilliant series of forays

---

* He later described his amazing adventures in *Scouting on Two Continents*.

and escapes he was wounded and invalided back to England. On the boat was another famous veteran, Winston Churchill. King Edward awarded Major Burnham the D.S.O. and a permanent majority in the British Army. There followed years of exploration and prospecting in Africa and Mexico under the auspices of the American mining magnate John Hays Hammond, who had been the first to head Rhodes' mining empire, Consolidated Gold Fields of South Africa.

The writer first met Burnham at his Pasadena home in 1926, shortly after the major had made a fortune in oil. Twenty years later when the writer was sitting in his Santa Barbara real estate office, a woman came in waving an advertisement and said, "I am Mrs. Frederick Russell Burnham and would like to see this property." (She was his second wife.)

After introducing himself the author asked, "How long ago did Major Burnham die?"

"Oh, he's not dead," she replied. "He's sitting right out in the car."

The Burnhams bought two acres on a hilltop in Santa Barbara with inspiring ocean and mountain views. They put a rustic redwood fence around the property, built a small house, and hung up a sign reading "The Outspan." At this beautiful place the author enjoyed many long talks with the wily scout.

As a boy in Los Angeles, Burnham had known the charming old Mexican, Pio Pico, ex-governor of California. He was amused by the ritual Pico went through when giving money to beggars. Whenever one of the latter accosted the governor, he would reach into his pocket and, with true Spanish courtesy, offer the man a handful of coins. The mendicant, equally bound by polite tradition, would invariably select the smallest coin.

At thirteen Burnham was a mounted messenger for Western Union and delivered the telegram to Lucky Baldwin accepting the latter's offer of $1.50 per acre for the Santa Anita ranch near Pasadena. Everyone thought Baldwin was crazy to pay such an exorbitant price.

When asked what were the most difficult aspects of scouting, the major remarked, "The capacity to withstand solitude and to remain absolutely motionless in the face of the enemy."

He was fond of reminiscing about King Lobengula who, next to Rhodes and Kruger, was the most powerful leader in South Africa. In his palmy days the great king lived beside the River of White Stones in Bulawayo, naked except for a girdle of monkey skins, and surrounded by piles of offal, putrefying carcasses of slaughtered animals, and a multitude of wives and retainers. Majestic, obese, cruel, and suspicious, he dispensed a terrible justice by ordering his victims tossed to the crocodiles which infested the pools in the river.

One day an impecunious Irishman* arrived in Bulawayo and implored Lobengula for a trade concession. The king, who disliked and distrusted white traders, refused as he had done with many others. When the desperate visitor pleaded that he would do anything to win a concession, Lobengula replied, "You can have your concession if you will swim across the big hole in the river where the crocodiles live."

Without hesitation the Irishman peeled off his clothes, jumped in, swam across the pool, and lived to make a fortune. Burnham said the only possible explanation was that the crocodiles, which are naturally cowardly, had never before seen white skin and hesitated just long enough for the man to get across.

* Not to be confused with Charles D. Rudd, who obtained a mineral concession for Cecil Rhodes in 1888.

When asked who was the most impressive personality he had ever met, the major answered without hesitation:

"Cecil Rhodes—for strength of character, force of intellect, ability to lead men, Rhodes even surpassed Theodore Roosevelt, whom I also knew fairly well."

The author asked Burnham how he happened to get into the oil business. Burnham explained that he and his son, Roderick, had done some geological work on Dominguez Hill near Los Angeles and were convinced that it contained oil. Since three dry holes had already been drilled there, they were unable to raise any money for several years. Finally in 1921, at the old Arlington Hotel in Santa Barbara, Burnham sold the idea to John Hays Hammond. The latter wired Harry Payne Whitney and Ogden Mills, and the three financiers each put up $100,000, and with the Burnhams formed the Burnham Development Company. They struck a gusher on the first try.* The other three wells would have struck oil too had they gone a few hundred feet deeper. By 1947 the Burnham Development Company had paid $25,-000,000 in dividends.

The author had the pleasure of introducing the president of Yale University, Dr. Charles Seymour, to Major Burnham. Seymour wanted to thank him personally for donating his fine collection of books on Africa to the Yale Library.

In a presentation copy of his second book, *Taking Chances,* the major wrote:

To Marshall Bond, Jr., a son who is worthy of perpetuating the name of his father and my valiant sourdough pioneer friend, I am,

Yours sincerely,
F. R. Burnham

*John Hays Hammond in his *Autobiography* says that their first well was drilled jointly with the Union Oil Co., and came in for 1,500 barrels a day.

On September 1, 1947, at the age of eighty-six, Major
Frederick Russell Burnham lay down for a nap after lunch
and never woke up. One can only hope that he had joined
his heroes, Cecil Rhodes and Major Allen Wilson. Mrs.
Burnham was especially proud of one of her many letters of
condolence—from Sir Winston Churchill.

After returning to Bulawayo from Rhodes' tomb, the
Denison party arrived at Mafeking on June 21. Two days
later in Johannesburg they visited the Village Deep Gold
Mine situated on the world's most productive gold reef, the
Witwatersrand. At that time this mine was the deepest in
the world, 7,300 feet. They watched the endless procession
of ore skips coming up the shaft, the chemical extraction
process using both cyanide and mercury, and the final melt-
ing of the gold into bars.

On June 25 they went to see a large diamond mine at
Kimberley. The ore was first reduced to gravel by iron roll-
ers, then washed, sorted, and flushed over vibrating tables
covered with grease. Diamonds can be made wet only by
petroleum, not by water, and hence stick to greased tables,
the rest of the material getting washed off. Forty tons of
gravel were passed over the tables daily, producing a pound
and a half of diamonds of all colors and sizes, a total of 3,000
carats, which the mine sold on contract to De Beers Consolidated for a flat $24 a carat regardless of size or quality.
The annual output was $20,000,000. Bond, like most tour-
ists, had the pleasure of hefting a bucket of diamonds.

On the mornng of June 27 everyone arose early as the
train sped through the mountain basins and broad valleys
of the Cape Colony. Suddenly at 10 A.M. Table Mountain
appeared with Capetown lying at its feet and the gray At-

lantic stretching out beyond. The trip was finally over except for sightseeing at the Cape and the voyage back to England.

While in Capetown the party was invited to tea at the delightful old colonial farmhouse of H. E. V. Pickstone, fruit king of South Africa and former head nurseryman of Cecil Rhodes. Bond was amused to recall that Pickstone had worked for Judge H. G. Bond, in 1895 at New Park, where he had learned the fruit business. After that he got a job as waiter in the Palace Hotel in San Francisco, but was demoted to silver polisher for spilling soup down a lady's neck. In the kitchen he and a Greek got into a fight and threw most of the silver in the hotel at each other. Both were thrown out the back door and fired.

From San Francisco, Pickstone worked his way to South Africa on a freighter. He recognized the similarity of South Africa to California as a potential fruit center and sought funds to start a nursery. It was Cecil Rhodes who in 1897 finally gave him £500. Within a few years, when he had become wealthy, he tried to repay the money, but Rhodes refused, saying, "Anything that is good for South Africa is all right with me."

In 1906 Pickstone* returned to California to see what was new in the fruit business. As he stood in front of the Palace Hotel being interviewed by a group of reporters and photographers he was thinking of how he had been thrown out the back door ten years before.

In 1932 the writer told this story to John Hays Hammond, who was wintering in Santa Barbara. The latter remarked,

---

* H. E. V. Pickstone, an Englishman, first went to South Africa in 1892, but came to California to seek business opportunities. According to Mrs. P. S. Pickstone he was, upon his return, introduced to Rhodes by Charles D. Rudd.

"I was the one who introduced Pickstone to Cecil Rhodes."†

Seventeen days after sailing from Capetown, Bond was met by his family at Southampton. He was so ill with malaria and amoebic dysentery that they took him to the French Riviera where, at the villa of his classmate Richard M. Hurd, he gradually regained his health.

John H. Denison, who had bought stock in General Motors before the expedition, sold it upon his return at enough profit to pay for the entire trip.

† Harry H. Webb of Santa Barbara, who succeeded Hammond as head of Consolidated Gold Fields of South Africa, also said it was Rudd who made the introduction and added that Hammond had the bad habit of stealing center stage and of portraying himself emerging from every scene smelling like a rose. In spite of his immense fame and fortune, he impressed the author as a dynamic but smallish sort of man, ever anxious to appear a little bigger than he was.

Mojave

AFTER MARSHALL BOND returned from Africa he became a stockbroker in Santa Barbara. On the day of the big crash in 1929 his margin account was wiped out along with nine-tenths of his money. He remarked at the time that he enjoyed the excitement so much that it was almost worth it. In 1932 one of the New York partners of his brokerage house was discovered to have embezzled so much money from the customers that the firm failed. Disgusted with the stock market, Bond decided to return to gold mining, which was the only business to thrive in time of depression.

The California Desert was becoming active and, since it was nearby, seemed the logical place to start. He set up a camp near Mojave (pronounced Mo-Harvey by the natives) and began examining prospects and making friends with numerous prospectors in the hope of obtaining favorable options to sell to qualified mining interests. He arrived just in time to witness the last important gold rush in California and soon became friendly with George I. Holmes, discoverer of the celebrated Golden Queen Mine.

In September of 1933 this bright young prospector found

a thirty-pound piece of float near the apex of a ravine between the old Queen Esther and Starlight Mines on Soledad
Mountain. With this momentous discovery a mining boom
swept the desert, which ended in 1942 only because the War
Priorities Board and rising costs forced most gold and silver
mines out of business.

Of his discovery Holmes said to a *Los Angeles Times*
reporter:

Every time I recall how near I came to missing that big strike
the cold chills run over me. I came within an ace of passing up
that piece of float that led me to the big bonanza. That afternoon I was looking around up in the little canyon and had
picked up a dozen pieces of worthless rock and thrown them
away because they were not worth a test. Finally I cast my eye
on that big piece of float. It was hard as a bar of iron. I hit it
several whacks with my sampling hammer to knock off enough
for an assay. It didn't budge, but the head of the hammer kept
flying off. I kept putting it back on but it was too weak to handle
the rock. Just when I was about to turn away in disgust the
hammer chipped off a piece about the size of my little finger.
I picked it up and the assay resulted in finding the mine.

Soledad Mountain is a rhyolitic intrusion rising majes-
tically above the floor of the desert about halfway between
the communities of Rosamond and Mojave. The Queen
Esther Mine had been discovered on its north slope in 1894
and was worked by Col. Seeley W. Mudd for the Guggenheims till 1910, producing $1,200,000. The Elephant Mine*
was found in 1896 and was worked sporadically by leasers
for many years, producing around $250,000 in gold and
silver. George Holmes by the age of sixteen had already
worked as a mucker in several mines, including the Ele-

---

* Now called the Elephant-Eagle and owned by ex-Governor Goodwin J.
Knight.

phant. Prospectors generally feel that the best place to find mines is where others have already been discovered. With this in mind Holmes returned to Mojave in 1932, firm in the belief that Soledad Mountain held fame and fortune for anyone willing to undertake the hard work of prospecting it.

Holmes was a painstaking, persistent, and experienced miner. He took a lease on part of the Elephant and soon uncovered forty tons of $50 ore, which he hauled to the Tropico Mill some eight miles distant. He then leased the Echo claims and again found a short vein of milling ore. However, the modest profits from these pay chutes hardly kept him in groceries and dynamite. Lacking capital for further development underground, he resorted to surface prospecting. The eighteen-acre claim upon which he made his discovery had been held for twenty-eight years by an old-timer named Radovich, but the latter had died, and his executors had failed to file the necessary notice to keep the claim in his estate. Since the title had lapsed on July 1, 1933, Holmes relocated the claim for a filing fee of one dollar and called it the Silver Queen.

Martin C. Engel, assayer and postmaster at Cantil, twenty-five miles north of Mojave, told the author he was in Roy Snow's barbershop in Mojave when Holmes came in, showed him the float, and said, "Martin, I haven't got any money, but please assay this float for me." Later Holmes gave Engel a larger piece, which he showed the author. It was white quartz with dark streaks of silver sulphide (argentite) and some free gold.

"I ran the assay," Engel said, "and it went $50 in silver and $50 in gold. Times were so tough that I couldn't afford to risk a three-cent stamp on a credit assay, so I didn't tell Holmes till I saw him a few days later in Mojave."

There is some disagreement among old-timers on what the float really assayed. A few years ago Holmes had it on display at the "Mojave Gold Rush Days" and reminded Engel that the latter had run the first assay on it. In a recent letter Engel wrote:

I had a long talk with Bruce Minard on the Silver Queen float. He insists it ran 43 ounces of gold and 800 ounces of silver but admitted his could have been a picked sample. I believe a piece of ore from the strike was run at the Tropico Mill and did go this high. I am quite sure, however, that Holmes' large piece of float never ran at such a fabulous figure but around $100.

With Holmes when he picked up the float were Bruce Minard and Virgil Dew, who were living in a shack near the Elephant Mine. Minard was a well-known prospector and desert rat suffering from tuberculosis. Dew was a wino who had been a truck driver for the Los Angeles Water and Power Commission but had recently been fired for drunkenness. Holmes said: "I'll cut you fellows in for a half-interest if you'll go to work looking for the vein this float came from." Being broke and having nothing else to do, the two men accepted. Holmes then made out the filing notice giving a 25 per cent interest each to his father, M. A. Holmes, himself, Dew, and Minard, then mailed it to the County Recorder in Bakersfield.

For the next two months Dew and Minard drove an inclined shaft into the talus slope at the spot where the float was found. Six feet below the surface they uncovered a six-foot quartz vein in rhyolite porphyry which assayed $12 a ton with values being 70 per cent in gold and 30 per cent in silver. Then they each gave Holmes a 5 per cent interest with the understanding that he build a road up to the claim. Holmes gave his father 5 per cent so that he and his father now owned 30 per cent each. According to Minard, the road was finally put in, not by Holmes, but by N. W. Sweetzer and Lou Emerick who had leased the upper part of the claim.

Early in 1934 Dew and Minard became so discouraged that they then sold their interests to C. W. "Cy" Townsend, a jovial gas station operator and Justice of the Peace in Mojave. Minard got $500 for his, and Dew, who drove a harder bargain, received $1,000. Martin Engel was in Mojave with his wife and daughter when Minard staggered up quite drunk and offered to sell them his share for $500. Engel said, "I liked Bruce and didn't want to take advantage of a friend in that condition and didn't think it would be legal if I did. I heard later that he had sold to Townsend."

A year later Minard was the unhappiest man Bond had ever met. When asked why he and Dew had sold so cheaply, Minard said:

"We were flat broke and needed the money to eat. We had to carry water and tools up on our backs and pack down any ore the same way. We couldn't make a dime trying to ship $12 ore under those conditions. It was too hard work, and the prospect looked discouraging."

With some justice Minard considers himself the true discoverer of the Silver Queen Vein, since he was the one who actually uncovered it.

Dew eventually sued the Holmeses on the grounds that they had neither put in nor paid for the road, which they had agreed to do, and was awarded a judgment of $113,684. According to Minard he moved to Inglewood, stayed drunk for eighteen years, and when that failed to finish him, committed suicide when his money ran out. Minard did not join in the suit, being too ill at the time, and because Holmes had brought him to Mojave in the first place and looked after him when he was sick. Later he did sue M. A. Holmes, but the case was thrown out of court.

George Holmes began to deepen the shaft begun by Dew

and Minard and gave short leases to three pairs of miners to help develop the property. By December, 1934, he was down 125 feet, and the vein had widened to 24 feet. Representatives of Gold Fields American Corporation, a subsidiary of Consolidated Gold Fields of South Africa, came to Mojave to inspect the property and paid $5,000 for a sixty-day option. Further exploration by its engineers revealed that the vein was truly spectacular, attaining a width of thirty to fifty feet. On January 16, 1935, Gold Fields American exercised its option to purchase the mine for $3,170,000 and, according to the deeds on record in Bakersfield, made a cash down payment of $533,500. The balance was to be paid by a sliding gross royalty starting at 2½ per cent with a maximum of 10 per cent on ore of $10 per ton or over.

Jay C. Stoel, a close friend of Holmes and later foreman of the Golden Queen, explained that this sliding royalty greatly increased the output of the mine by enabling the company to utilize large blocks of low-grade ore assaying $4 to $6 which were "sweetened" by higher quality ore to bring most of the mill heads to just under $10. Since mining and milling costs were less than $6 a ton, nearly all of the vein could in this way be mined at a profit. Holmes' claim was consolidated with adjacent claims and the enlarged property renamed the Golden Queen. Charles Kumpke was put in charge of mining operations, and development soon began in earnest. A 300-ton mill was erected which was later increased to a daily capacity of 500 tons, part of which was allocated to custom milling.

Bond wrote in his diary on February 16, 1935:

Spent the afternoon on Soledad Mountain. The Consolidated Gold Fields of South Africa Company is preparing for large operations. They are starting to cut a 2500 foot tunnel into the mountain on the Sailor Boy claim. They struck a vein in another tunnel in three feet—said to be 14 feet wide. With little data to go on I believe this to be the Silver Queen Vein and that it will be found at depth under the flat at the foot of the mountain. I think the outlook for a big gold mine is good.

The report on the minerals of Kern County published in 1962 by the California Division of Mines and Geology states:

This discovery led to a revival of mining activity throughout the Mojave District, and to the foundation of the Golden Queen Mining Company in 1935. This company acquired claims totaling about 300 acres embracing most of the northwest slope of Soledad Mountain.* By mid-1937, three hundred tons of ore per day were being produced. Extensive development and exploration work, including several thousand feet of diamond drilling, was done. . . . In output it ranks second to the Yellow Aster among the gold mines of Kern County.

Convenient to the Golden Queen mill an 8 foot by 8 foot tunnel was driven 2,500 feet into the mountain underneath the orebodies which could then be loaded by gravity into the ore cars and run out to the mill.

In March of 1936 Bond and an associate, E. L. Blanck, obtained an option for one week on a property of considerable speculative interest, the northeast quarter of section #7 on Soledad Mountain. They felt that there was a reasonable probability that the Silver Queen and Starlight Veins might extend into this nearby quarter section. In time of depression, however, it was difficult to find anyone bold enough to

* The Golden Queen Mine included the Silver Queen, Queen Esther, Echo, Gray Eagle, Soledad Extension, and in 1940 the Starlight (also called the Lodestar).

put up hard cash for a property on which no development
had been done nor any values uncovered and then be faced
with the added expense of exploration. At the end of the
week they lost the option. On October 18, 1936, Bond wrote
in his diary about telling some friends of the subsequent
history of this property:

I told them of my week's option on the NE quarter of section
#7 into which both the Silver Queen and Starlight Veins strike,
and of my interesting Edward Sykes of Santa Barbara sufficiently
to come to see it. He liked it but asked me, if positions were re-
versed, would I make a down-payment of $25,000 before being
allowed to do any work. I said I wouldn't. Shortly thereafter
Consolidated Gold Fields, which owns the Golden Queen, took
it on similar terms and made the $25,000 payment. Trenches
have already disclosed 400 feet of vein 25′ to 40′ wide averaging
$12 to $14 in gold.

In the fall of 1937 the author joined his father in the mining business. Shortly thereafter they received a letter from
Dwight L. Sawyer, one of the Golden Queen engineers, inviting them to lunch and a trip through the mine. Bond's
diary of January 22, 1938, reads:

We went to the Golden Queen at noon and lunched with
Sawyer and his fellow officials and afterward went through the
mine and mill.
The 600′ level is the haulage tunnel with a single track and
storage battery engines hauling ten car trains. Near the end of
the tunnel we went up an inclined shaft in a stope to the 200′
level. Here the ore, a light colored quartz, was 20′ to 50′ wide.
They mine by running up square set raises from the lower levels
leaving large pillars of ore which they later draw down and fill
up again with waste. A good deal of timbering is required. Diamond drilling has discovered other minor veins from 2′ to 6′
wide.

A tour through a large gold mine was an enviable experience, especially for a greenhorn such as the writer was then. Hard hats with miners' lanterns were provided at the portal of the tunnel. As the electric train progressed into the depths of the mountain, the dot of daylight at the mouth of the tunnel grew smaller and smaller until all one could see were the eerie patterns of light and shadow made by the lanterns flickering along the rocky walls. Here and there were small side tunnels where drills, air compressors, lumber, and tools were stored. A frightful din echoed and reechoed down the corridors as dozens of men with pneumatic drills bored holes in the rock in preparation for blasting. Miners received $5.50 a day for an eight-hour shift and worked six days a week. The size of the vein and the vast tonnage of ore being handled were truly impressive.

After inspecting the various levels the party returned to see the reduction process at the mill. A series of crushers reduced the ore to a small enough size to be introduced into the revolving cylindrical ball mills which in turn pulverized the material to a fine mud. This mud was then stirred in huge vats of a cyanide solution which dissolved the gold and silver. A zinc compound was then introduced to precipitate the metal. The concentrate was melted in a furnace and poured into molds. The author lifted a brick which had just cooled. It was silver in color with just a tint of gold, weighed seventy-seven pounds, and was worth $30,000.

There is a mystery that haunts the history of the Golden Queen and provides a favorite topic of speculation among old-timers—just how much did Townsend and the Holmeses make on the deal? They seem to have confided in nobody. One thing is certain—the mine was not rich enough to even come close to completing the royalty payments on the price of $3,170,000.

In the museum at the Tropico Mine is a photostat copy of

Holmes's first pay check, dated January 16, 1935, and drawn on the Security First National Bank of Los Angeles in the amount of $135,500. M. A. Holmes received the same, and the Townsend interests $262,500,* which included payment for a half interest in the Sailor Boy, Sailor Girl, Ben Hur, and Grand Prize claims which Townsend seems to have acquired.

The writer received production figures on the Golden Queen from both the Selby Smelter** and the Gold Fields American Corporation† which shed some light on the mystery but which are inconclusive and hence open to several interpretations. All other pertinent records have been destroyed. However, using these figures and a few logical assumptions to fill in the gaps, the writer is convinced that Townsend and the Holmeses received a total remuneration of approximately $1,000,000. Jay Stoel expressed the opinion that, after down payments and royalties were paid to the various owners, the profits realized by Gold Fields American were quite modest, especially in view of the size of the operation.

George Holmes bought a diamond drill and spent many

---

* Townsend was broke when he bought out Dew and Minard, but raised the money by giving a half interest to a dozen friends and relatives whose names appear on the deed to the Golden Queen Company.

** Before selling the mine Holmes shipped 3,893 tons (78 cars) of ore running $21.504 per ton, which produced $83,717. The settlement figure was approximately $50,000, but from it mining and shipping costs and payments to leasers had to be deducted.

† Separate tonnages were given for the Golden Queen ore and custom ore, but they were bulked together for yield and given an average per ton value of $10.905. Total tonnage handled and total bullion produced from both classes of ore were 903,185 and $10,227,933. However, because of the sliding royalty scale Golden Queen ore probably ran under $10 and custom ore closer to $12. Approximately 335,000 tons of custom ore was handled producing about $4,000,000. According to Lou Killian, 250,000 tons of this came from the nearby Starlight Mine, of which he was foreman. The Golden Queen therefore produced approximately $6,227,933 upon which Holmes and Townsend may have received average royalties of 8 percent in addition to the down payment.

years mining and prospecting. He produced over $1,000,000 from the Padre-Madre and Cargo Mines near Yuma but found nothing comparable to the Golden Queen. He bought a forty-acre orange ranch on the outskirts of Yuma for $40,000. Eventually the town spread out to the ranch, and prior to his death in 1966 he told the Stoels that he had just sold a commercial corner on Highway 80 for five times the original cost of the ranch, or $180,000.

Cy Townsend's subsequent career was equally spectacular. Martin Engel, who knew him well, said,

"Cy was the luckiest man I ever met. He could make more money in one day by accident than you and I could working the rest of our lives. As soon as he cashed that big down payment he started playing the horses, which worried his wife. She said, 'Cy, if you're going to lose your money betting on the ponies, go down to Los Angeles and buy an interest in one of the race tracks so you can get some of it back.' "

Prodded by her insistence, Townsend went to Los Angeles and bought some of the original stock in the newly formed Santa Anita Race Track at $5,000 a share. It turned out to be one of the most phenomenal bargains in the history of American enterprise. From the opening day the track was swamped with customers, and profits rose so precipitously that, by the end of the first year, the entire cost of the stock was repaid with a dividend of $5,000 a share. Except during the Second World War, it continued to pay as much or more each year with the value of the shares soon soaring to $85,000.

On a visit to Cantil at the time of the Korean War, Townsend arrived in a brand-new Packard limousine with a chauffeur behind the wheel. When Engel admired the sumptuous car, Townsend said, "I got stuck with an old jalopy in the last war so I bought a couple of these Packards this time just in case."

Engel then asked if the car had six or eight cylinders. Townsend replied, "I don't know whether it has six or eight but watch this." He pressed a button and up shot the radio aerial. With boyish delight he exclaimed: "Martin, ain't that the damnedest thing you ever saw!"

Another person who made some money out of the Golden Queen in a rather curious way was R. B. Potticary, a Greek dishwasher at the Manhattan Cafe in Mojave. Shortly before Holmes made his discovery, Potticary had been laid off by the owner of the cafe and decided to hole up for a while and take it easy. He filled a cardboard carton with $2.50 worth of food and went to the Elephant Mine with the intention of moving into the shack occupied by Dew and Minard. Since neither was home he shoved the groceries under a bed and sat down to wait.

In the meantime the other dishwasher at the Manhattan got roaring drunk and was fired by the owner, who then sent for Potticary and gave him back his old job. He had not spent a single night in the shack but did leave the groceries. When the first shipments of ore were made from the Silver Queen Vein, Potticary brought suit for a one-sixth interest on the grounds that Dew and Minard had eaten the food, which constituted a grubstake.

He lost the case, but Townsend gave him $5,000 for a release from further claims lest he appeal to a higher court. According to Minard this lawsuit was instrumental in getting the California State Legislature to pass the Wagy Act requiring future grubstake agreements to be in writing and duly recorded. "Before that," he said, "you could give a man a can of sardines and, if he made a strike, claim you had a grubstake."

While the Golden Queen was being developed in 1934 and 1935, more prospectors were flocking to the Mojave District. Excitement soon centered on Middle Buttes, a low rhyolitic group of hills half a mile to a mile wide and two miles long lying some four miles west of Soledad Mountain.

In January, 1934, Clyde Westfall found a piece of rich float on a patented section on the east end of Middle Buttes. He showed it to T. L. Brite, the latter's two sons Dick and Jack, and Clifford Burton. The discovery was kept secret for nearly a year until a lease on the northwest quarter of the section could be obtained. Clifford Burton put up $5,000 as a down payment, for which he received a half interest in the lease. Early in 1935 enough high-grade float was gathered on the surface to yield $20,000 in gold.

Bond's first mention of this discovery was on February 19, 1935:

Bruce Minard came into camp and said he had just returned from Middle Buttes where he had seen the Brite strike. He said it was the biggest thing in the district, 40 feet of $20 ore. Minard is inclined to exaggerate. I went there immediately. Quartz slide rock covered the mountain side. Brite claimed the quartz and dirt went $15 a ton.

In May Bond noted in his diary that Ernie L. Blanck had bought a one-third interest in the mine for $100,000 payable over a period of four years. The only cash involved was $2,500 which Blanck put up for shallow development work. Brite had in February taken a lease on eighty acres of the newly discovered Rogers-Gentry Mine at Neenach fifty miles southwest of Mojave and was glad enough to turn the management of the lease on Middle Buttes over to Blanck. So began the short but colorful history of the Burton, Brite, Blanck Mine which led to intensive prospecting on Middle Buttes and further important discoveries.

For months Bond closely followed the development of this mine, even to the point of panning the diggings, in the hope of accumulating sufficient favorable data upon which to make a deal.

On April 10, 1935, he wrote:

Brite showed me a piece of rock as large as his two fists heavily impregnated with gold.

May 5:
Spent the morning panning the ground where Blanck is carrying on development. When I returned to camp I found Clifford Burton and Ernie Blanck there, and we talked over their proposed development of the claim.

May 11:
Went up to the Red Dirt Glory Hole on the B.B.B. property and made some pannings which seemed phenominally rich. Dick Brite then took them to town for assaying. . . . At 5 P.M. I got the assays which were disappointing. The one I thought would go $1000 a ton only went $295. Still that is good.

This was a particularly difficult mine to evaluate as it gradually became evident that the rich specimens found on the surface and in shallow glory holes had, in ages past, been broken off from outcroppings of the nearby Trent property. A five-foot vein was found underground but of relatively low grade, and the values were spotty and discontinuous. Bond was unable to get an option on favorable enough terms to make a deal on this highly speculative mine. According to Dick Brite it eventually produced $100,000, with the ore averaging $28 a ton.

Bond had renewed his long friendship with Ernie L. Blanck. In 1933 Charis Denison Crockett (she had been on the African trip in 1927) and her husband were camping near Mojave. On a walk they met a bedraggled-looking man who, although the weather was cold, explained that he couldn't afford to buy an overcoat. When he said his name was "Blanck," they thought he was giving a false name, probably to cover a shady past. However, when they told him they were camping with Marshall Bond, he became very excited, saying that he had known him twenty-five years ago at the Seattle Athletic Club. He accompanied them back to camp and was warmly received by Bond, who gave him an old but serviceable overcoat.

Since leaving Seattle, Blanck had become an oil and mining scout with considerable success, but had eventually gone broke in the Depression. He was a plunger, and in 1937 when Bond and the author were trying to make a deal on the famous Kelly Silver Mine near Randsburg* he told them that when the mine was discovered in 1919, he had rushed over and plunked down $50,000 in cash for an option, only to find that he had been one hour too late.

After getting the overcoat from his friend, Blanck's luck seemed to change. He made a deal with an oil company to take over the operation of a group of wells at Maricopa. Production had dropped below the point of profitability for the oil company, but Blanck, with no labor costs, was able to make a pretty fair living. He also fell in with a wily old Scotchman named McDonald who had made several million dollars wildcatting and who was willing to give Blanck cautious backing in some of his deals. Handsome, intelligent, and soft spoken, Blanck was always pleasant company. During the ensuing six years he and Bond worked together on more than a dozen mining deals, all of which eventually fell through. Either the price was too high, conditions of the contracts offered being unreasonable, or the examinations

---

* The Kelly produced $16,000,000. One of Bond's principals, B. Golson, wanted to option the Kelly, Santa Fe, and several adjacent silver properties which he would combine for a big operation. Bond was unable to obtain the options.

in the field showed that values and ore tonnages were considerably less than claimed by the owners.

It was only a thirty-three-mile drive from Blanck's home in Maricopa to Cuyama Valley. When oil was discovered there after the Second World War, Ernie L. Blanck got there fast enough this time to purchase a favorable option. The field turned out to be far more extensive than most geologists had anticipated, and Blanck's lease was valued at more than $2,000,000.

When T. L. Brite began working his lease on Middle Buttes, Walter Trent of Tonopah, an associate of Senator Key Pittman of Nevada, leased the property adjacent to and south of Brite's strike. At the same time he sent for his prospector friend Clyde Garrett, from Fallon, and made a deal with him to prospect the lease. Bond's diary of February 26, 1935, says:

Went to the camp a quarter mile west of my own and found it occupied by Mr. & Mrs. Clyde Garrett. He has prospected since he was seventeen and made many strikes. He carries a small mortar, a gold pan, and a bucket of water and pans the hillsides systematically using four pails of water a day. He is an interesting man of fifty-eight who has done nothing but shoot, fish, and prospect all his life. He doesn't drink or smoke and is in fine condition. He impressed me as an unusually able and fine man.

It wasn't long before Garrett too discovered gold. In March, Bond wrote:

Up early and out to Middle Buttes at 8 A.M. Found Clyde Garrett ready to go to work. I took a heavy mortar in my rucksack, a pint of milk, a box of soda crackers, and my prospecting pick. In one hand I carried a heavy pestle and in the other a shovel. Over my shoulders I threw a drill parka as protection against the wind. Clyde devoted himself to trenching and panning the dirt. He constantly got colors. From a piece broken from a rhy-olite boulder I got a fine panning—perhaps the value of $50 a ton. No other rock I tried for the rest of the day showed any gold, but Clyde continued getting values from his trench dirt. Shall we find a vein? Quien sabe!

Three days later Garrett told Bond that two assays run by Trent went over $4,000 and $5,000 each and that the dirt went $17. On April 2 the diary continued:

Late in the afternoon I went up on the Trent property with Jim Clifford, a prospector camped near me. We got big pannings in the shaft and also in the open cut tunnel below it. Jim thinks they now have a vein. I think it may be a concentration of values from meteoric waters in a sheared zone in the rhyolite. The values are high, running from $50 to $500 or better. They have possibly $25,000 or more sacked and are not down 30 feet. The east end of the mountain both on Trent's and the Burton, Brite, Blanck ground seems very promising for ore.

In April, 1935, the author drove to Mojave and spent the weekend visiting his father and the mines on Middle Buttes. Clyde Garrett showed them the open cuts on the Trent property and the sacks of rich ore awaiting shipment to the Selby Smelter. Jack Brite took them through his workings and gave them several pieces of high-grade ore which speck-led their pan with tiny particles of gold.

Few sights are more beautiful and inspiring than the bril-liant sparkle of wet gold under the rays of the desert sun. These samples did not show much to the naked eye, but un-der a ten-power lens they appeared shot through with gold and ran about $700 a ton. Curiously enough, Brite said that these specimens had just been found by him in an old claim monument which had been erected at the time of the first discovery of gold in the Mojave District. The prospector had gathered up rocks of a convenient size to build the corner posts to his claim. Had he bothered to pan any one of them, he would have made a fortune.

Bond's diary of June 11, 1935, reads:

George Holmes, the discoverer of the Golden Queen, arrived about 2 P.M. I went down the Trent shaft with him and Ernie Blanck. Holmes said it looked better than the Queen did at the depth—60 feet. He said the Queen faulted 10 feet in 10 feet of depth and 30 feet at the 75 foot level. He said: "I packed 75 sacks of ore down the mountains and shipped them to the Selby Smelter and got $1700 which seemed like a million to me."

During the early development of the Trent lease, which became the Middle Buttes Mine, Clyde Garrett made $10,000 from one carload of ore averaging better than $500 per ton. Then he sold his interest to Walter Trent for $15,000 cash. The latter drove a tunnel from a shelf about halfway down the hill to the crosscut and tapped the vein at the 400-foot level in the same manner being used by the Golden Queen. Unfortunately this work was a dead loss, for his rich deposit pinched off at 36 feet below the surface. He should have followed it down with greater care and avoided tunneling.

When Trent gave up his lease it was taken over by that imaginative and resourceful miner George Holmes. An article in the *Los Angeles Times* of February 7, 1938, said he was shipping one hundred tons of ore a month from Trent's diggings to the Tropico Mill. Holmes told Bond that all he did was shovel the loose material Trent had left through a screen mesh and haul the fines to the mill. A couple of months of simple shoveling netted him $3,000.

Marshall Bond took an endless delight in the curious assortment of characters who flocked to mining camps under the romantic illusion that they too, like George Holmes, would strike it rich. He enjoyed hearing the colorful experiences of offbeat personalities whose backgrounds differed so widely from his own. Mojave was no exception, having its full compliment of con men, shysters, hobos, millionaires, habitual desert rats, and old-timers, many of whom he had known in former days and whose fortunes had had as many ups and downs as a stock market chart.

Among the well-to-do were Dr. Baruch, brother of the famous Bernard; Dr. A. H. Giannini, brother of the founder of the Bank of America; and John J. Raskob, who had made millions in General Motors but lost money leasing the Rogers-Gentry Mine.

Among the old-timers who worked in or visited Mojave were Death Valley Scotty, whom Bond regarded as a publicity hound and a faker as far as mining was concerned, and George Winkler, an able prospector and friend from Goldfield days, who found a million-dollar mine but didn't live to enjoy a penny of it. There was a Belgian, Alphonse ("Mike") de Graves who, with a couple of rounds of dynamite, blasted $45,000 from a rich pocket in the Yellow Dog Mine.* He and his wife went on an extended bat for three months and then lost most of what they hadn't drunk up by sinking a prospect shaft on the south side of Soledad Mountain. Another was an elusive desert rat, Seldom Seen Slim Ferge, who occasionally drifted by—and, of course, that indefatigable hard-rock enthusiast, Bob Montgomery.

Bond had not seen Gentleman Bob for some years but had read in the *Los Angeles Times* of June, 1934, that Montgomery had acquired an interest in the Garrett Gold Mine†

---

* Bert Wegeman, from whom de Graves got his lease, said, "Mike went only a few feet beyond where I stopped when he hit that pocket. In one year he took out $60,000."

† Clyde Garrett told the author in 1967 that Bob Montgomery and Verne Winter took out $150,000 but spent $155,000 in the process and encountered hot water at seventy feet which drowned the mine. He also told of a miner's ball at Silver City, Nevada, where Montgomery was the life of the party and danced all night at the age of seventy-eight.

in Dixie Valley, Nevada, which Clyde Garrett had discovered shortly before he came to Mojave.

Bond wrote on March 13, 1935:

After lunch I went to Clyde Garrett's strike and got my mortar and pestle. Just as I was leaving, Bob Montgomery, Verne Winter, and Clyde Garrett arrived. Bob asked me to dine with him and Winter in town. He was a famous prospector in the Goldfield days and made a large fortune then. He is over eighty, but is still active and doesn't look his age. We had a very good dinner at the French Cafe and an interesting talk. He has had a large mining experience, has nice manners, and is very kindly. He has evolved from a desert prospector to a man of considerable distinction and charm.

The last Bond heard of Bob Montgomery was from an article in the *Los Angeles Times* of December 2, 1940, reporting that he had just acquired an interest in a couple of tungsten mines forty miles northwest of Bishop, California. The veins were said to be 12 to 40 feet wide and to run $18 to $140 a ton. The ore was to be processed at the Pine Creek mill of the U.S. Vanadium Company. At the age of eighty-six the redoubtable Bob was ever confident that another fortune lay just around the corner.

Unlike Montgomery, Seldom Seen Slim never left the desert except to cool off in the Sierras during the summers. In 1913 he had moved into an abandoned shack in the old ghost town of Ballarat and had lived there ever since, roaming from one mining camp to another as the spirit moved until he had become a legend. He told Bond that he had acquired his nickname in Randsburg when a miner asked another if he had seen Slim and the other answered, "He's seldom seen here." He claimed to be a scientific prospector and to know where a lot of gold was buried, but, strangely enough, never seems to have dug it up.

Since water was a rare commodity in Ballarat, Slim used to perform a symbolic ablution once a month by splashing a little of the precious fluid over his skinny torso, but boasted that he hadn't had a real bath in years. Slim told Martin Engel, "I got sick once and they put me in the hospital and then they washed me, so I left."

Bond once asked him if he missed women. "Hell, no," replied Slim. "I fell for a girl once, but when I put my hand on her leg, all I felt was a bunch of splinters; I didn't know she had a wooden leg. That cured me once and for all."

Marshall Bond loved camp cooking and often invited his mining friends to dinner. The low cost of food in those days is indicated by a note he wrote on October 24, 1936: "I bought four filet mignon steaks for 90¢ and three pounds of green peas for a quarter." Filet mignon was one of the least expensive cuts to be had on the desert and was sometimes sold as low as 15 cents apiece. When Bond asked the butcher in Lancaster why this was so, the latter replied, "I practically have to give them away because the miners don't know what they are and couldn't pronounce it if they did."

Raising money for prospecting and development work was the most difficult problem confronting the would-be miner. Bond was not only short of cash, but his wealthy associates had had so much practical experience with the risks of mining (which exceed most other businesses) that they were seldom willing to speculate unless the price was reasonable and considerable tonnages of ore blocked out —two conditions which, by the very nature of the game, seemed mutually exclusive. Of course every conceivable device was used by the unscrupulous to con the unwary into parting with either his mine or his money, as the case might be, usually with disastrous results. An amusing example of reverse psychology was to be seen in Mint Canyon, where some operators were sinking a shaft on ground which appeared to offer poor prospects of mineralization. The sign read:

APEX GOLD MINE

KEEP OUT

ABSOLUTELY NO MONEY WANTED

Through the gold mining business Bond had another brief encounter with Major Frederick Russell Burnham, who owned the Iron King Mine near Prescott, Arizona.* Bernard Golsan, a Frenchman who had made a million dollars in the 1920's from the Guadalupe Silver Mine† at Inde, in Mexico, wanted to buy Burnham's mine. Franklin W. Smith was Golsan's geologist and highly recommended his old associate Marshall Bond as a go-between. On November 17, 1937, Bond met Golsan at the Biltmore in Los Angeles and wrote:

Golsan said he would like a proposition from Major Burnham on the Iron King and asked me if I would conduct the negotiations, offering me $100 an hour. I accepted even though I hadn't seen Burnham since December, 1929, at the Boone and Crockett Club meeting in New York.

On November 22 the encounter took place.

I went to Major Burnham's office in the Union Oil Bldg. at 10:30 and had an hour's chat with him. We talked of cattle, Africa, his experiences as a scout in the Matabele Wars, and finally got down to business. Would he sell the Iron King Mine in Arizona? He would not. He is shipping 300 tons of ore a day to the smelter and making a profit of $3 a ton. The ore is very

* Burnham and his son, Roderick, had been interested in mining near Prescott for years. Bond's diary tells of dining there with young Burnham on November 23, 1907.

†Golsan bought the Guadalupe Mine for $200,000 from Alexander Baring of Santa Barbara.

complex, but he thinks he will succeed in solving the metal-
lurgy so he can mill it at the mine.

Bond never saw the major again, and the $100 fee was the
only hard cash he actually earned during the entire Mojave
gold rush.

At almost the same time that George Holmes discovered
his famous piece of float an eccentric roustabout, W. J.
"Bill" Rogers, came down to Neenach from Gorman to pick
up some schoolchildren. While waiting for the students he
walked up a canyon behind the school and panned the
gravel in a spring. To his complete amazement he washed
out an ounce of gold. Rogers had no money but knew a man
named Tom Gentry in Fairmont who did.

Rogers gave Gentry a half interest in his discovery, provided the latter would put up the money to buy the 160
acres upon which the former had panned the gold. Rogers
then went posthaste to Los Angeles to see the owner, a former storekeeper from Lancaster, named Leo Harris, and told
him he wanted to start a goat ranch and that his quarter
section was the most suitable property he had found for the
purpose. Harris, who knew his hilly acreage wasn't worth
much, was happy to unload it for $10 an acre, or $1600.
However, as soon as the presence of gold became known,
Harris sued Rogers on the grounds that the reason for pur-
chasing the ranch had been fraudulently presented. After a
long hilarious lawsuit, in which the subject of goats was
fully explored, Harris was awarded a 7 per cent royalty on
all ore mined and recovery of his property when mining
ceased.

When the author visited Tom Gentry in Bakersfield, he
was ninety years old and his memory had begun to fail.
However, Mrs. Gentry, who was Bill Rogers' step-daughter,
was eloquent on the subject of Rogers and his operation of

the mine. She said that it had produced about $300,000 including the $110,000 the Brites took out of the southwest acres. Rogers produced $100,000 and various leasers the balance.

On the subject of Rogers, Mrs. Gentry stated firmly:

"He was crazy, outrageous, and unpredictable. He liked having people around, but was terribly suspicious of everybody. He would welcome you with open arms one day and throw you off the property the next. Everything that could possibly go wrong with a mine happened to ours because of his antics. He even boasted of how he had gypped Harris. When I think of the fortune he spent on lawyers! We had eight lawsuits against us all going at the same time. He loved the publicity and invited all his neighbors to come to Los Angeles and paid their travel expenses and hotel bills so they could watch him on the witness stand."

When asked if Rogers really was a crook, she said:

"That's putting it mildly. He'd have robbed his own mother if she had been around, and even hid money from himself. His favorite trick was to lend jack hammers to leasers, steal them back at night, and then force the leasers to replace the lost hammers with new ones."

"Do you mind if I quote you?" the writer asked.

"Go right ahead," she replied. "You couldn't say anything bad about Rogers that wouldn't be true. He was a colorful character, all right, especially his language. You wouldn't believe it, but in spite of everything Rogers did, we eventually got our money back and a small profit besides."

About this mine Bond wrote on January 21, 1935:

Pulled out at 9 A.M. for Neenach—the little mining camp a man named Rogers developed. His ore, which he ships to Burton's Mill, runs $40 a ton in gold. He has produced, it is said,

$200,000 and is not down 100 feet. The camp is less than half a mile from the highway on a range of low hills which show decomposed granite and lime beds.

Dick Brite said that in spite of taking out $110,000 in eleven months from the Rogers-Gentry property, only a modest profit was realized. The ground was so unstable that costly square-set timbering had to be installed throughout to prevent cave-ins. However, due to the richness of the ore, excitement ran high.

Bond kept posted on developments at Neenach but was never able to effect a deal. He wrote on December 16, 1938:

Stopped at Neenach to see Sol Camp, the manager of the Rogers-Gentry Mine, now being developed under bond and lease by John J. Raskob of New York. Bill Rogers was there and he and Sol Camp disapproved of the manner and method of development under Raskob's engineer. A 200 foot shaft had been put down in 40 days. We went to the top of the hill to see Raskob's drilling outfit. It was a churn drill, and casing was set in the hole as in oil drilling.

It appeared that Rogers and previous lessees had already extracted most of the ore, for even with unlimited capital, Raskob's drilling and tunneling got him nowhere. He told Tom Gentry that there were 25,000 tons of good ore at the bottom but that it would be too costly to get it out. Shortly thereafter Raskob abandoned the mine.

One of the most interesting gold mines in the area was the Governor (formerly called the New York Mine) only an hour out of Los Angeles on the way to Palmdale. It was situated on a hill a mile north of the highway at Acton and had been worked in the late nineteenth century by Governor Henry T. Gage of California. The vein of white sugar quartz was very strong, four to fifteen feet wide, and ran around $20 a ton. Gage had taken out $100,000, but when he reached the 400-foot level the vein suddenly disappeared. A crosscut was driven forty feet to the east in a half-hearted attempt to relocate the vein. Since most desert mines seldom exceed a few hundred feet in depth, Governor Gage must have concluded that his mine had bottomed, because he abandoned the property without even cleaning out the debris in the crosscut from the last round of explosives.

Some thirty-five years later Francis Gage, the governor's son, lost his job during the Depression and, since he couldn't find another, came to Acton to look at his father's old mine. He shoveled out the debris and at the end of the crosscut discovered the continuation of the vein. A reverse fault had thrown it forty feet to the east.

Francis Gage lost no time in relocating the Governor Mine and also the Red Rover* on a nearby hill. He took in a couple of partners to get enough money to begin mining, but almost from the start the Governor proved rich enough to pay its own way. Bond liked the looks of these properties and proposed their purchase to Bernard Golsan. His diary of December 29, 1937, reads:

Marshall Jr. and I went to Palmdale, got Franklin Smith and Charles Lees, Golsan's engineers, and went to the Governor Mine. Gage took us through it. On the 400 foot level they had a chute of ore which they said ran $40 to $50 in gold. From there we went to the old Red Rover Mine. Smith and Lees think these orebodies will go deep and want us to see what they can be had for.

Smith thought that, unlike most desert mines, the well-defined Governor vein which lay between monzonite and Pelona schist would continue to considerable depth. Sub-

* The Red Rover, a less valuable property, had also been worked and abandoned. When the price of gold was raised to $35 an ounce by President Roosevelt in 1934, it too was made to pay. According to Gage its total production was $550,000.

sequent development proved him correct, for Bond recorded in his diary of October 14, 1940, that the Governor was down one thousand feet and that a ten-foot face of heavy sulphides had been encountered that assayed $74.

Bond spent several months trying to get Gage to put a price on his mines, but he insisted that Golsan make an offer. Consequently Bond and the writer spent three days underground helping Smith and Lees cut, sack, and label samples. There were no reserves of ore blocked out beyond that exposed by blasting on the previous day, but the assays were good.

A week later Golsan made two propositions. He offered to buy the mines for $180,000 with $50,000 cash and the balance from a 10 per cent royalty, or to take a lease for fifteen years at $1,000 a month. Gage turned down both offers. It was well for him that he did, for it was reported some years later that the Governor and the Red Rover had produced $1,500,000 (more than half the total production of gold in Los Angeles County) and that Gage and his partners had made a profit of $500,000.

When the huge orebodies of the Golden Queen were uncovered most observers concluded that the climax had been reached in the mining boom at Mojave.* However, they were sadly mistaken, for there lay buried on the west end of Middle Buttes a deposit of gold and silver which would prove the most profitable mine in the entire Mojave District. It was to become known as the Cactus Queen, and Bond just missed getting an option on it by a few days.

Among the more successful operators at Mojave were the Mudds and the Burtons. Clifford and Cecil Burton had

* The author has purposely left out descriptions of other productive mines, such as the Standard, Whitmore, Wegman, and Pride of Mojave, because they did not particularly concern his father. A half interest in the last named was owned by Bing Crosby, Clark Gable, Gary Cooper, and Jackie Coogan, but they seem to have sold out toward the end of 1938.

emigrated from England in 1900 and in 1912 went to work at the Tropico Mine. By the mid-1930's these two farsighted and industrious Englishmen had not only acquired the whole of Tropico Hill* but a number of other properties throughout the district, among which was a half-section of railroad land situated along the western escarpment of Middle Buttes. George Ward, an uncle of Mrs. Clifford Burton, had found a piece of float there in 1934 and persuaded the Burtons to buy it for nine dollars an acre from the Southern Pacific Company.

The Burtons spent some time and money prospecting it, but finding nothing of commercial value and being desirous of terminating their business relationship with Ward, sold the property to Joseph A. Otto for $40,000. The southerly 40 acres was called the Blue Eagle and was later renamed the Cactus Queen. By selling this property the Burtons for once had missed the boat.

At about the same time the Southern Pacific Company sold 320 acres east of the Blue Eagle to a couple of miners, Henry Shumake and J. W. Beery, for $8.60 an acre. They in turn sold the northerly 120 acres to Otto and his partner, Fred I. Wright† for $25,000. Of course these deals were nearly always on credit, with only small amounts of cash down. This property, called the Silver Prince, revealed at intervals for at least two thousand feet the outcroppings of the extension of the Cactus Queen Vein.**

* The Burtons mined the Tropico Vein themselves, leased out the rest of the hill, and ran a 150-ton custom mill. From 1900 to 1952 the Tropico Mine produced $4,000,000 from ore averaging $13.50.

† Wright had had the distinction of producing the richest carload of ore in history—$574,958.39 at the old price of gold—when he was in charge of the Hayes-Monnette lease on the Mohawk Mine in Goldfield.

** The state mining bulletin on Kern County says: "The vein lies along a major fault which, at the surface, separates Mesozoic quartz monzonite on the northwest from Tertiary quartz latite porphyry on the southeast."

The curious thing about the Cactus Queen Vein was that, being a true quartz fissure vein twenty feet wide in places, it was clearly visible and had been panned and assayed by numerous prospectors, including the Burtons, since the turn of the century, but on the surface it only assayed $3.40 a ton. Apparently no qualified geologist had studied this quartz, for if he had, he must have seen that it was heavily fractured and would have concluded that the surface values had probably been leached out by rainwater and redeposited below. In fact such was eventually shown to have been the case.

While Otto and Wright were trying to find commercial ore on the Silver Prince,* an alert prospector, George Weyman, who had been leasing on Soledad Mountain, made a detailed examination of the Blue Eagle and decided it merited underground exploration. He must have sensed the possibility of secondary enrichment, for he obtained a lease and took it to a couple of prosperous ranchers in Ojai, Alan Kempe and George B. Kimball. They were not only interested but persauded two neighbors, Theodore Pratt and Rawson B. Harmon, to go in with them, each putting up $5,000 for development. Work progressed slowly and was plagued by labor troubles. Weyman became discouraged and sold his interest to the ranchers at what he imagined was a reasonable profit. Finally, when the shaft reached the sixty-foot level, it began running into commercial ore.

In May, 1935, Kimball told Bond that they had a large and satisfactory body of ore on the 100-foot level. On June 17 the *Los Angeles Times* reported that the men from Ojai had purchased the Blue Eagle for $161,700. In September Bond wrote: "Kempe showed me the mill and smelter returns on their shipments thus far. They total about $5,000

---

* Like the Burtons, Otto and Wright also missed the boat on the Cactus Queen.

with an average value of $15 a ton." Alan Kempe told the author some years later that although the Cactus Queen was basically a silver mine, the ratio of gold to silver increased with every foot of depth.

By October sufficient development had been done to indicate the probability of a big mine. However, the ranchers were also faced with large capital expenditures, especially for the construction of a mill. Since they seemed unwilling to risk more of their own money, it appeared to Bond and Blanck that the occasion was favorable for making a sale. Consequently, during October and November Bond had a series of conferences with Kempe and his partners at the former's home in Ojai. Unfortunately, at the first conference the ranchers revealed that only a few days previous their engineer, Major Julian Boyd, had approached Harvey S. Mudd regarding a sale. They expected an early decision and promised Bond an option should Mudd turn down their proposition. But by the end of November Kempe reported that L. Webster Wicks, head of the Mudd office, was so impressed with the formation and the values that Mudd and his associates had decided to take over the Cactus Queen.

According to Kempe the Mudds received 51 per cent, the ranchers 44 per cent, and Major Boyd 5 per cent as payment for his services as entrepreneur. Harvey S. Mudd insisted that the ranchers share in the cost of further development, which they did. He also tried to buy them out, which they refused. He then generously allowed a number of his employees to buy stock in the mine at his own cost. By the time the 150-ton mill was erected a three-year supply of ore had been blocked out and a total of $600,000 expended on development and the mill.

Several years later a wealthy associate of the Mudds, Wil-

liam A. Honnold, told Bond that before they had even begun building a mill they had uncovered enough ore to pay
for both the mine and the mill. By May, 1937, the richness
and magnitude of the mine became fully apparent. Kempe
stated that the orebody on the 600-foot level was 50 feet
wide, ran $70 to $100 a ton, and that the value of the ore in
sight was estimated at $4,000,000.

The Cactus Queen proved a very profitable operation for
the Mudds, but was only one of their many mining ventures.
Col. Seeley W. Mudd, a brilliant graduate in mining engi-
neering from Washington University in St. Louis, began his
career in the 1880's working for the Guggenheims in the Little Jonny and Ibex Mines at Leadville. Later he and Philip
Wiseman made a fortune in gold at Oatman, Arizona, in the
United Eastern Mine. In 1910 C. Godfrey Gunther, who was
sponsored by Mudd and Wiseman, visited the Island of Cyprus because he had read that Cyprus meant "copper" in
Greek and that the ancients had mined there. He found they
had left large low-grade deposits of copper and pyrites which
could only be handled by modern technological methods.
Colonel Mudd organized Cyprus Mines Corporation, and
commenced production shortly after the close of the First
World War. At the time of the Cactus Queen discovery, the
colonel's son, Harvey S. Mudd, headed the corporation and
was assisted by his brother Dr. Seeley G. Mudd. Today that
company is a $150,000,000 enterprise with worldwide activ-
ities in mining, shipping, and lumber. After the death of
Harvey S. Mudd, his family founded the college which bears
his name.

The Cactus Queen eventually bought the Silver Prince
but, according to Kempe, it didn't amount to much. A real
bonanza, however, which the Cactus Queen also acquired,
was found just to the east on the Shumake and Beery prop-

erty by Bond's old friend, George Winkler. On May 22, 1937, Bond wrote:

Had George Winkler to dinner. I had a fine beef stew. The meat was a thick tenderloin cut, so it was tender and delicious. George consumed three large helpings. I also had stewed tomatoes and strawberries and cream for desert. The entire dinner cost $1.00 exclusive of the beer we drank. I knew George in Goldfield 24 years ago. He is a good prospector and an indefatigable worker.

Winkler never had a lease on the two-hundred-acre Shumake and Beery property but prospected it anyway. He found a boulder filled with gold that was worth $15,000.* Spurred on by this, he next discovered a spot less than a yard square where the whitish rhyolite was so rich that it assayed as high as $3,500 a ton. Since it was not a vein and looked exactly like the rest of the formation, it could not be detected visibly. Winkler carefully mapped his strike and shortly thereafter died of a heart attack.

In April, 1937, the *Los Angeles Times* reported that Shumake and Beery's two hundred acres had been leased by the Cactus Queen. Mrs. Shumake told the author that it was sold to the Cactus Queen for $75,000 before her husband knew of Winkler's discovery. Winkler must have died during the summer of 1937, for the Cactus Queen seems to have bought the map from his widow before the end of that year for a price reported as $5,000.

During the winter of 1937-38 the Cactus Queen paid Clyde Garrett a salary and a percentage to prospect the balance of this property. The author recalls spending a day in

---

* What became of this boulder is a mystery. Mrs. Shumake has no recollection of it. Kempe wrote that it went $3,500 a ton, but the author believes he was confusing it with Winkler's other discovery. Winkler may have highgraded the rich boulder.

January, 1938, with Garrett,* observing his method of prospecting and helping him do some of the panning. He had a map checkerboarding the entire two hundred acres (except for the Winkler strike, which he was told to bypass) into ten-foot squares and was panning every corner. He said he had never prospected a claim so thoroughly in his life. With this methodical system he found two more pay streaks but said that they either didn't amount to much or proved to be extensions of the Winkler strike because he never received any royalties on them.

Winkler's deposit proved to be phenomenal. It was an enriched zone, completely irregular in shape, and was mined by the open pit method. The *Los Angeles Times* reported in January, 1938: "The glory hole on the Shumake and Beery claim of the Cactus Queen produced $75,000 from a space the size of a boxcar." Alan Kempe said some years later that Winkler's strike produced over $1,000,000 and was used to sweeten the mill heads of some of the lower grade ore from the Silver Prince.

On May 11, 1938, Bond wrote:

Marsh and I went to the Middle Buttes and climbed up to see the new strike made by the Cactus Queen. It is on the brow of a hill half a mile east of their mill. The ore is in rhyolite much like the Trent Lease on the east end of Middle Buttes and is said to run $500 a ton.

Dr. Seeley G. Mudd wrote in 1967 that the total production of the Cactus Queen exceeded $9,000,000, and that a

* Clyde Garrett, discoverer of numerous gold and mercury mines, was ninety when the author visited him in Silver City, Nevada, in 1967. He told of buying a Geiger counter in 1952 and of prospecting with it for a single day. He located the Mound House uranium mine less than three miles from his home and sold it for $10,000 cash. "Not bad for one day's work," he said. Garrett died January 16, 1968.

profit of $5,000,000 was realized. Kempe stated that the ore averaged better than $20 a ton and that the cost of mining and milling came to $9.50 a ton. The margin was so wide that he and the ranchers received approximately $550,000 each, Colonel Boyd $250,000, and the Mudds and their associates $2,550,000. Alan Kempe was not exaggerating when he said of the Cactus Queen, "It was the answer to a miner's prayer."

Conclusion

Unlike ALEC McDonald, Bob Montgomery, or Alan Kempe, Marshall Bond never found the answer to a miner's prayer. He retired from mining in 1940 and died the following year, a victim of cancer. On March 10, 1935, he had written a brief evaluation of his life:

This is my 68th birthday. Good fortune, a restless nature, love of adventure, and accident have given me a more interesting life than that which falls to most men. However, instead of making my life my own I wasted precious years in business for which I have no liking. My early experience with cattle when I rode on the round-up on the plains of Colorado in the days of the open range was probably the most thrilling and interesting of my life. The rest of what I value most are shooting, fishing, camping, and people. My greatest blessings have been my mother, my wife, and my children. Marshal Foch said in his last speech in Paris at the grave of the Unknown Soldier: "Regardez le crepuscule." I behold the twilight with equanimity and gratitude.

In 1887, as a boy, Bond had camped in the South Park of Colorado in what was called in Mexican days the Bayou Salado. Forty years earlier a courageous young Englishman,

George F. Ruxton, had camped there too. In his book *Adventures in Mexico and the Rocky Mountains*, Ruxton described his experience in one of the finest passages in the literature of the West, which poignantly expresses the deepest meaning of Bond's life.

Although liable to an accusation of barbarism, I must confess that the very happiest moments of my life have been spent in the wilderness of the Far West; and I never recall but with pleasure the remembrance of my solitary camp in the Bayou Salado, with no friend near me more faithful than my rifle, and no companions more sociable than my good horse and mules, or the attendant coyote which nightly serenaded us. With a plentiful supply of dry pine logs on the fire, and its cheerful blaze streaming far up into the sky, . . . I would sit cross-legged enjoying the general warmth, and watch the blue smoke as it curled upward, building castles in its vapory wreaths, and, in the fantastic shapes it assumed, peopling the solitude with figures of those far away. Scarcely, however, did I ever wish to change such hours of freedom for all the luxuries of civilized life.

Index